PR
4381
. C66
1988

WITHDRAWN

Byron

The Making
of a Myth

Stephen Coote

THE BODLEY HEAD
LONDON

To
FRANCES KELLY
Literary agent and friend

All rights reserved. No part of this publication may be
reproduced, stored in a retrieval system, or transmitted in any
form or by any means, electronic, mechanical, photocopying,
recording or otherwise, without the permission of the copyright
holder.

Typeset by Hourds Typographica, Stafford
Origination by La Cromolito, Milan

A CIP catalogue record for this book
is available from the British Library

ISBN 0–370–31230–9

Printed in Spain for
The Bodley Head Ltd,
32 Bedford Square, London WC1B 3EL
by Cayfosa, Barcelona

First published in 1988

Contents

"A Byron all over"

The life of Lord Byron has taken its place among the myths of the modern world. Everyone has heard the story of the English poet and peer who, after a brief and reckless round of debauchery, went into exile and gave up his life to the cause of Greek freedom. How was the myth made? Why was it necessary?

In its origins it was tawdry enough. Early in the spring of 1785, a handsome army captain appeared at the Assembly Rooms in Bath. He had recently been widowed and now, once again, he was in search of an heiress. Among the many prospects dancing their way to marriage he saw a girl with a rolling gait who spoke with a broad Scots accent. When "Mad Jack" Byron learned she was worth £23,000, he set out to woo her with his practised skill. By 13 May he had secured his prize.

He began to spend it with a careless hand. In eighteen months his wife's estates had been squandered along with the £3,000 the sometime Miss Gordon had brought with her in cash. Her family castle at Gight was mortgaged and then sold, but when Captain Byron finally retreated to France, he was pursued by his still-besotted wife. She now informed him that she was "big with bairn".

Her declaration was of little interest, but her purse, replenished by her lawyer from her now slender means, was perhaps of some consolation to the captain and the actresses who made up his entourage. Its desperate owner, however, could speak no French, and when she at last decided to make her way back to England, the captain took the opportunity to divest himself of a further encumbrance: Mrs Byron was to chaperone his daughter by a previous marriage. "Mad Jack" heaved a sigh of relief and returned to his pleasures.

Money, however, was always his problem, and Mrs Byron was soon reluctantly trailed to London by her remittance man. While he hid himself to avoid his creditors, occasionally emerging to beg guineas from his wife, she rented some poor but respectable rooms behind Oxford Street. There, on 22 January 1788, she gave birth to a clubfooted child. Mrs Byron christened the boy George and gave him her maiden name. For the next ten years her son was to be plain George Gordon.

She then moved from London to the cheaper life of Aberdeen, but even here she was followed by her grasping husband. The captain's debts had multiplied. His wife's resources dwindled still further. Quarrels in their cramped lodgings became tempestuous and were to echo forever in the psyche of their son. Finally, Captain Byron, financed for the last time, left once again for France. Here, amid the self-destructive squalor of his life, he died, perhaps by his own hand. It might well have been a relief to all concerned, but his widow declared she would never recover from her grief.

The crippled boy had to be looked after however, and Mrs Byron set about her duties with erratic devotion. She hired a nurse and then found a school where her son began the obligatory chore of learning Latin, and the somewhat more difficult task of countering the taunts of his fellows with the sharpness of his fists, or the roughness of his broad Scots tongue. He pulsed with energy. He fought, he rode, he swam. He tried, in fact, to lead the ordinary and extrovert life of a little boy in a provincial town.

He also read. Left to himself, he devoured travel books and fed his imagination on the images of the East they contained. Meanwhile, with his nurse's sister, he began to study the Bible. The impression the Scriptures made on him was to be deep, lasting and ambiguous, for, though Byron was to remember their poetry all his life, he was also to associate the dour Calvinism of May Gray—her lurid emphasis on guilt and damnation—with something equally sinister. As they read verses from the Psalms together, the auburn locks and grey-blue eyes of the little boy aroused his teacher's interest. She began to caress and fondle her charge. As she told him of a harsh and judging God, so she roused him to physical pleasure. "My passions were developed very early—so early, that few would believe me," Byron wrote. For a long time this remained a gnawing secret. His mother, meanwhile, had had little George painted as Cupid.

She also began to tell him of his ancestry. She was herself descended from James I of Scotland, and her family were lairds of more ancient standing than ever the English Byrons were. He should be aware of the blood he had inherited. Often enough it boiled over. He had his mother's temper and there were violent scenes— either at school where the lame boy invariably fought for the underdog, or at home, where the distraught and foolish widow chased her son, hit him, and then, using her bitterest epithet, declared he was "a Byron all over".

She did not know how true this was. The Byron inheritance was to pass to her son in full, and in a surprising way. In 1794, after a life of shipwreck in the South Seas and amorous adventures on land, "Mad Jack's" father was killed by a cannonball. His brother was a peer with no legitimate offspring. The captain's son, therefore, became heir to the Byron title, and so to a role that forms part of the Byron myth.

PEERS, POWER AND POLITICS

"God will not always be a Tory"

Chance elevated Byron to the peerage, anger made him satirize its monopoly on power. Byron was a radical by nature, and in the last cantos of *Don Juan*, he created the cold and calculating figure of Lord Henry Amundeville on whom to vent the energies of his wrath.

He was a cold, good, honourable man,
    Proud of his birth, and proud of every thing;
A goodly spirit for a state divan,
    A figure fit to walk before a king;
Tall, stately, form'd to lead the courtly van
    On birth-days, glorious with a star and string;
The very model of a Chamberlain—
And such I mean to make him when I reign.

But there was something wanting on the whole—
    I don't know what, and therefore cannot tell—
Which pretty women—the sweet souls!—call *Soul*.
    Certes it was not body; he was well*
Proportion'd, as a poplar or a pole,
    A handsome man, that human miracle;
And in each circumstance of love or war
Had still preserved his perpendicular.

Byron inherited much of his mother's passionate and volatile temperament. She was by turns foolish, vulgar and loving. She was also one of the first to recognize her son's poetic genius.

Here Byron exposes the cant and calculation by which the old order in England held onto the reins of power. Lord Henry's urbanity and patriotism are shown to be merely a mask for self-interest. This is Byron's shrewd, cool portrait of ancient privilege and corruption.

Lord Henry was a great electioneerer,
    Burrowing for boroughs like a rat or rabbit.
But county contests cost him rather dearer,
    Because the neighbouring Scotch Earl of Giftgabbit
Had English influence, in the self-same sphere here;
    His son, the Honourable Dick Dicedrabbit,
Was member for the 'other Interest' (meaning
The same self-interest, with a different leaning).

Courteous and cautious therefore in his county,
   He was all things to all men, and dispensed
To some civility, to others bounty,
   And promises to all—which last commenced
To gather to a somewhat large amount, he
   Not calculating how much they condensed;
But what with keeping some, and breaking others,
His word had the same value as another's.

A friend to freedom and freeholders—yet*
   No less a friend to government—he held,
That he exactly the just medium hit
   'Twixt place and patriotism—albeit compelled,
Such was his Sovereign's pleasure (though unfit,
   He added modestly, when rebels railed)
To hold some sinecures he wished abolished,
But that with them all law would be demolished.

He was 'free to confess'—(whence comes this phrase?
   Is't English? No—'tis only parliamentary)
That innovation's spirit now-a-days
   Had made more progress than for the last century.
He would not tread a factious path to praise,
   Though for the public weal disposed to venture high;
As for his place, he could but say this of it,
That the fatigue was greater than the profit.

Heaven, and his friends, knew that a private life
   Had ever been his sole and whole ambition;
But could he quit his king in times of strife
   Which threatened the whole country with perdition?
When demagogues would with a butcher's knife
   Cut through and (oh! damnable incision!)
The Gordian or the *Geo*rdi-an knot, whose strings*
Have tied together Commons, Lords, and Kings.

Sooner 'come place into the civil list
   And champion him to the utmost'—he would keep it,
Till duly disappointed or dismissed:
   Profit he cared not for, let others reap it;
But should the day come when place ceased to exist,
   The country would have far more cause to weep it;
For how could it go on? Explain who can!
He gloried in the name of Englishman.

The poet's father was a callous philanderer, a rake in the true Byron tradition. Of Mrs Byron he declared: "I defy you and all the Apostles to live with her two months".

That an obscure Aberdonian schoolboy was certain of elevation to the ranks of the aristocracy meant far more than his admission to the colourful and ancient ceremonies of the House of Lords. It meant that Byron was to be part of a charmed circle of great families. These, by their possession of landed estates and a title, controlled the country through their patronage of its politics, church and army. They were the focus of power and the sources of influence. A complex web of unwritten rules ensured that the upbringing of their members fitted them to this role. It was they who by their education at one of the great public schools, by their desultory attendance at Oxford or Cambridge, and their participation in the Grand Tour of the classical sites of Europe, set standards of gentlemanly conduct. Through these, when they came into their estates, they supposedly maintained the structure of society. The solid guarantee that those estates also provided allowed for the most colourful and eccentric diversity of behaviour. However, aristocratic status was not impugned by holding radical views. The title was something all but eternal, the individual and his oddities were a passing phenomenon. To be a peer in such a society as this was to inherit a role that was powerful, infinitely flexible, and inescapable.

It descended on the poet a little after his tenth birthday. He was invited into his teacher's study and there offered cake and wine. A voice newly deferential in tone then told him that he was George Gordon, sixth Baron Byron of Rochdale. The little ceremony, Byron later declared, at once gave him high notions of his new dignity.

In August 1798, having sold her furniture to cover their expenses, Mrs Byron took the young peer to view his estate. She herself was in a flurry of excitement, and as they approached the tollgate at Newstead she could not forbear asking the keeper whose grand estate lay yonder. "It was Lord Byron's, but he is dead," the woman replied. "And who is the heir now?" "They say it's a little boy that lives in Aberdeen." May Gray, now Mrs Byron's maid, could contain herself no longer. "This is him, God bless him!" she declared, and turned to kiss her charge.

The two women and the boy then made their way between rundown farms and the stumps of fallen oaks to where the walls of Newstead Abbey reared up in gothic silhouette. The romantic ruins of the great west end of the church were particularly impressive. As they drew closer, they saw the fountain that guarded the entrance. Here Mr Hanson, Mrs Byron's agent, stood ready to receive them. It was all in awe-inspiring and romantic contrast to their cramped quarters in Aberdeen. Surely, Mrs Byron thought, the estate must be worth at least £2,000 a year. Mother and son would move in immediately. Nothing Hanson could say would deter them. He might argue that the buildings

*Newstead Abbey was a curiously apt ancestral home
for the poet. A gothic ruin associated with
debauchery, it also had great romantic appeal and
was a symbol of the poet's aristocratic status.*

at the rear of the court had no roofs and show them that the grand refectory was used as a hay barn. Such trifling matters would not discourage them.

But, as they slowly learned more, mother and son began to realize what the Byron inheritance meant. The felled oaks and dilapidated farms might have given them pause for thought, but an ornamental castle on one of the lakes spoke clearly of the extravagances of the fifth lord. It was here, so they were told, that the last Lord Byron had held unspeakable orgies until, having killed a neighbour in a duel, been acquitted by his peers, and then gone mad over the follies of his relations, he felled the trees on his estate and settled down to a life of misanthropy. Far from there being £2,000 a year, the old lord's creditors had seized much of his furniture to cover his debts. Repairs and legal fees would swallow anything else.

The little family, noble but penniless, stood amid the wreckage of their ancestors. Lord Byron had entered into his inheritance.

"A good sort of fellow"

Here was a new position, a new role. The complex little boy from Aberdeen must be made an English peer. Hanson, having shrewdly assessed the worth of Mrs Byron, realized much of the responsibility for this would fall upon him. There was, above all, the question of money. Hanson consulted with the Earl of Carlisle whom he had persuaded to be Byron's guardian. Lord Carlisle and the English aristocracy were not unfamiliar with poverty among their ranks, and a petition to the king eventually resulted in the granting of a pension of £300 a year from the Civil List. Mrs Byron and her son might live on charity, but they would maintain their status.

There was also the question of Byron's lame foot. Hanson discovered his mother was having it tended by a Nottingham quack whose treatment consisted of rubbing the foot with oil and then trying to screw it straight in some sort of vice. The process was excruciatingly painful and completely useless. Hanson promptly put a stop to it. He took his charge to London, where he had a special boot constructed. Byron, entering his deeply self-conscious adolescence, often refused to wear it.

Then there was the problem of May Gray. Clearly the fatherless boy had confessed to Hanson what had passed between them, and, rightly appalled, he tactfully insisted Byron's mother dismiss her maid for beating her son and entertaining low company in the house. Hanson himself, meanwhile, had introduced Byron to Mary Charworth, one of the young peer's neighbours. Perhaps he hoped the boy's evident affection for her would help heal the wound. In fact, it only opened another. Throughout his schooldays Byron was to be hopelessly in love with Mary Charworth. "She was the *beau idéal* of all that my youthful fancy could paint of beautiful," he wrote, and, as time went by, his feelings for her were to prostrate him.

Meanwhile, he had to be educated for his new position. Hanson found a small school in Dulwich where Byron's Latin (an essential passport to male gentility) was slowly brought up to standard. To preserve this small gain, Hanson then invited the boy to spend Christmas with his family in London. A visit from Mrs Byron showed how wise this was, for the exasperating gaucheness of her behaviour (perhaps she felt that, having lost her husband, she was now losing her son) managed to offend both Hanson himself and Lord Carlisle. When, pandering to her son's wishes, Mrs Byron kept the boy away from school and quarrelled with his headmaster on the issue, Hanson decided he must again take action. At the end of April 1801 he went with Lord Carlisle to interview the headmaster of Harrow. Dr Drury, though aware of the boy's deficient education, agreed to accept him. "I soon found," he wrote, "that a wild mountain colt had been submitted to my management."

The English public schools of the early 19th century had not yet suffered the evangelical earnestness of Dr Arnold, the great Victorian reformer, and still survived in their anarchic Georgian form: a combination of bullying and occasional riot, sodomy and classical grammar. Harrow was regarded as the best of them. Eton, so a contemporary declared, was full of dissipated youths, and Westminster of near blackguards, while the boys of St Pauls were the most depraved of them all.

Byron loathed his early years at Harrow. He was taunted for his lameness, while "the drilled dull lesson" was repugnant to his vivid imagination. He was determined, however, to prove himself as good at sports as the other boys and he became a reasonable cricketer, playing in the Eton-Harrow match of 1805. The resilience of the boy from Aberdeen would always win him friends. He was, wrote one, "a good sort of fellow".

The wildness of Mrs Byron's son was a constant problem, however. His energies were untamed, even by 18th century standards, and, by the time Byron was ready for university coaching, Dr Drury sternly suggested that he should find a private tutor. Byron would have none of it. The hint touched his quick sense of wounded honour. The teenage peer was acquiring the habits of his rank and he was now a leader in the school. He did not wish his companions to think he had been expelled. Dr Drury saw the sense in this and was shrewd enough not to send the rebellious boy away with a chip on his shoulder. Besides, he was himself due to retire. When the new headmaster appeared, Byron, loyally leading his juvenile troops, headed a rebellion against him.

But there were other sides to the volatile and touchy teenager, contradictory characteristics that were to grow and strengthen in his complex psyche. He might loathe his lessons, but this did not prevent him from reading widely. According to one of his undergraduate notebooks, by the time he was 15 he had devoured upwards of 4,000 novels (surely a somewhat generous estimate), including those of Cervantes, Fielding and Sterne. He also claimed to have read Rousseau's

*Byron's love for Mary
Charworth was cruelly
rebuffed. However, when he
was famous and her marriage
had staled, she approached
Byron and was rejected.*

Confessions, lives of Newton and Catherine the Great, and works by the philosophers Montesquieu, Locke and Hume. Perhaps he had. In a life of constant and tumultuous activity Byron acquired a very wide range of information even though he was rarely seen reading. "The truth is I read eating, read in bed, read when no one else reads." He was in fact that most committed of scholars, the autodidact, and his tastes were being developed by his enthusiasms. He had already discovered the works of Pope, and this great satirist of the 18th century, along with the other authors Byron listed, suggests the romantic and headstrong writer's lifelong attachment to the reasoned, revolutionary ideals of the 18th century Enlightenment. If school life was a ferment, so, too, was his mind.

And so, as always, were his emotions. Very young men are rarely happy for much of the time. Constant fantasy slides quickly into black despair. Such moods made themselves felt early on in Byron's adolescence, and on a flat limestone tomb beneath the elms of Harrow churchyard the poet often fell a victim to their power.

Harnessed in great verse, the swirling void of Byronic melancholy added something of lasting value to the temperament of Europe. There was much to feed it, even from the start. There were, in particular, the souring memories and new ideals of passion. As an infant in Scotland, Byron had formed a strong, if sexless, attachment for his cousin Mary Duff. Another cousin, Margaret Parker, had caused the sleepless 12-year-old's first rush into poetry. Now, deep in the toils of adolescence, Byron's hopeless attachment for Mary Charworth was frighteningly intense. Even his mother, writing to Hanson to explain her son's long absence from school, was surprised by its force. The love-sick Byron spent his time alternately mooning over his thoughts of the older woman and firing his pistols for hours at a time, something that was to become a lifelong habit. Mary Charworth, engaged to an elegant fox-hunting squire, was mildly amused, but she dashed his hopes with a careless sentence: "What! me care for that lame boy!" Byron limped home, furious and broken-hearted. "I cannot get him to return to school," his mother wrote, "though I have done all in my power for six weeks past. He has no indisposition that I know of, but love, desperate love, the *worst* of all *maladies* in my opinion."

But, although she indulged him over this, relations between mother and son were fast deteriorating. Her Civil List pension had been partly cut to help pay for Byron's education. Newstead Abbey had been rented out. Mrs Byron's life was ever more curtailed and frustrating. The love-sick boy faced a termagant mother. The least thing upset her. Matters grew so bad that Byron eventually moved into the lodge at Newstead in order to avoid her. Here for a time he was beguiled by his young tenant's moonlight shoots. However, there was more to Lord Grey de Ruthyn's friendship than an interest in country sports. Just before Byron's 16th birthday he seems to have made a pass at him. Byron was disgusted. He was ever the hunter, not the hunted. But when he told his mother of his new and cordial detestation of Lord Grey, there was a furious quarrel in which she let slip an odd phrase that suggested she was half in love with the sensual young lord herself.

Amid this tangle of squalor and despair there was one comfort. "Mad Jack's" daughter, the little girl Mrs Byron had been obliged to bring back from France, had grown into a kindly woman of 20. Her future father-in-law was putting obstacles in the way of her marriage however, and her pain was perhaps a little assuaged by the warm and brilliant letters she now began to receive from her half-brother. "I hope you will not attribute my neglect to want of affection," he wrote, "but rather to a shyness naturally inherent in my Disposition . . . . you are *the nearest relation* I have in *the world both by the ties of Blood* and *affection.*" Augusta was an older woman, a relation, a friend. Above all, she gave value to Byron's emotions in a world that had so far often snubbed and abused them. He could tell her almost everything, and so he did. His poetry from this time is so much boyish rhyming, but in his letters he is already showing his literary powers.

And if there was Augusta to write to, there were also friendships with younger boys at school. Such relationships were warmed by conventions of extreme emotion. "At school friendship is a passion. It entrances the being; it tears the soul," wrote Disraeli. Byron, too, declared that his school friendships were passions. They were also a dangerous consolation. The young Lords Delawarr and Clare exposed yet another complex need in the poet even as they innocently fed it.

"Hours of Idleness"

The period of Byron's formal schooling came to its inevitable close. He carved his name on his classroom wall, and, after the Eton-Harrow match, went on to London with the teams. Here they got drunk and "kicked up a row" in the Haymarket Theatre. It might be thought that Byron was becoming a Regency buck.

The truth was more painful. Harrow, for all its tumult, had sheltered him and offered love. Now, at 17, he had to face the complexities of his character alone. His mother's temper had not improved. Her house was a bitter sanctuary where she took a mean delight in telling her son of Mary Charworth's marriage. Nor did Byron's arrival at Cambridge improve matters. He had wanted to go to Oxford, but there was no place for him, and, despite his "*super*excellent" rooms and the gold-braided gown that marked his nobleman's status, he stared across the Great Court of Trinity with wolfish, unsocial eyes. He was intensely alone. The conventional dissipations of his peers, though he indulged in them, disgusted his more ardent temperament. He found greater pleasure swimming near Grantchester with his old school friend, Edward Noel Long.

Such compensations were a familiar comfort, yet they were no longer free from guilt. The fact that he was no longer a boy depressed him, for what had been, perhaps, the blameless experiments of early adolescence, were now not quite so innocent. The affection he had won at school and for which he still craved took on a sinister and dangerous edge. Though he returned to Harrow from time to time and, with a reckless and characteristic generosity, pressed £5 notes into the hands of Delawarr and his friends, the sexual element in such meetings could no longer be denied.

This portrait of Byron in his Albanian costume is one of the most famous images of the poet. It shows Byron as Childe Harold, the extravagant, romantic and aristocratic Englishman, familiar with exotic places and exotic people – a man living on the perilous edge of sensation and relishing the self-display. Byron describes his delight at buying the costume in the letter to his mother quoted on pp.38–43.

Charles Eastlake's "Lord Byron's Dream" evokes Byron the orientalist and freedom fighter. Extravagantly posed among classic ruins and attended by Greeks slumped in deep sleep, Byron alone has an inspiring vision of political independence: "I dreamed that Greece might yet be free". Hence the title of Eastlake's painting.

For several periods of his life, Byron was to be powerfully and physically attracted to younger males, and in Regency England the death penalty for "sodomites" was regularly invoked. The church and press demanded it; the Society for the Suppression of Vice ensured that victims were produced. On average, two a year were hanged. Those slightly more fortunate, pilloried before the screaming London mob, sometimes escaped with their lives. Neither money nor social position offered any sure defence. William Beckford, the richest man in England, was forced into exile and disgrace, then finally allowed to return. His friend, Lord Courtenay, was also hounded abroad. Byron knew the dangers of his burgeoning desires. To grow up aware of forbidden feelings was to watch passion mature in the shadow of the rope.

His depression deepened, and his natural energies could not always shake it off. Amid the riotous living and mounting expenses of Cambridge there was, it seemed, almost no one to whom he could confess his secret. He was evasive even with Augusta. In his letters, Byronic melancholy is often tinged with those ambiguous suggestions of guilt which were also a part of its public allure. "If I could explain at length the *real* causes which have contributed to this perhaps *natural* temperament of mine, the Melancholy, which hath made me a bye-word, nobody would wonder; but this is impossible without doing much mischief."

He sought release and excitement in London, recklessly spending money he did not have. From his lodgings at 16 Piccadilly the lame teenager set out in search of women—any women—in whose hired embraces he could prove his manhood or forget his troubles. He was beginning to find that a life of constant stimulation was his only remedy against the black void of inertia. His expenses mounted prodigiously as he threw himself into London life. He wrote to Augusta asking her to guarantee a loan. She refused, though she offered some of her own money, which Byron could not accept. He turned instead to his landlady.

<hr/>

CAMBRIDGE

"this place is the Devil"

Wit, self-mockery and a brilliant colloquial style are clearly evident even in Byron's earliest letters. Here, writing to his lawyer, he gives a vivid picture of the disillusion and dissipation experienced by a young aristocrat at Cambridge in 1805.

> Dear Sir.—Your advice was good but I have not determined whether I shall follow it, this place is the *Devil*, or at least his principal residence, they call it the University, but any other appellation would have suited it much better, for Study is the last pursuit of the Society; the Master eats, drinks, and Sleeps, the Fellows *drink, dispute* and *pun*, the *employments* of the under Graduates you will probably conjecture without my description. I sit down to write with a head confused with dissipation, which though I hate, I cannot avoid. I have only supped at home 3 times since my arrival, and my table is constantly covered with invitations, after all I am the most *steady* man in the College, nor have I got into *many* Scrapes, and none of consequence.

This idealized evocation of Harrow suggests something of the dreams of innocence with which the undergraduate Byron veiled his schooldays.

Mrs Massingberd was well aware of the advantages this gave her. No one could lend money to a minor without a guarantor, and in return for underwriting loans offered at ruinous rates of interest she received a handsome reward. At first Byron's borrowings were a matter of a few hundred pounds. These helped pay off his school and college bills—in his first term at Cambridge Byron had spent the very considerable sum of £20 on books alone—while also leaving room for a margin of fantasy. He would flee abroad . . . Germany . . . Vienna . . . St Petersburg. His mind revolved these desperate possibilities. Escape was a constant fantasy.

The truth was, he had fallen in love. In his Cambridge wretchedness he had approached a younger boy. John Edleston was 15, and a chorister in the college chapel. Byron was at first attracted by his voice, then by his fair hair and dark eyes. Edleston's docile and kindly nature, however, soon won him over completely.

There was much about the intensely sentimental but platonic relationship which followed the model of the aristocratic patron and his protégé. At various times in his life Byron was to take on other such handsome lads as his pages, and to stress his superior social standing may have left his feelings less vulnerable. He certainly provided

Edleston with money he could ill afford, and the embarrassed boy was unsure how he should show his gratitude. He eventually bought Byron a cornelian brooch in the shape of a heart, but when he offered his present he burst into tears, fearing its modest value might make it appear a tawdry gift. Byron, too, was moved to tears. It seemed to him that he was at last loved for his own sake, and he expressed his feelings in verse. "The Cornelian", sentimental and mannered though it is, was popular among Byron's friends.

Elizabeth Pigot, a neighbour of his mother's, certainly liked the poem, and Byron felt sufficiently confident to explain something of its origins to her. His letter, an early example of what was to develop into a genius for self-dramatization, coincided with Edleston's departure to a London business house. Byron, "with a *Bottle* of Claret in my *Head*, & *tears* in my *eyes*", told Elizabeth how he and Edleston had seen each other every day, how they had parted, and how they planned to be reunited and live as chastely as David and Jonathan. "I hope you will *one day* see *us* together," he wrote sentimentally. Events were to turn out sadly different.

For a peer of the realm, attendance at Cambridge was not usually a matter of acquiring scholarship. The dons at both universities were still largely under the sway of that bibulous and gossiping sloth which had appalled both Edward Gibbon and the poet Thomas Gray in the previous century. Consequently, there was nothing particularly remarkable about Byron's long absences either in London or, when funds were low, at his mother's house.

Relations with his mother were inevitably stormy. News of her son's debts brought back memories of "Mad Jack", and her anger was not allayed when Byron arrived with a carriage and horses, a groom and a valet. Peace was largely maintained by Byron's frequent visits to Elizabeth Pigot. But there was further evidence of his dissipations. Always prone to fat, by the autumn of 1806, Byron, who was a little over 5 foot 8 inches, weighed 202 pounds. What Mrs Byron may not have known is that heavy drinking had also seriously undermined her son's health. A strict regimen was clearly necessary and Byron threw himself into it with characteristic vigour. By playing cricket in seven waistcoats and a greatcoat, bathing, the use of emetics, and eating one meal a day, he was eventually able to boast that his tailor had taken in his clothes by nearly half a yard.

These were not his only exertions. Amid so much waste, Byron's commitment to his vocation was already absolute, and he wrote with that superabundant energy by which he lived. Sometimes, as now, it drove him to the silly, sometimes to the sham. Often it roused his wit, anger or spite. At his most interesting however, in his verse as in his life, Byron tested the conventions of his day to their hilt. When they cracked, he replaced them with his own.

Fugitive Pieces appeared at Byron's expense in 1806. It was immediately withdrawn. References to "love's exstatic posture" were not appreciated in the provinces, and another volume—"*vastly* corrected and miraculously chaste"—was soon produced. Henry Mackenzie, author of a sentimental novel called *The Man of Feeling*, was sent a copy and congratulated the author. He was probably being no more than polite; there is little in the book that suggests the masterpieces to come. It was Greece that made Byron a poet and turned an itch for rhyme into the compulsion of a genius. Hanson, more shrewd than tactful, wrote that Byron's true talent was for rhetoric. Notwithstanding, when the elated young poet returned to Cambridge in the summer he had yet another new volume proudly packed in his carriage. The title—*Hours of Idleness*—had been supplied by the printer who was to publish the book. Byron was now a fully-fledged author.

But Edleston was in London and Byron's old set had gone down. There seemed nothing to keep him at Trinity. Even his rooms had been given to another, an Etonian whose tutor had warned him not to damage the movables, "for Lord Byron, Sir, is a young man of *tumultuous passions*". Charles Skinner Matthews was amused by the tone of unworldly awe. He repeated the anecdote to John Cam Hobhouse, and when they both told the story to Byron, all three became friends in a morning. They were radicals and literary men, equals in age, rivals in wit, and became companions in dissipation.

Hobhouse was the most levelheaded of them and the longest lived. He was to harden in a world of Victorian values, but the Regency Hobhouse, Byron's Hobhouse, was liberal, warm and dependable. Politics were in his blood. His father was a Member of Parliament. He himself was a Whig, and he probably introduced Byron to their Cambridge club.

By temperament, Byron was born for opposition, and the Whigs were the natural party for an aristocratic rebel. In the Glorious Revolution of 1688 they had successfully defended the rights of the people (in reality their own aristocratic oligarchy) against the might of the crown. James II was sent into exile and the power of Parliament affirmed. In the following century they settled into the Palladian graciousness of country house politics, but by the 1790s the Whigs were in decline. Revolution in France had led to war in Europe, and it was the iron hand of Toryism that held Napoleon at bay. Forced into opposition, the Whigs projected an image of themselves that Byron was to absorb and develop. They were the guardians of liberty and true patriots. It was their duty, as men of education and property, to be the friends of the people and, by preserving themselves, to maintain the balance of the state. For youthful radicals like Charles Skinner Matthews, the ideals of the French Revolution were still a potent force. To Byron and his other admiring friends, Matthews was the "Citoyen".

A third of Byron's Cambridge friends was Scrope Beardmore Davies. Though he was a fellow of King's, Davies was most often seen at the green baize tables of the London clubs. He lived, quite literally, by hazard. For several years he was prodigiously successful at the game, and his winnings supported his dandy's lifestyle: the quietly elegant clothes, the days of apparent ease interspersed with fashionable boxing lessons and parties that flashed with wit, radicalism and erudite quotation. Davies was also five years older than Byron and the poet was at an impressionable age. Davies could not only show him the ways of a fast and dissolute world but could guarantee the loans its expense required. These were later to cause much pain, but in the meantime, as the debts mounted to £10,000, £12,000, £13,000, there was a flow of brilliant conversation. Stimulation was all. "Byron dined with me," Davies wrote, "and blazed forth with genius. I am unhappy."

Byron's genius still found its best expression in talk and in his gloriously spontaneous letters that are like talk transcribed. He was working hard at poetry, however. It was another stimulant. There were over a thousand more lines in manuscript as well as 214 pages of a novel, he reported. In his crowded London life, enervated, as he told Hobhouse, by his obsessive pursuit of sex, Byron found that two in the morning was the best time to write. The bottles were mostly empty, the carriages had rolled away, the girls were perhaps asleep. Thus are set the habits of a lifetime. *Hours of Idleness*, meanwhile, was in the bookshops.

It was also in the hands of the critics. They declared it to be schoolboy trash. An anonymous account in the *Edinburgh Review* was the cruellest of all. The setting up of this magazine was a landmark in English intellectual life. It was the vehicle of liberal opinion and was read by upwards of 50,000 people. When the critic declared that Byron's poems were flat, derivative and frivolous, his anguish was extreme. He had been publicly and crushingly humiliated by those he hoped might be his friends. For a while, only dissipation could provide an anaesthetic, but he eventually replied to the work in his first important poem, *English Bards and Scots Reviewers*. Here, in couplets imitating those of his admired Pope, Byron castigated the contemporary literary scene. The attacks on the leading romantic poets— Wordsworth, Southey and Coleridge in particular—though echoing contemporary opinion, suggest the accuracy with which Byron read. In his contempt, he began to find his own voice.

from ENGLISH BARDS
AND SCOTS REVIEWERS

*"Those poor idiots of the Lakes too—are diluting
our literature as much as they can."*

Byron's antipathy to the Lake poets—Wordsworth, Coleridge and Southey—was
marked through much of his career. He loathed them variously for what he considered
their banality, obscurity and hypocrisy. Southey, in particular, Byron regarded as little
more than a talentless time-server. He ridiculed him both here at the start of his career
and later with majestic sarcasm in *The Vision of Judgment.*

Oh! SOUTHEY, SOUTHEY! cease thy varied song!
A Bard may chaunt too often, and too long:
As thou art strong in verse, in mercy spare!
A fourth, alas! were more than we could bear.
But if, in spite of all the world can say,
Thou still wilt verseward plod thy weary way;
If still in Berkeley-Ballads most uncivil,*
Thou wilt devote old women to the devil,
The babe unborn thy dread intent may rue:
'God help thee', SOUTHEY, and thy readers too.

    Next comes the dull disciple of thy school,
That mild apostate from poetic rule,
The simple WORDSWORTH, framer of a lay
As soft as evening in his favourite May;
Who warns his friend 'to shake off toil and trouble,*
And quit his books, for fear of growing double';
Who, both by precept and example, shows
That prose is verse, and verse is merely prose,*
Convincing all by demonstration plain,
Poetic souls delight in prose insane;
And Christmas stories tortured into rhyme,
Contain the essence of the true sublime:
Thus when he tells the tale of Betty Foy,
The idiot mother of 'an idiot Boy';*
A moon-struck silly lad who lost his way,
And, like his Bard, confounded night with day,
So close on each pathetic part he dwells,
And each adventure so sublimely tells,
That all who view the 'idiot in his glory',
Conceive the Bard the hero of the story.

*Byron's early criticism of Coleridge's
poetry later mellowed to mature respect.*

    Shall gentle COLERIDGE pass unnoticed here,
To turgid ode, and tumid stanza dear?
Though themes of innocence amuse him best,
Yet still obscurity's a welcome guest.
If inspiration should her aid refuse,
To him who takes a Pixy for a Muse,*
Yet none in lofty numbers can surpass
The Bard who soars to elegize an ass:
So well the subject suits his noble mind,
He brays the Laureat of the long-ear'd kind!

Having attained his majority, Byron took possession of Newstead again, and assumed his seat in the House of Lords. He intended to regard his duties seriously. A large sum was spent on learned political tomes, and he told Hanson that a period of travel was a necessary preparation for the political life. This would also have the advantage of drastically reducing his expenses. Byron was now staggering under a ruinous burden of debt, and in the loneliness of Newstead (where a maid had conceived his illegitimate child) his mind divided itself between macabre fantasies and lurid jest. A skull was dug up in the grounds. He had it mounted as a silver goblet. Hobhouse, Matthews and others came to stay. Recalling the orgies of Byron's ancestors, they dressed up as monks and, drunk amid the gothic ruins, parodied the rites of the Hell Fire clubs, those associations of 18th century libertines who toyed with black magic. But beneath all this, deep and persistent, a sense of gloom, futility and cynicism fought with Byron's natural energies and love of freedom. It was time to get away, to find new excitements and shape another role. On 2 July 1809 Byron and Hobhouse set out on the Grand Tour.

CHILDE HAROLD

"I awoke one morning and found myself famous"

The first two cantos of *Childe Harold's Pilgrimage* are the record of Byron's Grand Tour. They caused a sensation when they first appeared and the poet found himself a celebrity overnight. This was partly because of the radical political views he expressed, and partly because his narrator and hero were emotionally so interesting. Childe Harold himself (the word "Childe" suggests his aristocratic status) is a dissolute, satiated and melancholy peer, a young man in need of the spiritual refreshment a pilgrimage might provide. Bryon's deliberately archaic language derives from the 16th century poet Spenser whose nine line stanza he also adopted.

> Childe Harold bask'd him in the noon-tide sun,
> Disporting there like any other fly;
> Nor deem'd before his little day was done
> One blast might chill him into misery.
> But long ere scarce a third of his pass'd by,
> Worse than adversity the Childe befell;
> He felt the fulness of satiety:
> Then loath'd he in his native land to dwell,
> Which seem'd to him more lone than Eremite's sad cell.*

For he through Sin's long labyrinth had run,
Nor made atonement when he did amiss,
Had sigh'd to many though he lov'd but one,
And that lov'd one, alas! could ne'er be his.
Ah, happy she! to 'scape from him whose kiss
Had been pollution unto aught so chaste;
Who soon had left her charms for vulgar bliss,
And spoil'd her goodly lands to gild his waste,
Nor calm domestic peace had ever deign'd to taste.

And now Childe Harold was sore sick at heart,
And from his fellow bacchanals would flee;
'Tis said, at times the sullen tear would start,
But Pride congeal'd the drop within his ee:*
Apart he stalk'd in joyless reverie,
And from his native land resolv'd to go,
And visit scorching climes beyond the sea;
With pleasure drugg'd he almost long'd for woe,
And e'en for change of scene would seek the shades below.

The Childe departed from his father's hall:
It was a vast and venerable pile;
So old, it seemed only not to fall,
Yet strength was pillar'd in each massy aisle.
Monastic dome! condemn'd to uses vile!
Where Superstition once had made her den
Now Paphian girls were known to sing and smile;*
And monks might deem their time was come agen,
If ancient tales say true, nor wrong these holy men.

Yet oft-times in his maddest mirthful mood
Strange pangs would flash along Childe Harold's brow,
As if the memory of some deadly feud
Or disappointed passion lurk'd below:
But this none knew, nor haply car'd to know;
For his was not that open, artless soul
That feels relief by bidding sorrow flow,
Nor sought he friend to counsel or condole,
Whate'er his grief mote be, which he could not control.*

And none did love him—though to hall and bower
He gather'd revellers from far and near,
He knew them flatt'rers of the festal hour;
The heartless parasites of present cheer.
Yea! none did love him—not his lemans dear—*
But pomp and power alone are woman's care,
And where these are light Eros finds a feere;*
Maidens, like moths, are ever caught by glare,
And Mammon wins his way where Seraphs might despair.

Childe Harold had a mother—not forgot,
Though parting from that mother he did shun;
A sister whom he lov'd, but saw her not
Before his weary pilgrimage begun:
If friends he had, he bade adieu to none.
Yet deem not thence his breast a breast of steel;
Ye, who have known what 'tis to doat upon
A few dear objects, will in sadness feel
Such partings break the heart they fondly hope to heal.

His house, his home, his heritage, his lands,
The laughing dames in whom he did delight.
Whose large blue eyes, fair locks, and snowy hands
Might shake the saintship of an anchorite,
And long had fed his youthful appetite;
His goblets brimm'd with every costly wine,
And all that mote to luxury invite,
Without a sigh he left, to cross the brine,
And traverse Paynim shores, and pass Earth's central line.*

"*Childe Harold's Pilgrimage*"

By the end of October Byron and Hobhouse had reached Albania. Hobhouse was taking notes for his travel book. Byron, he observed, was writing a long poem in Spenserian stanzas. This was *Childe Harold's Pilgrimage*. It was to establish Byron's fame and mould the tastes of Europe.

The purpose of the Grand Tour itself had long been established. As early as 1693, the English philosopher Locke had seen it as an educational process. The young traveller should broaden his mind by acquaintance with different social customs and then return to take up his position in society, marry and propagate. So much was decent. Dr Johnson, slightly more ironically, declared that the grand object of travel was merely to see the shores of the Mediterranean. In fact, the Tour was often regarded as a mixed blessing. While some travellers confined themselves to the role of the monied and salacious booby—Pope expressed the common lament that all classic learning was lost on classic ground—others were permanently transformed and returned to build gracious houses and fill these with fine collections. Byron, as one of the last grand tourists, recast the whole convention.

He was obliged to shape this new image by one of his heroes. Napoleon—forever widening the boundaries of his French empire—had redrawn the map of Europe by 1800. France itself and Italy were closed to English travellers, but Wellington's exertions in the Peninsular War were opening up Portugal and Spain. Byron first sailed to Lisbon. In addition to Hobhouse (who had quarrelled with his father and whose expenses were covered by a loan from the all-but-bankrupt poet), Byron was accompanied by a longtime Newstead retainer; by William Fletcher, his grumbling but dogged valet; and by Robert Rushton, a handsome boy from Byron's estate who probably shared his master's bed and certainly had a hold on his heart. Others were to join the group, some were to quit, or be sent home. But always, at its centre, there was Byron: Byron cynical, witty and salacious; Byron vigorously in love with harsh countries and their bright and strident peoples; Byron standing moodily at the taffrail, his eyes on a dark sea wrinkling beneath the moon. The myth was beginning to form.

In Lisbon he ate oranges and spoke bad Latin with the monks. He visited Cintra and, with a peculiar *frisson* of interest, climbed to the Moorish palace of Monserrat where Beckford had lived in luxurious, if bitter, exile. But the poverty of the country and what he considered as the supine nature of its people oppressed him. His servants and baggage were sent on to Gibraltar while Byron himself, Rushton and a local guide, rode off across the peninsula towards Seville and Cadiz. The freedom of the wide, sunburned plains was exhilarating. The horses were excellent, and the tourists rode upwards of 70 miles a day, stopping only to rest in the hard beds of the local inns and refresh themselves with eggs and wine. Byron's health improved considerably. At Seville he saw a bullfight and, like many later English tourists, was revolted by it. The sombre and cavernous vaults of the cathedral impressed him however. In Cadiz he flirted with the women.

But his emotions were also engaged at a deeper level. This was the Spain of the Peninsular War. As he recreated it in *Childe Harold's Pilgrimage*, Byron's itinerary followed the wake of the campaign. He became a political poet, depicting the horrors of war. He was aware of its pageant, bloodshed and futile bungling. He also valued its moments of supreme personal heroism. As he developed such responses through his later work, so, in the central cantos of *Don Juan*, Byron becomes the most interesting English poet of warfare between Shakespeare and Wilfred Owen. This is a neglected facet of his genius, but an essential aspect of his criticism of world events.

Byron knew that as part of Napoleon's plan to control western Europe, he had given the throne of Spain to Joseph Bonaparte. His own mission, Napoleon told the Spaniards, was to restore their nation to its youth, but the people took the initiative themselves. They developed the concept of guerilla warfare, and, in Aragon, after three months of street fighting, the French were obliged to leave Saragossa to its rightful inhabitants. Byron was thrilled by such stirrings of popular and national independence. They appealed to his vivid, patrician sense of freedom. Here were action, colour and a cause.

But if Byron expressed a Whig's delight in national freedom, he also exposed the Whigs' distrust of the British military involvement in Spain. Wellington (still only Sir Arthur Wellesley at this time) was beginning to show the iron strengths of careerism and class pride that were to make him the saviour of Europe and place him among the most hated of Byron's satirical butts, a figure on whom he was to lavish vituperation.

THE SIEGE OF ISMAIL

"A proper mixture of siege—battle—and adventure"

In an age of constant warfare, Byron was the supreme and most critical
poet of battle. This is revealed by these stanzas from the eighth canto of
Don Juan. Here, after a variety of adventures, Byron's hero has become
a soldier of fortune. He and his friend Johnson, a bluff Englishman, are
present at the siege of Ismail. This is shown to be an event of great cruelty
and dreadful bungling, motivated solely by the greed of those in power.
Such was Byron's view of nearly all contemporary warfare, and his disgust
shows through his humour. He also manages to convey, however, a moment
of great human pity and kindness. Amid the carnage, Juan saves a little
girl whom he then adopts. This combination of savagery and kindness,
blood lust and charity, suggests how Byron's art allowed him to "sketch
your world exactly as it goes".

*Byron delighted in the romance of Spanish cities
like Seville, but travelling in the wake of the
Peninsular War he began to discover that warfare
itself was a great and necessary poetic theme.*

The city's taken—only part by part—
    And Death is drunk with gore: there's not a street
Where fights not to the last some desperate heart
    For those for whom it soon shall cease to beat.
Here War forgot his own destructive Art
    In more destroying Nature; and the heat
Of Carnage, like the Nile's sun-sodden Slime,
Engendered monstrous shapes of every Crime.

A Russian officer, in martial tread
    Over a heap of bodies, felt his heel
Seized fast, as if 'twere by the serpent's head
    Whose fangs Eve taught her human seed to feel:
In vain he kicked, and swore, and writhed, and bled,
    And howled for help as wolves do for a meal—
The teeth still kept their gratifying hold,
As do the subtle snakes described of old.

A dying Moslem, who had felt the foot
    Of a foe o'er him, snatched at it, and bit
The very tendon, which is most acute—
    (That which some ancient Muse or modern Wit
Named after thee, Achilles) and quite through 't
    He made the teeth meet, nor relinquish'd it
Even with his life—for (but they lie) 'tis said
To the live leg still clung the severed head.

However this may be, 'tis pretty sure
   The Russian officer for life was lamed,
For the Turk's teeth stuck faster than a skewer,
   And left him 'midst the invalid and maimed:
The regimental surgeon could not cure
   His patient, and perhaps was to be blamed
More than the head of the inveterate foe,
Which was cut off, and scarce even then let go.

But then the fact's a fact—and 'tis the part
   Of a true poet to escape from fiction
Whene'er he can; for there is little art
   In leaving verse more free from the restriction
Of truth than prose, unless to suit the mart
   For what is sometimes called poetic diction,
And that outrageous appetite for lies
Which Satan angles with, for souls, like flies.

The city's taken, but not rendered!—No!
   There's not a Moslem that hath yielded sword:
The blood may gush out, as the Danube's flow
   Rolls by the city wall; but deed nor word
Acknowledge aught of dread of death or foe:
   In vain the yell of victory is roared
By the advancing Muscovite—the groan
Of the last foe is echoed by his own.

The bayonet pierces and the sabre cleaves,
   And human lives are lavished every where,
As the year closing whirls the scarlet leaves
   When the stript forest bows to the bleak air,
And groans; and thus the peopled City grieves,
   Shorn of its best and loveliest, and left bare;
But still it falls with vast and awful splinters,
As Oaks blown down with all their thousand winters.

It is an awful topic—but 'tis not
   My cue for any time to be terrific:
For chequered as is seen our human lot
   With good, and bad, and worse, alike prolific
Of melancholy merriment, to quote
   Too much of one sort would be soporific,
Without, or with, offence to friends or foes,
I sketch your world exactly as it goes.

John Cam Hobhouse, Byron's companion on the Grand Tour, was a lifelong friend. Though involved in the destruction of Byron's memoirs, he at least salvaged many of the poet's finest letters.

And one good action in the midst of crimes
    Is 'quite refreshing,' in the affected phrase
Of these ambrosial, Pharisaic times,*
    With all their pretty milk-and-water ways,
And may serve therefore to bedew these rhymes,
    A little scorched at present with the blaze
Of conquest and its consequences, which
Make Epic poesy so rare and rich.

Upon a taken bastion where there lay
    Thousands of slaughtered men, a yet warm group
Of murdered women, who had found their way
    To this vain refuge, made the good heart droop
And shudder:—while, as beautiful as May,
    A female child of ten years tried to stoop
And hide her little palpitating breast
Amidst the bodies lulled in bloody rest.

Two villainous Cossacques pursued the child
    With flashing eyes and weapons: matched with them
The rudest brute that roams Siberia's wild
    Has feelings pure and polished as a gem,—
The bear is civilized, the wolf is mild:
    And whom for this at last must we condemn?
Their natures? or their sovereigns, who employ
All arts to teach their subjects to destroy?

Their sabres glittered o'er her little head,
    Whence her fair hair rose twining with affright,
Her hidden face was plunged amidst the dead:
    When Juan caught a glimpse of this sad sight,
I shall not say exactly what he *said*,
    Because it might not solace 'ears polite;'
But what he *did*, was to lay on their backs,
The readiest way of reasoning with Cossacques.

One's hip he slashed, and split the other's shoulder,
    And drove them with their brutal yells to seek
If there might be chirurgeons who could solder
    The wounds they richly merited, and shriek
Their baffled rage and pain; while waxing colder
    As he turned o'er each pale and gory cheek,
Don Juan raised his little captive from
The heap a moment more had made her tomb.

Continuing on his Grand Tour, Byron was appalled to find that the marbles of the Parthenon were being bought up by Lord Elgin and shipped to London.

And she was chill as they, and on her face
   A slender streak of blood announced how near
Her fate had been to that of all her race;
   For the same blow which laid her Mother here,
Had scarred her brow, and left its crimson trace
   As the last link with all she had held dear;
But else unhurt, she opened her large eyes,
And gazed on Juan with a wild surprise.

Just at this instant, while their eyes were fixed
   Upon each other, with dilated glance,
In Juan's look, pain, pleasure, hope, fear, mixed
   With joy to save, and dread of some mischance
Unto his protégée; while hers, transfixed
   With infant terrors, glared as from a trance,
A pure, transparent, pale, yet radiant face,
Like to a lighted alabaster vase;—

Up came John Johnson: (I will not say '*Jack*,'
   For that were vulgar, cold, and common place
On great occasions, such as an attack
   On cities, as hath been the present case:)
Up Johnson came, with hundreds at his back,
   Exclaiming:—'Juan! Juan! On, boy! brace
Your arm, and I'll bet Moscow to a dollar
That you and I will win St George's collar.*

'The Seraskier is knocked upon the head,
   But the stone bastion still remains, wherein
The old Pacha sits among some hundreds dead,
   Smoking his pipe quite calmly 'midst the din
Of our artillery and his own: 'tis said
   Our killed, already piled up to the chin,
Lie round the battery, but still it batters,
And grape in volleys, like a vineyard, scatters.

'Then up with me!'—But Juan answered, 'Look
   Upon this child—I saved her—must not leave
Her life to chance; but point me out some nook
   Of safety, where she less may shrink and grieve,
And I am with you.'—Whereon Johnson took
   A glance around—and shrugged—and twitched his sleeve
And black silk neckcloth—and replied, 'You're right;
Poor thing! what's to be done? I'm puzzled quite.'

Byron's meeting with Ali Pasha was one of the highlights of his Grand Tour. He was enthralled by the tyrant's exotic court and fascinated by the Turks' sexual ambivalence. Ali's actions led to the War of Greek Independence.

Said Juan—'Whatsoever is to be
　　Done, I'll not quit her till she seems secure
Of present life a good deal more than we.'—
　　Quoth Johnson—'*Neither* will I quite ensure;
But at the least *you* may die gloriously.'—
　　Juan replied—'At least I will endure
Whate'er is to be borne—but not resign
This child, who is parentless and therefore mine.'

Johnson said—'Juan, we've no time to lose;
　　The child's a pretty child—a very pretty—
I never saw such eyes—and hark! now choose
　　Between your fame and feelings, pride and pity;—
—Hark! how the roar increases!—no excuse
　　Will serve when there is plunder in a city;—
I should be loth to march without you, but,
By God! we'll be too late for the first cut.'

But Juan was immoveable; until
　　Johnson, who really loved him in his way,
Picked out amongst his followers with some skill
　　Such as he thought the least given up to prey;
And swearing if the infant came to ill
　　That they should all be shot on the next day;
But, if she were delivered safe and sound,
They should at least have fifty roubles round;

And all allowances besides of plunder
　　In fair proportion with their comrades;—then
Juan consented to march on through thunder,
　　Which thinned at every step their ranks of men:
And yet the rest rushed eagerly—no wonder,
　　For they were heated by the hope of gain,
A thing which happens every where each day—
No Hero trusteth wholly to half-pay.

Byron immortalized his affair with Theresa Macri in his lyric "The Maid of Athens". This caught the popular imagination and associated Byron's concern for Greek freedom with his exotic love life.

Wellington could already see the necessity for decisive action in the Peninsula, and he took it. He reformed the army and turned confusion into bloody victory. As Byron pursued his pilgrimage, watching, commenting, criticizing, the future of a Europe he was to find intolerably autocratic was being largely shaped by the other Englishman's ambition. "I . . . went abroad and took command of the Army," Wellington wrote, "and never returned, or even quitted the field, till the nations of the Peninsular . . . were delivered from the French armies: till I had invaded France . . . till the general peace was signed at Paris; and the British cavalry, sent by sea to Portugal, Spain and the south of France, marched home across France, and embarked for England in the ports of France in the British Channel." Against such an absolute conviction that Britain must return Europe to the status quo, Byron was to shape his own revolutionizing and personal myth.

WELLINGTON

"I have simplified my politics into an utter detestation of all existing governments"

Byron's love of liberty sprang from his own exuberance. So did his savage capacity for hatred, a quality in which he approaches his revered 18th century master Pope. The illiberal views of Wellington, the "Iron Duke", roused Byron's wholesale contempt. At the start of the ninth canto of *Don Juan* he reveals the vanquisher of Napoleon as petty, authoritarian, money-grubbing and vain. Above all, Wellington is shown to be the man whose victories could have made Europe free, but who deliberately chose to re-enslave her to her old tyrants.

Though Wellington had saved Europe from Napoleon, Byron despised the "Iron Duke" for his autocratic manner. Wellington became the butt of some of his sharpest satire on a Europe settling back into tyranny.

Oh, Wellington! (or 'Vilainton'—for Fame
    Sounds the heroic syllables both ways;
France could not even conquer your great name,
    But punned it down to this facetious phrase—
Beating or beaten she will laugh the same)—
    You have obtained great pensions and much praise;
Glory like yours should any dare gainsay,
Humanity would rise, and thunder 'Nay!'*

I don't think that you used Kinnaird quite well
    In Marinêt's affair—in fact 'twas shabby,*
And like some other things won't do to tell
    Upon your tomb in Westminster's old abbey.
Upon the rest 'tis not worth while to dwell,
    Such tales being for the tea hours of some tabby;
But though your years as *man* tend fast to zero,
In fact your Grace is still but a *young Hero.*

Though Britain owes (and pays you too) so much,
    Yet Europe doubtless owes you greatly more:
You have repaired Legitimacy's crutch,—
    A prop not quite so certain as before:
The Spanish, and the French, as well as Dutch,
    Have seen, and felt, how strongly you *restore*;
And Waterloo has made the world your debtor—
(I wish your bards would sing it rather better).

You are 'the best of cut-throats:'—do not start;*
    The phrase is Shakespeare's, and not misapplied:—
War's a brain-spattering, windpipe-slitting art,
    Unless her cause by Right be sanctified.
If you have acted *once* a generous part,
    The World, not the World's masters, will decide,
And I shall be delighted to learn who,
Save you and yours, have gained by Waterloo?

I am no flatterer—you've supped full of flattery:
    They say you like it too—'tis no great wonder:
He whose whole life has been assault and battery,
    At last may get a little tired of thunder;
And swallowing eulogy much more than satire, he
    May like being praised for every lucky blunder;
Called 'Saviour of the Nations'—not yet saved,
And Europe's Liberator—still enslaved.

I've done. Now go and dine from off the plate
    Presented by the Prince of the Brazils,
And send the sentinel before your gate
    A slice or two from your luxurious meals:
He fought, but has not fed so well of late.
    Some hunger too they say the people feels:—
There is no doubt that you deserve your ration,
But pray give back a little to the nation.

I don't mean to reflect—a man so great as
    You, my Lord Duke! is far above reflection.
The high Roman fashion too of Cincinnatus,*
    With modern history has but small connection:
Though as an Irishman you love potatoes,
    You need not take them under your direction;
And half a million for your Sabine farm*
Is rather dear!—I'm sure I mean no harm.

This fine portrait of Byron and his servant by the fashionable painter George Sanders was commissioned by the poet as he was setting out on the Grand Tour.

Great men have always scorned great recompenses:
  Epaminondas saved his Thebes, and died,
Not leaving even his funeral expenses:
  George Washington had thanks and nought beside,
Except the all-cloudless Glory (which few men's is)
  To free his country: Pitt too had his pride,
And, as a high-soul'd Minister of State, is
Renowned for ruining Great Britain gratis.

Never had mortal Man such opportunity,
  Except Napoleon, or abused it more:
You might have freed fall'n Europe from the Unity
  Of Tyrants, and been blest from shore to shore:
And *now*—What *is* your fame? Shall the Muse tune it ye?
Now—that the rabble's first vain shouts are o'er?
Go, hear it in your famished Country's cries!
Behold the World! and curse your victories!

Byron spent some of the happiest days of his Grand Tour at the Franciscan Convent in Athens. He was now on his own and could enjoy the affection of the schoolboys there. In England sodomy was punishable by death.

It was time to explore this further, and he sailed from Spain to Malta. Here he formed one of countless "eternal" attachments—in this case for Constance Spenser Smith. But his mind was troubled, and observers began to notice the typical features of Byronic melancholy. He had already written a will leaving an annuity to Robert Rushton. Now he sent the boy back to England. He was himself bound for the illicit pleasures of Turkey and Greece. The Levant, he wrote knowingly, "is too dangerous a state for boys to enter".

Byron's travels in the eastern Mediterranean were to make him a poet and shape many of his interests as a man. It was a fateful, enriching encounter. On his first day, as the *Spider* anchored off Patras, Byron glimpsed the little town of Missolonghi. Here, 15 years later, he was to die in the cause of Greek freedom. Now, however, he must meet the Greeks' Turkish masters.

The travellers made their way through the vibrant but impoverished landscape towards Jannina, Hobhouse grumbling at the discomfort, but rousing himself to some enthusiasm as he spied the domes and minarets of the city glittering through the cypress groves. He and Byron were to travel through the country under the protection of Ali Pasha, a local client prince of the Sultan, and as they entered the suburbs of his capital they gauged the measure of the man: hanging from a tree were the arm and torn side of a victim of Ali's justice. Ali ruled his considerable dominions by numerous acts of cruelty and deception, and he regarded himself as virtually independent of the capital of the Turkish empire at Constantinople. In this he was wrong, but for the moment he had gone "to finish a little war" and begged his distinguished visitors to join him at his castle. This was more than courtesy. Ali was wholly a politician and he wanted to counter French influence in the Ionian Sea. The arrival of this young English lord and his friend suited his purpose well.

Byron and Hobhouse were now in a landscape no other Englishman besides Leake (the starchy British Resident) had ever traversed, and the excitement and dangerous novelty reached a climax in their reception at Tepelene. This Byron described in a letter to his mother. It is a masterly example of travel writing, alive with colour and movement, the beating of kettledrums and the wailing cries of the imams.

ADVENTURES IN TURKEY

"one day in the palace of the Pacha & the next perhaps in the most miserable hut of the Mountains"

Byron wrote this letter to his mother in 1809. It is a masterly picture of a young traveller's excitement. The letter is enthusiastic and vivid, full of life, humour and self-mockery. It is also carefully designed to flatter Mrs Byron. It was to be some years, however, before Byron discovered that this artfully casual tone was also the true voice of his poetry.

When I reached Yanina the capital after a journey of three days over the mountains through a country of the most picturesque beauty, I found that Ali Pacha was with his army in Illyricum besieging Ibraham Pacha in the castle of Berat.—He had heard that an Englishman of rank was in his dominions & had left orders in Yanina with the Commandant to provide a house & supply me with every kind of necessary, *gratis*, & though I have been allowed to make presents to the slaves &c. I have not been permitted to pay for a single article of household consumption.—I rode out on the viziers horses & saw the palaces of himself & grandsons, they are splendid but too much ornamented with silk & gold.—I then went over the mountains through Zitza a village with a Greek monastery (where I slept on my return) in the most beautiful Situation (always

excepting Cintra in Portugal) I ever beheld.—In nine days
I reached Tepaleen, our Journey was much prolonged by
the torrents that had fallen from the mountains &
intersected the roads. I shall never forget the singular scene
on entering Tepaleen at five in the afternoon as the Sun was
going down, it brought to my recollection (with some
change of *dress* however) Scott's description of Branksome
Castle in his lay, & the feudal system.—The Albanians in
their dresses (the most magnificent in the world, consisting
of a long *white kilt*, gold worked cloak, crimson velvet gold
laced jacket & waistcoat, silver mounted pistols &
daggers,) the Tartars with their high caps, the Turks in
their vast pelisses & turbans, the soldiers & black slaves
with the horses, the former stretched in groupes in an
immense open gallery in front of the palace, the latter
placed in a kind of cloister below it, two hundred steeds
ready caparisoned to move in a moment, couriers entering
or passing out with dispatches, the kettle drums beating,
boys calling the hour from the minaret of the mosque,
altogether, with the singular appearance of the building
itself, formed a new & delightful spectacle to a
stranger.—I was conducted to a very handsome apartment
& my health enquired after by the vizier's secretary "a la
mode de Turque."—The next day I was introduced to Ali
Pacha, I was dressed in a full suit of Staff uniform with a
very magnificent sabre &c.——The Vizier received me in
a large room paved with marble, a fountain was playing in
the centre, the apartment was surrounded by scarlet
Ottomans, he received me *standing*, a wonderful
compliment from a Mussulman, & made me sit down on
his right hand.—I have a Greek interpreter for general use,
but a Physician of Ali's named [Seculario?] who
understands Latin acted for me on this occasion.—His first
question was why at so early an age I left my country? (the
Turks have no idea of travelling for amusement) he then
said the English Minister Capt. Leake had told him I was of
a great family, & desired his respects to my mother, which
I now in the name of Ali Pacha present to you. He said he
was certain I was a man of birth because I had small ears,
curling hair, & little white hands, and expressed himself
pleased with my appearance & garb.—He told me to
consider him as a father whilst I was in Turkey, & said he
looked on me as his son.—Indeed he treated me like a

child, sending me almonds & sugared sherbet, fruit &
sweetmeats 20 times a day.—He begged me to visit him
often, and at night when he was more at leisure—I then
after coffee & pipes retired for the first time. I saw him
thrice afterwards.—It is singular that the Turks who have
no hereditary dignities & few great families except the
Sultan's pay so much respect to birth, for I found my
pedigree more regarded than even my title.—His Highness
is 60 years old, very fat & not tall, but with a fine face, light
blue eyes & a white beard, his manner is very kind & at the
same time he possesses that dignity which I find universal
amongst the Turks.——He has the appearance of any
thing but his real character, for he is a remorseless tyrant,
guilty of the most horrible cruelties, very brave & so good
a general, that they call him the Mahometan
Buonaparte.—Napolean has twice offered to make him
King of Epirus, but he prefers the English interest &
abhors the French as he himself told me, he is of so much
consequence that he is much courted by both, the
Albanians being the most warlike subjects of the Sultan,
though Ali is only nominally dependent on the Porte. He
has been a mighty warrior, but is as barbarous as he is
successful, roasting rebels &c. &c.—Bonaparte sent him a
snuffbox with his picture[;] he said the snuffbox was very
well, but the picture he could excuse, as he neither liked *it*
nor the *original*.—His ideas of judging of a man's birth
from ears, hands &c. were curious enough.—To me he
was indeed a father, giving me letters, guards & every
possible accommodation.—Our next conversations were of
war & travelling, politics & England.—He called my
Albanian soldier who attends me, and told him to protect
me at all hazards.—His name is Viscillie & like all the
Albanians he is brave, rigidly honest, & faithful, but they
are cruel though not treacherous, & have several vices, but
no meannesses.—They are perhaps the most beautiful race
in point of countenance in the world, their women are
sometimes handsome also, but they are treated like slaves,
beaten & in short complete beasts of burthen, they plough,
dig & sow, I found them carrying wood & actually
repairing the highways, the men are all soldiers, & war &
the chase their sole occupations, the women are the
labourers, which after all is no great hardship in so
delightful a climate, yesterday the 11th. Nov. I bathed in

the sea, today It is so hot that I am writing in a shady room of the English Consul's with three doors wide open no fire or even *fireplace* in the house except for culinary purposes.—The Albanians [11 lines crossed out] Today I saw the remains of the town of *Actium* near which Anthony lost the world in a small bay where two frigates could hardly manoeuvre, a broken wall is the sole remnant. — On another part of the gulph stand the ruins of Nicopolis built by Augustus in honour of his victory.———Last night I was at a Greek marriage, but this & 1000 things more I have neither time or *space* to describe.—I am going tomorrow with a guard of fifty men to Patras in the Morea, & thence to Athens where I shall winter.—Two days ago I was nearly lost in a Turkish ship of war owing to the ignorance of the captain & crew though the storm was not violent.—Fletcher yelled after his wife, the Greeks called on all the Saints, the Mussulmen on Alla, the Captain burst into tears & ran below deck telling us to call on God, the sails were split, the mainyard shivered, the wind blowing fresh, the night setting in, & all our chance was to make Corfu which is in possession of the French, or (as Fletcher *pathetically* termed it) "a *watery* grave."—I did what I could to console Fletcher but finding him incorrigible wrapped myself up in my Albanian capote (an immense cloak) & lay down on deck to wait the worst, I have learnt to philosophize on my travels, & if I had not, complaint was useless.—Luckily the wind abated & only drove us on the coast of Suli on the main land where we landed & proceeded by the help of the natives to Prevesa again; but I shall not trust Turkish Sailors in future, though the Pacha had ordered one of his own galleots to take me to Patras, I am therefore going as far as Missolonghi by land & there have only to cross a small gulph to get to Patras.—Fletcher's next epistle will be full of marvels, we were one night lost for *nine* hours in the mountains in a *thunder* storm, & since nearly wrecked, in both cases Fletcher was sorely bewildered, from apprehensions of famine & banditti in the first, & drowning in the second instance.—His eyes were a little hurt by the lightning or crying (I dont know which) but are now recovered.—When you write address to me at Mr. *Strané's* English Consul, Patras, Morea.———I could tell you I know not how many incidents that I think would amuse you, but they crowd on my mind as much as would swell my paper, & I can neither arrange them in the one, or put them down on the other, except in the greatest confusion & in my usual horrible hand.—I like the Albanians much, they are not all Turks, some tribes are Christians, but their religion makes little difference in their manner or conduct; they are esteemed the best troops in the Turkish service.—I lived on my route two days at once, & three days again in a Barrack at Salora, & never found soldiers so tolerable, though I have been in the garrisons of Gibraltar & Malta & seen Spanish, French, Sicilian & British troops in abundance, I have had nothing stolen, & was always welcome to their provision & milk.—Not a week ago, an Albanian chief (every village has its chief who is called Primate) after helping us out of the Turkish Galley in her distress, feeding us & lodging my suite consisting of Fletcher, a Greek, Two Albanians, a Greek Priest and my companion Mr. Hobhouse, refused any compensation but a written paper stating that I was well received, & when I pressed him to accept a few sequins, "no, he replied, I wish you to love me, not to pay me." These were his words.—It is astonishing how far money goes in this country, while I was in the capital, I had nothing to pay by the vizier's order, but since, though I have generally had sixteen horses & generally 6 or 7 men, the expence has not been *half* as much as staying only 3 weeks in Malta, though Sir A. Ball the governor gave me a house for nothing, & I had only *one servant*.—By the bye I expect Hanson to remit regularly, for I am not about to stay in this province for ever, let him write to me at Mr. Strané's, English Consul, Patras.——The fact is, the fertility of the plains are wonderful, & specie is scarce, which makes this remarkable cheapness.—I am now going to Athens to study modern Greek which differs much from the ancient though radically similar.—I have no desire to return to England, nor shall I unless compelled by absolute want & Hanson's neglect, but I shall not enter Asia for a year or two as I have much to see in Greece & I may perhaps cross into Africa at least the Ægyptian part.—Fletcher like all Englishmen is very much dissatisfied, though a little reconciled to the Turks by a present of 80 piastres from the vizier, which if you consider every thing & the value of specie here is nearly worth ten guineas English.—He has suffered nothing but from *cold*, heat, & vermin which those who lie in cottages & cross mountains in a wild country must undergo, & of which I have equally partaken with himself, but he is not valiant, & is afraid of robbers & tempests.——I have no one to be remembered to in England, & wish to hear nothing from it but that you are well, & a letter or two on business from Hanson, whom you may tell to write.——I will write when I can, & beg you to believe me,

yr affect. Son
BYRON

P.S.——I have some very "magnifique" Albanian dresses the only expensive articles in this country they cost 50 guineas each & have so much gold they would cost in England two hundred.——I have been introduced to Hussein Bey, & Mahmout Pacha both little boys grandchildren of Ali at Yanina. They are totally unlike our lads, have painted complexions like rouged dowagers, large black eyes & features pefectly regular. They are the prettiest little animals I ever saw, & are broken into the court ceremonies already, the Turkish salute is a slight inclination of the head with the hand on the breast, intimates always kiss, Mahmout is ten years old & hopes to see me again, we are friends without understanding each other, like many other folks, though from a different cause;——he has given me a letter to his father in the Morea, to whom I have also letters from Ali *Pacha*.——

But the oriental flavour shows more than a gift for literary pictorialism. Byron conveys the feelings of a young man fascinated by an exotic and wicked power and flattered by an intimacy that shades into the ambiguous. This combination is significant. As Byron stood before the wily despot, dressed in his scarlet "Windsor uniform" and with thoughts of *Childe Harold* already forming in his mind, so he became the first 19th century example of the literary pilgrim to the Orient.

Like the later French romantic writers Chateaubriand and Lamartine, Flaubert and de Nerval, Byron's journey to the East was partly a private pilgrimage into the exotic recesses of his own mind, a pilgrimage stimulated by the harsh landscape, the unfamiliar customs and the suggestions of a lush sexuality at once perverse and extreme.

European restrictions broke down in the face of a world both barbarous and highly civilized. Byron was fascinated. "In England the vices in fashion are whoring & drinking, in Turkey, Sodomy and smoking, we prefer a girl and a bottle, they a pipe and a pathic." Byron's flippancy hid deeper interests however. The cruel and the illicit were to find expression in his *Oriental Tales*, which were to be translated from Spain to St Petersburg, influencing artists as diverse as Pushkin and Verdi. But the political element, largely unrecognized for the moment, was soon to be just as important. When Byron saw the effects of Turkish rule in Greece his revolutionary ideals were set forever.

He and Hobhouse now made their adventurous way south to Athens, adding a storm and a dinner with brigands to Byron's fund of traveller's tales and poetic images. His awareness of the Greeks' barely concealed longing for freedom was heightened on Christmas Eve 1809 when he entered Athens. The distant view of the Acropolis impressed him, but its serenity was in sharp contrast to the cowed inhabitants of the dirty streets surrounding it. The golden, classical age of Pericles had vanished and, with it, liberty. "Where are thy men of might? thy grand in soul?" Nowhere, it seemed. Worse, the last vestiges of the Greeks' ancient culture were being plundered by those with whom Liberty herself supposedly dwelt. Lord Elgin was shipping the marbles of the Parthenon back to London. Byron revolted against what he saw as the crudest form of cultural imperialism. His loathing of the established order in England combined with his love of Greek independence.

THE ELGIN MARBLES

"I know no motive which can excuse, no name which can designate, the perpetrators of this dastardly devastation"

Centuries of Turkish rule in Greece had sunk many of the Greeks themselves in political apathy. From the first, Byron was deeply sympathetic to those who yearned for independence. However, when he discovered that the English, the supposed guardians of freedom, were looting the remains of the Greek's ancient inheritance, he was appalled. In these bitter lines from the second canto of *Childe Harold's Pilgrimage*, he satirizes Lord Elgin, who was removing the threatened sculptures of the Parthenon and transporting them to London where they remain.

Here let me sit upon this massy stone,
The marble column's yet unshaken base;
Here, son of Saturn! was thy fav'rite throne:
Mightiest of many such! Hence let me trace
The latent grandeur of thy dwelling place.
It may not be: nor ev'n can Fancy's eye
Restore what Time hath labour'd to deface.
Yet these proud pillars claim no passing sigh,
Unmov'd the Moslem sits, the light Greek carols by.

But who, of all the plunderers of yon fane
On high, where Pallas linger'd, loth to flee
The latest relic of her ancient reign;
The last, the worst, dull spoiler, who was he?*
Blush, Caledonia! such thy son could be!
England! I joy no child he was of thine:
Thy free-born men should spare what once was free;
Yet they could violate each saddening shrine,
And bear these altars o'er the long-reluctant brine.

But most the modern Pict's ignoble boast,
To rive what Goth, and Turk, and Time hath spar'd:
Cold as the crags upon his native coast,
His mind as barren and his heart as hard,
Is he whose head conceiv'd, whose hand prepar'd,
Aught to displace Athena's poor remains:
Her sons too weak the sacred shrine to guard,
Yet felt some portion of their mother's pains,
And never knew, till then, the weight of Despot's chains.

This portrait of Byron was painted by Richard Westall in 1813. In its dreamy evocation of melancholy passion it exactly captures an aspect of Childe Harold that accounted for Byron's popularity in Regency England.

What! shall it e'er be said by British tongue,
Albion was happy in Athena's tears?*
Though in thy name the slaves her bosom wrung,
Tell not the deed to blushing Europe's ears;
The ocean queen, the free Britannia bears
The last poor plunder from a bleeding land:
Yes she, whose gen'rous aid her name endears,
Tore down those remnants with a Harpy's hand,
Which envious Eld forbore, and tyrants left to stand.*

The ruins of the Parthenon provided the classically educated of Byron's time with an image of the glory that was Greece. For Byron, they were a symbol of a nation in servitude.

Where was thine Aegis, Pallas! that appall'd
Stern Alaric and Havoc on their way?*
Where Peleus' son? whom Hell in vain enthrall'd,
His shade from Hades upon that dread day,
Bursting to light in terrible array!
What? could not Pluto spare the chief once more,
To scare a second robber from his prey?
Idly he wander'd on the Stygian shore,
Nor now preserv'd the walls he lov'd to shield before.

Cold is the heart, fair Greece! that looks on thee,
Nor feels as lovers o'er the dust they lov'd;
Dull is the eye that will not weep to see
Thy walls defac'd, thy mouldering shrines remov'd
By British hands, which it had best behov'd
To guard those relics ne'er to be restor'd.
Curst be the hour when from their isle they rov'd,
And once again thy hapless bosom gor'd,
And snatch'd thy shrinking Gods to northern climes abhorr'd!

Hobhouse was less indignant. He thought the Elgin marbles would be of great use to English artists and antiquaries. He rather hoped to be counted among the latter himself, an attitude that was beginning to irritate Byron. At Marathon, Hobhouse busied himself with measuring the site and plotting out the course of this antique battle for liberty. Byron, with aristocratic disdain, seemed merely to stare at the view:

The mountains look on Marathon—
    And Marathon looks on the sea;
And musing here an hour alone,
    I dreamed that Greece might still be free.

There are different types of truth and sometimes they must part company. Byron and Hobhouse would soon do so, but for the moment, they made their way to Smyrna, Ephesus and Constantinople, as well as visiting the plain of Troy. On 3 May, while their ship rode at anchor, Byron swam the Hellespont, a distance of slightly over four miles. It was a feat of which he was often to boast. However, the warmth of his stay in the Greek capital—he was having a mild affair with Theresa Macri, the daughter of his landlady whom he was to make famous as the "Maid of Athens"—had confirmed him in his dislike for the crushing barbarism of Turkish rule. Besides, news from home was bad: Hanson was finding it difficult to pay the mounting interest on Byron's debts; worse, "the *Edleston* is accused of indecency", in other words of homosexual activities. Byron was deeply depressed. Perhaps, too, he was worried personally. Certainly he badly needed to be on his own. He finally parted with Hobhouse and returned to Athens.

But the spontaneity had gone out of the life he had enjoyed there. Mrs Macri was happy enough that an English lord should make advances to her daughter, but she now wanted these to lead further. Byron was not so easily trapped: "the old woman, Theresa's mother, was mad enough to imagine I was going to marry the girl; but I have better amusement".

That amusement was Eustathios Georgiou. Even Fletcher, who had been privy to many of his master's less orthodox affairs, was put out by the parasol with which the boy protected his peach-like skin. However, Fletcher was soon to be sent home, leaving Byron to explore this side of his nature alone, and he was later to boast of over 200 conquests.

SONG

*"The old woman . . . was mad
enough to imagine I was going
to marry the girl"*

This delightful and deservedly famous lyric was written for Theresa Macri, whom it immortalized as the "Maid of Athens". The depth of Byron's attachment to Theresa is uncertain, but the affair itself became a popular element in the Byron myth.

Maid of Athens, ere we part,
Give, oh, give me back my heart!
Or, since that has left my breast,
Keep it now, and take the rest!
Hear my vow before I go,
Ζωή μου, σᾶς ἀγαπῶ.*

This Bonnington watercolour of a Turk reclining suggests the oriental atmosphere Byron discovered and popularized.

By those tresses unconfin'd,
Woo'd by each Aegean wind;
By those lids whose jetty fringe
Kiss thy soft cheeks' blooming tinge;
By those wild eyes like the roe,
Ζωή μου, σὰς ἀγαπῶ.

By that lip I long to taste;
By that zone-encircl'd waist;
By all the token-flowers that tell
What words can never speak so well;
By Love's alternate joy and woe,
Ζωή μου, σὰς ἀγαπῶ.

Maid of Athens! I am gone:
Think of me, sweet! when alone.
Though I fly to Istambol,
Athens holds my heart and soul:
Can I cease to love thee? No!
Ζωή μου, σὰς ἀγαπῶ.

David Allan portrays Byron with the "Maid of Athens" in a picture that conveys an indolent and sensual exoticism.

Meanwhile, he went with Eustathios to visit the son of Ali Pasha (another lover of boys), but Byron eventually became so exasperated with his Greek friend that he sent him home. On his own return to Athens, Byron moved out of the troublesome Macri household and took up residence in the Capuchin monastery at the foot of the Acropolis. Here, amid the laughter and foreign tongues of the boys at the monastery school, he fell quite seriously in love. Nicolo Giraud was 15. For Byron, a period of carefree happiness ensued as he learned Italian with his new friend and went bathing with him in the Piraeus. Nicolo, he assured Hobhouse, swam nude.

The year Byron spent in Athens was one of the most untroubled of his life. He had been avid for experience and found adventure. Childe Harold, the cynical and satiated Regency buck of his poem, had travelled Europe from Lisbon to Turkey. A continent had come between Byron and his alter ego. Now, beneath the Acropolis, he found pleasure without guilt. He also glimpsed his cause. Across the Iberian peninsula people were struggling for their freedom. Could not the Greeks as well? He was unsure. In his poem he urged them to self-expression; in his notes to the poem he suggested that foreigners alone could emancipate the country. But neither poetry nor notes alone cause revolutions. In his palace at Jannina, the despotic Pasha still mutilated his victims. It was to be 11 years before his own scheming and defeated head was sent as a present to the Sultan and the War of Greek Independence could begin. Meanwhile the Greeks themselves could only wait, plot, and watch the English, who were to save them, ravaging their past. It was time for Childe Harold to return home. He boarded the *Hydra* for Malta, sailing with the last shipment of the Elgin marbles. The draft of his poem was in his pocket. But one further tone, one more experience was wanting before his image was complete and Byron could wake to find himself famous.

BYRONIC MELANCHOLY

*"it was one of the deadliest and heaviest feelings
of my life to feel that I was no longer a boy"*

The reverse of Byron's exuberance was an intense inwardness and a despair sometimes bordering on panic, which became a constant theme in his work. In the first two cantos of *Childe Harold's Pilgrimage*, for example, he offers a picture of a satiated and disillusioned hero. This brief note written in Malta shows how intensely Byron experienced these feelings himself.

1st At twenty three the best of life is over and its bitters double. 2ndly I have seen mankind in various Countries and find them equally despicable, if anything the Balance is rather in favour of the Turks. 3dly I am sick at heart.

"Me jam nec *faemina* . . .
Nec *Spes animi credula mutui*
Nec *certare* juvat *Mero*"*

4thly A man who is lame of one leg is in a state of bodily inferiority which increases with years and must render his old age more peevish & intolerable. Besides in another existence I expect to have *two* if not *four* legs by way of compensation.
5thly I grow selfish & misanthropical, something like the "jolly Miller" "I care for nobody no not I and Nobody cares for me."
6thly My affairs at home and abroad are gloomy enough.
7thly I have outlived all my appetites and most of my vanities aye even the vanity of authorship.

"*Mad, bad and dangerous to know*"

He returned to discover grief. While he was trying to publish *Childe Harold* and sort out his financial worries, a servant arrived to inform Byron that his mother was seriously ill. Such was the gravity of Byron's financial position that he had to turn to Hanson for the money to cover his journey to Newstead, but before he could set off he was told that Mrs Byron was dead. The love Byron could not show in life expressed itself in sorrow. He was unable even to follow his mother's coffin to the church. Later, as he sorted through her effects, he discovered a bound volume of his reviews. Mrs Byron, gauche and unloving as she so often seemed, had written notes in the margins prophesying her son's greatness.

News then reached him that Matthews had died—the brilliant and witty "Citoyen" had got tangled in weeds while out swimming and died in grotesque agony. But the cruellest blow was the death of Edleston. It seemed that the supports of his youth were falling one by one. Though Byron recognized that the affair had long been over—his hopes that he and the boy might live together had been as transient as boyhood itself—his imagination was once more plagued by loss and remembered joy. This time, he sought relief in verse.

It was impossible that Byron should publicly express his intense feelings for a boy, especially one who had perhaps fallen foul of the law. So, in the brooding isolation of Newstead, he transformed Edleston into "Thyrza" and wrote lyrics of a taut power he had not previously achieved. His grief even spilled over into his revisions of *Childe Harold*. The cynical hints of atheism Byron had expressed in his Turkish drafts of the poem now gave way to a chastened, questioning hope of immortality. But it was the grief—absolute, mysterious, numbing—that added the last intriguing shadow to the portrait of the Childe and so gave pathos to the Byron myth. John Murray, advised by the best critics of the poem's qualities, prepared his presses. Byron, meanwhile, returned to thoughts of Greece.

TO THYRZA

"Thou too art gone thou loved and lovely one!"

Byron's intense attachment to John Edleston, a Cambridge choirboy, was the first of a number of such relationships. Edleston's death affected the poet profoundly. Byron disguised the nature of his passion by giving the boy the biblical and female name of "Thyrza" in his elegies to him. The secrecy and depth of passion these poems reveal were an essential aspect of the mystique of "Childe Harold".

One struggle more, and I am free
 From pangs that rend my heart in twain;
One last long sigh to love and thee,
 Then back to busy life again.
It suits me well to mingle now
 With things that never pleas'd before:
Though every joy is fled below,
 What future grief can touch me more?

Then bring me wine, the banquet bring;
 Man was not form'd to live alone:
I'll be that light unmeaning thing
 That smiles with all, and weeps with none.
It was not thus in days more dear,
 It never would have been, but thou
Hast fled, and left me lonely here;
 Thou'rt nothing, all are nothing now.

In vain my lyre would lightly breathe!
 The smile that sorrow fain would wear
But mocks the woe that lurks beneath,
 Like roses o'er a sepulchre.
Though gay companions o'er the bowl
 Dispel awhile the sense of ill;
Though pleasure fires the madd'ning soul,
 The heart—the heart is lonely still!

On many a lone and lovely night
 It sooth'd to gaze upon the sky;
For then I deem'd the heav'nly light
 Shone sweetly on thy pensive eye:
And oft I thought at Cynthia's noon,*
 When sailing o'er the Aegean wave,
'Now Thyrza gazes on that moon—'
 Alas, it gleam'd upon her grave!

When stretch'd on fever's sleepless bed,
 And sickness shrunk my throbbing veins,
'Tis comfort still', I faintly said,
 'That Thyrza cannot know my pains':
Like freedom to the time-worn slave,
 A boon 'tis idle then to give;
Relenting nature vainly gave
 My life, when Thyrza ceas'd to live.

My Thyrza's pledge in better days,
 When love and life alike were new!
How different now thou meet'st my gaze!
 How ting'd by time with sorrow's hue!
The heart that gave itself with thee
 Is silent—ah, were mine as still!
Though cold as e'en the dead can be,
 It feels, it sickens with the chill.

Thou bitter pledge! thou mournful token!
 Though painful, welcome to my breast!
Still, still, preserve that love unbroken,
 Or break the heart to which thou'rt prest!
Time tempers love, but not removes,
 More hallow'd when its hope is fled:
Oh! what are thousand living loves
 To that which cannot quit the dead?

He was also preparing for his first venture into English politics. Harold, the critic of Tory absolutism, must have his say, and an issue lay near to hand.

The war with France had severely curtailed the markets for English goods. Mechanical innovation had proceeded apace however, and the gulf had widened dangerously between the manual labourers and those who owned the machinery. An unquestioning belief in market forces led rival manufacturers to think there would always be a sale for their goods, particularly if machines could make them ever more cheaply. The result was widespread bankruptcy, unemployment, and disaffection. This was particularly true of the stocking-weaving district of Nottinghamshire, where a new technique which made more efficient use of existing machinery had been developed. As a result, wages had fallen, and among the 50,000 families reduced to starvation the mythical "King Ludd" emerged as a potential saviour. Ludd was a shadowy figure whom it was believed was responsible for organizing the well-drilled raiding parties who began smashing the manufacturers' looms. Byron's gothic pile of Newstead lay near the heart of that unfettered capitalism which was among the earliest products of the industrial revolution.

The fear of industrial unrest and insurrection was immediate and widespread. Troops were assembled at Nottingham. The Tory cabinet, confusing economic problems with issues of law and order, wished to make machine-breaking a capital offence. Byron resolved to speak against the bill. As a Whig, he saw the Tories' policies tightening like a dead man's grip. As a peer, he had a right to express his view. Though as penniless as those he claimed to support, Byron wrote to Lord Holland as one titled gentleman to another. Lord Holland was both a leader of the Whigs and the Recorder of Nottingham, which meant that he was involved on both a national and a local level. In true party tradition, an issue of liberty was to be handled by a benevolent élite. The Luddite cause appeared to concern the traditional rights to resistance, to petition, to public meeting and to association. In fact, the Luddites themselves had no such coherent policy of revolt; they were just desperately hungry men.

The Whigs, however, were a fragmented opposition. By 1811, the rights they had secured in the Glorious Revolution looked dangerously close to the ideals of the French Revolution. Liberty, equality and brotherhood were unpopular terms, and the suspension of Habeas Corpus (the right to no imprisonment without trial) was only six years away. As the owners of great estates, many of the Whigs were forced into the anomalous position of holding increasingly radical views in order to frame their policy. Byron, keen to join them, took a young man's common course; he aped their vocabulary, but in somewhat over-simplified terms.

A RADICAL IN THE HOUSE OF LORDS

"parliamentary mummeries"

When Byron returned to England from the Grand Tour he was burning with a lifelong concern for freedom and human dignity. Here, in a letter to the Whig leader Lord Holland, he expresses his outrage at the suffering inflicted on working-class people by the forces of the early Industrial Revolution. Byron was to express similar ideas when he opposed the introduction of the death penalty for machine-breakers in the House of Lords. He was soon to realize, however, that parliament was not his true political platform.

My Lord,—With my best thanks I have the honour to return the Notts letter to your Lordship.—I have read it with attention, but do not think I shall venture to avail myself of it's contents, as my view of the question differs in some measure from Mr. Coldham's.—I hope I do not wrong him, but *his* objections to ye. bill appear to me to be founded on certain apprehensions that he & his coadjutors might be mistaken for the *"original advisers"* (to quote him) of the measure.——For my own part, I consider the manufacturers* as a much injured body of men sacrificed to ye. views of certain individuals who have enriched themselves by those practices which have deprived the frame workers of employment.—For instance;—by the adoption of a certain kind of frame 1 man performs ye. work of 7–6 are thus thrown out of business.—But it is to be observed that ye. work thus done is far inferior in quality, hardly marketable at home, & hurried over with a view to exportation.—Surely, my Lord, however we may rejoice in any improvement in ye. arts which may be beneficial to mankind; we must not allow mankind to be sacrificed to improvements in Mechanism. The maintenance & well doing of ye. industrious poor is an object of greater consequence to ye. community than ye. enrichment of a few monopolists by an improvement in ye. implements of trade, which deprives ye workman of his

The oppressed working people of Nottinghamshire, organized into the Luddite movement, caused widespread fear. This cartoon shows a Luddite leader disguised as a woman, while behind is a burning factory.

bread, & renders ye. labourer "unworthy of his hire."—My own motive for opposing ye. bill is founded on it's palpablè injustice, & it's certain inefficacy—I have seen the state of these miserable men, & it is a disgrace to a civilized country.—Their excesses may be condemned, but cannot be subject of wonder.—The effect of ye. present bill would be to drive them into actual rebellion.—The few words I shall venture to offer on Thursday will be founded upon these opinions formed from my own observations on ye. spot.—By previous enquiry I am convinced these men would have been restored to employment & ye. county to tranquillity.—It is perhaps not yet too late & is surely worth the trial. It can never be too late to employ force in such circumstances.——I believe your Lordship does not coincide with me entirely on this subject, & most cheerfully & sincerely shall I submit to your superior judgment & experience, & take some other line of argument against ye. bill, or be silent altogether, should you deem it more adviseable.——Condemning, as every one must condemn the conduct of these wretches, I believe in ye. existence of grievances which call rather for pity than punishment.——I have ye honour to be with great respect, my Lord, yr. Lordship's most obedt. & obliged Servt.

BYRON

P.S.—I am a little apprehensive that your Lordship will think me too lenient towards these men, & *half* a *framebreaker myself*.

The fashionable society hostess Lady Holland was an inspiration to the liberal Whig movement at their headquarters in Holland House. It was here that she introduced Byron to Lady Caroline Lamb.

It was the vocabulary—the style—that was most important to him. Byron at this time was temperamentally unsuited to patient committee work and the shrewd, slow accumulation of allies that form so large a part of a conventional political career. He did not even care to research matters thoroughly. When he rose to make his maiden speech in the House of Lords he filled the chamber with his drawling and mannered radical oratory. The Nottinghamshire stocking weavers, he declared, having given a vivid picture of their undeserved suffering and compared them to the peoples oppressed by the Turks, were victims of greed and new machinery. This last statement, however, was simply untrue—there was no new machinery. Byron had adopted the Whig line and repeated it without question. The performance was all.

When it was over he praised himself to Tom Moore (the author of *Irish Melodies* and one of a growing number of influential literary friends) and declared how he had defended the people against a dreadful grievance with the greatest eloquence. "But what was the dreadful grievance?" Moore asked. "The grievance?" Byron repeated and paused. "Oh, *that* I forget." His politics were an attitude, and, with some loss of self-esteem, Byron came to recognize that he would never triumph in what he soon dismissed as "Parliamentary mummeries". Lord Holland also realized that his young neighbour's temperament was too volatile for a long-term parliamentary career. Byron's political influence was to be expressed in other ways and on a broader stage.

But his acquaintance with Lord Holland brought Byron one great benefit—entrance to the Whigs' glittering headquarters at Holland House. This was the centre of London's intellectual society. Here Lady Holland inspired, chivied and organized the most brilliant men of her day. Here, to the strains of the newly-introduced waltz, peers and poets discussed the latest scandal or chatted about the liberation of Spain. And here, limping in his evening dress, came Byron.

The author of *Childe Harold's Pilgrimage* was suddenly the most famous writer in England. He was the dark-haired Adonis who had visited barbarous lands, the rake who was gnawed by a secret grief. Excited conversation at once embroidered the Byron myth. What though his poem was poorly constructed and often confused. It was exciting. It was new. It said the right things. Byron was willed into instant stardom. He *was* Childe Harold. His cantos were on every table and his every post contained anonymous letters from doting female admirers. "I have read your Book & . . . think it beautiful," wrote one. "You deserve to be and shall be happy," she promised. Later, at Lady Westmoreland's, she was offered an introduction. She declined it. Byron was surrounded by other women. He was piqued. She was thrilled. His beautiful, pale face was her destiny, she wrote. Her excitement was unbounded. Bored with her husband and in the floodtide of her womanhood, she longed for an encounter with a poet whom she thought "mad—bad—and dangerous to know". At last, at Holland House, his hostess introduced Byron to the blonde and lisping Lady Caroline Lamb.

She summoned him to her home at Melbourne House. He went. He went again, and on his second visit he was observed by Lady Caroline's cousin, a quiet provincial girl with a religious bent. She thought it clever to be unimpressed by him. She confided to her diary that she had watched his lips thicken with disdain and his eyes roll in his head. This was all part of the myth. Miss Milbanke, however, would make no offering at the shrine of Childe Harold.

REGENCY LONDON

"It is a damned place"

In the eleventh canto of *Don Juan* Byron recreates with
great vividness the crowded, gilded, febrile days of his
triumph among the Whig aristocracy in London.

Then dress, then dinner, then awakes the world!
   Then glare the lamps, then whirl the wheels, then roar
Through street and square fast flashing chariots, hurled
   Like harnessed meteors; then along the floor
Chalk mimics painting; then festoons are twirled;
   Then roll the brazen thunders of the door,
Which opens to the thousand happy few
An earthly Paradise of 'Or Molu'.*

There stands the noble Hostess, nor shall sink
   With the three-thousandth curtsey; there the Waltz,
The only dance which teaches girls to think,
   Makes one in love even with its very faults.
Saloon, room, hall o'erflow beyond their brink,
   And long the latest of arrivals halts,
'Midst royal dukes and dames condemned to climb,
And gain an inch of staircase at a time.

Thrice happy he, who, after a survey
   Of the good company, can win a corner,
A door that's *in*, or boudoir *out* of the way,
   Where he may fix himself, like small 'Jack Horner,'*
And let the Babel round run as it may,
   And look on as a mourner, or a scorner,
Or an approver, or a mere spectator,
Yawning a little as the night grows later.

But she did listen to the gossip. Her friend, Mrs Knight, told her
"authentic things" about the poet that made him appear dreadfully perverted. These, no doubt, concerned the affair with Lady Caroline, who,
despite being married and a peeress, was flaunting her latest prize with
the utmost abandon. Miss Milbanke was alarmed. She thought Christian principles were at stake. She would have to meet him. There were

*The politics of liberation were much discussed at Holland House.
Goya's "The Third of May, 1808", however, is a searing comment on
revolution and repression. Just as the Bourbon tyranny was being
restored, he depicted those Spaniards murdered by the French during
their invasion of the country. He asks what hope is there for liberty.*

comforts she could bring. She found him at Lady Cowper's and talked.
She had, Byron noticed, very pretty skin. For her part, Miss Milbanke
was convinced he had a noble heart and had been perverted by unkind-
ness alone. She returned home. As she scribbled letters and entries in
her diary her mission began to form. Surely Byron repented what he
had done, even if she had no very clear idea of what this might be. It
was just that he was not strong enough to reform without her help. It
was her Christian duty to bring him succour, she decided. She believed
he was not a danger to her. She was armed in her righteousness. She
would fight spiritual wickedness in high places, and if the whole
armour of God was no more than a bodice and a fan, then with these
she would shield his passage to salvation. Meantime, she would wait.

Caroline, too, was deep in the madness of infatuation. Reckless, impulsive, a child of nature as well as of a peer, she allowed her feelings to take complete control, even lingering at the lodge gates when Byron was at parties to which she had received no invitation. At Melbourne House she cancelled the dancing, for her lame lover could not waltz and Childe Harold preferred to stay reading with her out of the crowd. Here he would grow bitter and self-pitying. Byronic melancholy reached an hysterical pitch. The yawning void of self-disgust constantly opened before him. He was deformed. He was ugly. He was sinful. Caroline's husband was a god compared to him. But she loved her poet more, didn't she? He desperately needed the stimulus of her attention and a pause was fatal. A second's delay and he would round on her. "My God, you shall pay for this, I'll wring that obstinate little heart." But she loved him better than virtue or reputation, and she flaunted her obsession with an abandon that was finally to repel him. Even her mother-in-law, Lady Melbourne, was alarmed. A great society hostess, a woman of 62 and reared with the poise of a previous age, Lady Melbourne had the wit to see that it was the volatile and motherless poet whom she might bend to her will. For her, Childe Harold was still, in part, a child. But even Lady Melbourne did not realize how far Caroline had gone in her extravagant behaviour.

For Byron, she had gone far enough. On 29 July 1812 he planned to escape from London with the faithful and dependable Hobhouse. It was midday. Hobhouse was waiting in Byron's lodgings when there was a thunderous rapping at the door. The door was opened. Out of the crowd that had gathered emerged a person in strange disguise. The figure entered and made her way to the bedroom. Here Caroline pulled off a layer of her clothes and stood revealed in her page's livery. To Hobhouse, the catastrophe of an elopement seemed inevitable. He remained calm. A maid's cloak and bonnet were fetched. There were

Holland House was the London centre of the Whig party. It was here that politicians and high society met. Byron evokes this life in the stanzas quoted on p 56.

entreaties. There were arguments. Hobhouse insisted she should leave. Her eyes blazed. She produced a knife. She would kill herself there and then. She would do no such thing. Hobhouse talked. Eventually Caroline let him accompany her to her coach wrapped in the maid's clothes, but on one condition—she must see Byron before he left town.

Eleven days later she sent him the bloodied clippings of her pubic hair. In her enthusiasm, she had cut them too close.

Byron became increasingly convinced she was mad; in addition, trapped in the rushing and gilded hell of Piccadilly, his own worries were driving him to despair. The stimulation was extreme. Across the swirl of desire, between late-night bouts of compulsive versifying, he watched his financial problems becoming ever more acute. Newstead was put up for sale. It was eventually bought by a Lancashire lawyer, but Mr Claughton at once repented his dash into landed dignity. Happier searching for anomalies in the deeds, he soon found this a useful means of deferring payment even of the deposit. Childe Harold was hopelessly broke.

LADY CAROLINE LAMB

"the cleverest, most agreeable, absurd, amiable,
perplexing, dangerous, fascinating little being that lives"

Byron's affair with Lady Caroline Lamb is one of the most famous incidents in English literary history. The meeting of these two people so openly passionate and recklessly emotional outraged polite society. The depth of Byron's feeling is clear in the hatred with which he reflects on the pain Caroline had caused him.

> A word to you of Lady [Caroline Lamb]—I speak from experience—*keep clear of her*—(I do not mean as a woman—that is all fair) she is a villainous intriguante—in every sense of the word—mad & malignant—capable of all & every mischief—above all—guard your *connections* from her society——with all her apparent absurdity there is an indefatigable & active spirit of meanness & destruction about her—which delights & often succeeds in inflicting misery—once more—I tell you keep her from all that you value—as for *yourself*—do as you please—no human being but myself knows the thorough baseness of that wretched woman—& now I have done.———

His thoughts turned briefly to the waiting Miss Milbanke, perhaps because she presented such a contrast to her wild cousin. Her aunt, Lady Melbourne, could not believe he was serious, but while the poet, hungry for sensation, found relief in the ageing arms of Lady Oxford, a correspondence began. Miss Milbanke liked letters. Lady Melbourne delicately attempted to sound out her feelings. Miss Milbanke was gently but ambiguously evasive. She could wait a little longer.

Meanwhile, the hysterical Caroline was demanding vengeance, the return of her trinkets, attention at any price. With almost operatic insanity she burned copies of her lover's letters (the originals she could not destroy) and, to the accompanying chant of little children, threw an effigy of her lover to the flames. "All bolts, bars, and silence can do to keep her away are done daily and hourly", he wrote desperately. One day she managed to get into his rooms in Albany when he was out and wrote "Remember me!" on the first page of his copy of the horror novel *Vatheck*. These enraged lines were Byron's response:

REMEMBER THEE!

Remember thee! remember thee!
  Till Lethe quench life's burning stream
Remorse and shame shall cling to thee,
  And haunt thee like a feverish dream!

Remember thee! Ay, doubt it not.
  Thy husband too shall think of thee!
By neither shalt thou be forgot,
  Thou *false* to him, thou *fiend* to me!

Byron grasped at any form of release. His letters to Lady Melbourne, full of irony and self-revelation, were one source of escape. But there was something else to which he could not as yet confess.

Byron had not seen his half-sister since his return from the Grand Tour. Augusta was now unhappily married and the mother of three children. Each found relief in the other's company. To the harassed poet, made cynical by the shyness he had once confessed to her as a schoolboy, by his lameness, and by the mauling he had received at the hands of the volatile, brilliant women of high society, Augusta's simple warmth was very welcome. She was like himself and yet was another. As he pursued his women, sheltered from the tempests of Lady Caroline, or read the priggish correspondence of Miss Milbanke (she had just invented a rival for his affections) so Augusta's family intuitions reached down to soothe Byron's deepest hurts. He began, imperceptibly, to fall in love. And with passion came guilt. Augusta's tenderness drove Byron to excitement, relief, self-torture and to verse. He was on the edge of hell and for a time he relished it. The lava of his imagination burst from its black and fiery depths. In his hastily scribbled *Oriental Tales*, the Byronic hero—the outcast wracked by nameless and dreadful crimes—first fully emerges.

---

from LARA

"Lara . . . I wrote while undressing after coming home from balls and masquerades in the year of revelry 1814"

The Byronic hero was to have a profound influence on the European romantic movement. The following passages from *Lara* are the most succinct expression of his contradictory qualities. Isolation, mystery, and hatred of mankind mingle with appearances of conviviality, and even mirth. The Byronic hero is cynical, softhearted, and corrupted by secret guilt, yet he somehow preserves the traces of a noble spirit and even the ability to inspire love. He is essentially Byron's alter ego—an image of which the poet, if not his public, soon tired.

17

In him inexplicably mix'd appeared
Much to be loved and hated, sought and feared;
Opinion varying o'er his hidden lot,
In praise or railing ne'er his name forgot;
His silence formed a theme for others' prate—
They guess'd—they gazed—they fain would know his fate.
What had he been? what was he, thus unknown,
Who walked their world, his lineage only known?
A hater of his kind? yet some would say,
With them he could seem gay amidst the gay;
But own'd that smile if oft observed and near,
Waned in its mirth and withered to a sneer;
That smile might reach his lip, but passed not by,
None e'er could trace its laughter to his eye:
Yet there was softness too in his regard,
At times a heart as not by nature hard,
But once perceiv'd, his spirit seem'd to chide
Such weakness, as unworthy of its pride,
And steel'd itself, as scorning to redeem
One doubt from others' half withheld esteem;
In self-inflicted penance of a breast

Leopold Robert's "Bandit on the Watch" conveys the romantics' fascination with the turbulent outsider, the melancholy, passionate victim of injustice, who was also the hero of Byron's "Oriental Tales".

Which tenderness might once have wrung from rest;
In vigilance of grief that would compel
The soul to hate for having lov'd too well.

*Lady Caroline Lamb described Byron as "mad—bad—
and dangerous to know". Each was fascinated by the
other. Their volatile affair was the talk of
London and destroyed Caroline's precarious sanity.*

18

There was in him a vital scorn of all:
As if the worst had fall'n which could befall
He stood a stranger in this breathing world,
An erring spirit from another hurled;
A thing of dark imaginings, that shaped
By choice the perils he by chance escaped;
But 'scaped in vain, for in their memory yet
His mind would half exult and half regret:
With more capacity for love than earth
Bestows on most of mortal mould and birth,
His early dreams of good outstripp'd the truth,
And troubled manhood followed baffled youth;
With thought of years in phantom chase misspent,
And wasted powers for better purpose lent;
And fiery passions that had poured their wrath
In hurried desolation o'er his path,
And left the better feelings all at strife
In wild reflection o'er his stormy life;
But haughty still, and loth himself to blame,
He called on Nature's self to share the shame,
And charged all faults upon the fleshly form
She gave to clog the soul, and feast the worm;
'Till he at last confounded good and ill,
And half mistook for fate the acts of will:
Too high for common selfishness he could
At times resign his own for others' good,
But not in pity, not because he ought,
But in some strange perversity of thought,
That swayed him onward with a secret pride
To do what few or none would do beside;
And this same impulse would in tempting time
Mislead his spirit equally to crime;
So much he soared beyond, or sunk beneath
The men with whom he felt condemned to breathe.
And longed by good or ill to separate
Himself from all who shared his mortal state;
His mind abhorring this had fixed her throne

Far from the world, in regions of her own;
Thus coldly passing all that passed below,
His blood in temperate seeming now would flow:
Ah! happier if it ne'er with guilt had glowed,
But ever in that icy smoothness flowed!
'Tis true, with other men their path he walked,
And like the rest in seeming did and talked,
Nor outraged Reason's rules by flaw nor start,
His madness was not of the head, but heart;
And rarely wandered in his speech, or drew
His thoughts so forth as to offend the view.

19

With all that chilling mystery of mien,
And seeming gladness to remain unseen:
He had (if 'twere not nature's boon) an art
Of fixing memory on another's heart:
It was not love perchance—nor hate—nor aught
That words can image to express the thought;
But they who saw him did not see in vain,
And once beheld, would ask of him again:
And those to whom he spake remembered well,
And on the words, however light, would dwell:
None knew, nor how, nor why, but he entwined
Himself perforce around the hearer's mind;
There he was stamp'd, in liking, or in hate,
If greeted once; however brief the date
That friendship, pity, or aversion knew,
Still there within the inmost thought he grew.
You could not penetrate his soul, but found,
Despite your wonder, to your own he wound;
His presence haunted still; and from the breast
He forced an all unwilling interest;
Vain was the struggle in that mental net,
His spirit seemed to dare you to forget!

While Caroline Lamb courted Byron with extravagant fervour, Annabella Milbanke pursued him with a zealot's fire to convert him. Their disastrous marriage led to Byron's exile from England.

Culled from Milton, Rousseau, Goethe and Schiller, the Byronic hero was mixed with a little of the villains of the popular thriller writer Mrs Radcliffe and much of Byron's own moods. Under whatever name he happens to go—Selim, Conrad, Hugo, Alp—the Byronic hero of this period is a fiery and lawless outsider, smitten with melancholy, burning with remorse, and activated by fierce political passions. He lives in the outer reaches of exotic and distant countries (usually those visited by Childe Harold) and, having either saved his women or condemned them to horrible punishments, found revenge or been revenged upon, he dies as a monk or a freedom fighter.

The likeness to Byron's image of himself in all this is obvious and was to become more so. Nowhere is it clearer than in his portrait of the Corsair. As the poet enthuses over Conrad's high and pale forehead (Lady Caroline had noted this) and goes on twice to describe his snarling lip (Miss Milbanke had noted that) there comes upon the reader the perhaps slightly uncomfortable feeling of having interrupted a very young man posing in front of the bathroom mirror.

The Byronic pose, however, was a huge commercial success. The myth was a money-spinner, and Byron became one of the first bestsellers. By the middle of 1813, *The Giaour* had run through over five editions. When *The Bride of Abydos* (originally a tale of incest) was published at the end of that year 6,000 copies were sold in a month. The success of the snarling Corsair, however, was staggering. "I sold, on the day of publication,—a thing perfectly unprecedented—10,000 copies," wrote John Murray. A little over a month later the poem had run through seven editions and sold 25,000 copies. Hair-raising advances were discussed. In 1812 Byron had been offered £600 for the first two cantos of *Childe Harold's Pilgrimage*. The following year he matched the popular poet and novelist Walter Scott with £1,000 for *The Giaour* and *The Bride of Abydos*.

Such sums reflect in part the new professionalism of publishers who had largely separated themselves from the booksellers to whom they now sold their wares at trade fairs. Murray was a leader in this development and he priced his copies high. *The Corsair* cost 6s and 6d. Byron, deeply in debt, for the moment took not a penny—it was beneath the dignity of Childe Harold to write for money.

But shrewd marketing and careful pricing are only one aspect of the making of a bestseller. It is the public who buys, and in his *Oriental Tales* Byron hit upon an eternally popular formula—exotic sex among exotic people in exotic places. The mystique and scandal that surrounded the author increased their popular appeal. In addition, there was a third element. Bestselling writers frequently draw attention to the care they have taken over their research, and Byron was no exception. He gave his readers a new vocabulary of Mamelukes, Caiques and Tophaiks (people usually like to think that what they are reading is improving) and told them that "the ataghan [is] a long dagger worn with pistols in the belt, in a metal scabbard, generally of silver; and, among the wealthier, gilt or of gold." He took such matters very seriously. "I don't care one lump of sugar for my *poetry*," he wrote to Murray, "but for my *costume* and my *correctness*; on these points I will combat lustily."

Yet none of this wholly explains the popularity of the early Byronic hero. Why was so large a public crying out for such melodrama as *Lara* and *The Corsair* provided? How was it that the Byronic hero could become a myth?

Wordsworth had given part of the answer over a decade before. He believed the horrors of the long-drawn-out Napoleonic Wars and the increasing accumulation of large numbers of people drearily employed in great cities had led to a jading of the appetite and a craving for extra-ordinary incident. Newspapers partly satisfied this hunger, and it was what Wordsworth consequently diagnosed as a "savage torpor" of the mind, a blunting of the finer faculties, that had led to a taste for "frantic novels, sickly and stupid German tragedies, and deluges of idle and extravagant stories in verse". Byron was at one with his times. Just as the paralysing inertia of inactivity drove him to lead a life of almost continual emotional frenzy, so his poems, reflecting this private dilemma, expressed the mood of the age. Publishers and literary journals had promoted an interest in literature, thus creating a greatly enlarged readership. National events had created a need for emotional release. Here was a market, and Byron supplied it. He wrote for many thousands of people who, like Jane Austen's Captain Benwick, wondered "how ranked *The Giaour* and *The Bride of Abydos*; and moreover, how *The Giaour* was to be pronounced". The myth of the Byronic hero was successful because it answered a national need.

But even in tumultuous success Byron found despair. The coarsened palates of the Regency public might tingle with the fare he offered, but the poet in him—unable as yet fully to emerge—knew that the Byronic hero was largely an attitude and, as such, was rather too often a bore. He had grave doubts about his own abilities. The poems had been written with unnerving speed after attendance at late night balls. This shows clearly. Though there are passages where the melodrama is quite effective, much of the versification is abominable. Yesterday's best sellers are rarely a good read, and Byron's *Oriental Tales* belong as much to the history of publishing as to literature. The self-acknowledged truth spilled out to Tom Moore: "I have lately begun to think that my things have been strangely over-rated," he declared, "I have done with them for ever". He went on to confess that *The Bride of Abydos* had been written in four days, *The Corsair* in ten. This "I take to be a most humiliating confession, as it proves my own want of judgement in publishing, and the public's in reading things, which cannot have stamina for permanent attention". The *Oriental Tales* had been a brilliant sensation, but they made the ensuing darkness seem more bleak.

Not only did Byron doubt his vocation but his feelings were in torment. Augusta still held him with a ruthless gentleness. He needed her and he needed to part from her. Lady Melbourne saw this clearly and was concerned. When Byron declared he wanted to fly from England with his half-sister, Lady Melbourne put a stop to it. Miss Milbanke, meanwhile, renewed her correspondence. She was a little more forthcoming now, and she shrewdly asked Byron to veil her secrets from her aunt. But Lady Melbourne was now determined to forward the affair, and she encouraged Byron in his pursuit. While Caroline still raved, Augusta lured, and new sensations were explored with Lady Frances Wedderburn Webster, Byron's interest in Miss Milbanke was expressed almost entirely by post.

But it *was* an interest. Perhaps for them both, moving towards their cruel and tragic encounter, the combination of intimacy and distance was what they most required. She could sermonize and hint, he could preen himself before his cold admirer. But whether it was through art or carelessness, it was for Miss Milbanke that Byron provided his most telling passage of self-revelation. "The great object of life is Sensation," he wrote, hoping to shock her, "—to feel we exist—even though in pain—it is this 'craving void' which drives us to Gaming—to Battle—to Travel—to intemperate but keenly felt pursuits of every description whose principal attraction is the agitation inseparable from their accomplishment."

This is a terrible statement. In his *Oriental Tales* Byron had provided a coarse image of the romantic hero; in his correspondence, with the deft spontaneity that is the measure of its genius, he outlines the agony of the romantic soul. Here, half a century before Baudelaire, is the craving for stimulus, the terror and self-destruction of the flight from blank despair. Here, too, is the mission of the Russian poet, Lermontov's rebellious hero seeking a storm as though in storms there were tranquillity. And here, above all, is Byron, the dandy of anguish and the would-be liberator of Greece, exposing his heart in a hurried sentence and finding a vocabulary that from time to time defines us all.

Miss Milbanke was shocked, as she was meant to be, but with a naïvety bordering on genius she continued to send her prim and pretty letters. She was attracted to him. Then she was unsure. He need not fear his rival, but did he really love her? Perhaps out of cowardice, he told her, rather formally, that he did. She was certain, she replied, that she ought not to accept him. But "if we could have met, all my apparent inconsistencies would have been dispelled". With the artifice of a schoolgirl, more subtly lethal than the ranting of Caroline or the siren songs of Mayfair, Miss Milbanke was getting her way. She raised hopes, she raised objections. While his other women tempted Byron to the tempest-tossed oceans of their passion, Miss Milbanke was luring him to the shallower waters of her virtue. He seemed impelled towards her. "Are the 'objections' to which you alluded insuperable?" he wrote. They were not. She was sure she could save him, and she replied to London by return of post. "I am and have long been pledged to myself to make your happiness the first object in my life." She sent a similar letter to Newstead, just in case. Byron, who was there with Augusta, went pale as he handed her the missive. Then he capitulated. Poor Annabella Milbanke—she had won.

SHE WALKS IN BEAUTY

"There is something to me very softening in the presence of a woman . . ."

This is one of Byron's most famous and perfect lyrics. It was written in June 1814 for his cousin Anne Wilmot when he saw her, for the first time, at a London party.

She walks in beauty, like the night
    Of cloudless climes and starry skies;
And all that's best of dark and bright
    Meet in her aspect and her eyes:
Thus mellow'd to that tender light
    Which heaven to gaudy day denies.

One shade the more, one ray the less,
    Had half impair'd the nameless grace
Which waves in every raven tress,
    Or softly lightens o'er her face;
Where thoughts serenely sweet express
    How pure, how dear their dwelling place.

Cruikshank's cartoon shows Byron as the leader of fashionable and rakish London, but it was engraved in the very year of his fall from grace and his enforced exile in Europe.

And on that cheek, and o'er that brow,
    So soft, so calm, yet eloquent,
The smiles that win, the tints that glow,
    But tell of days in goodness spent,
A mind at peace with all below,
    A heart whose love is innocent!

"My disastrous marriage"

Almost at once Annabella began to repent. Though their correspondence was voluminous, and Byron, in his episolary moods, was preparing to surrender his vices to her correction, she was fearful of meeting him face to face. And he, too, delayed. There were practical reasons for this—Newstead had to be sold to provide a wedding settlement, and though Claughton had paid up some of the deposit, Hanson now took it into his head to slip away on another matter. Weeks passed, and with them the deeper reasons for the delay began to emerge. Byron's strongest affections were still for Augusta. Though her sisterly feelings were largely unpossessive, the wrench was hard for him to make. Besides, what were the implications of marriage to such an obtuse and innocent girl as Annabella? Byron's ambiguous desires ran very deep, and bachelor freedom had become a habit. The young poetesses who besieged his lodgings were not always without attraction. One of them, who called herself "Eliza", charmed him into giving her £50 towards the publication of her works. To his fiancée, when they finally met, he gave nothing.

Annabella's self-consciousness made her awkward, silent. The blackness of Byron's moods frightened her. For a week the couple avoided each other's glances while under the watchful eyes of her parents. He did not love her, she thought. There was a scene when she offered to break off the engagement. And she was inhibited, too, by the force of her feelings. Sensing this, Byron tried to caress her into kindness. She could only urge him to leave. After a fortnight, he went, "as comfortable as a pilgrim with peas in his shoes, and as cold as Charity, Chastity or any other virtue".

But their correspondence continued. Her parents, naturally, wanted a church wedding. He sharply insisted on a special licence so that they could be married at her home. In his London lodgings, meanwhile, he said farewell to "Eliza" who, "with a desperate effort", tore herself forever from "the truly noble Lord Byron". On Christmas Eve 1814 he set off for the Milbankes' home. "Never was lover less in haste," wrote Hobhouse.

There was no reception after the plain little service, just a carriage waiting to take the couple on the 40-mile drive to their Yorkshire honeymoon. It was a winter of perishing cold. During the lumbering and draughty silence of the journey—interrupted, the bride later reported, by her husband's hysterical singing—Lady Byron was on the verge of tears. Then it began to snow. They arrived at Halnaby Hall, and though Byron "*had* Lady B. on the sofa before dinner", he loathed the idea that she should sleep with him. He was, as always, self-conscious about his lame foot. She insisted, however, and the red curtains were closed round their marriage bed. During the night, Byron woke in a state of panic. The firelight was playing on the hangings, and for a moment he thought he was in hell.

The following morning the lake had frozen and the landscape was silenced with snow. Annabella was again on the point of tears. She was afraid of him and he despised her for it. We must feel we exist, he had written, "even though in pain". He now began to inflict it upon them both. His moments of tenderness—in the library, perhaps, as they read together, or he worked on *Hebrew Melodies*—made the anguish worse.

His financial affairs were now desperate. Claughton's money settled only a few of Byron's debts, and the worried poet was now drinking heavily—drinking for escape, drinking for stimulus. He rose from besotted dreams to stalk their honeymoon nights with a dagger and a gun in his hands. He was the Corsair of his imagination. With great finesse, he even began to torture his wife with hints of his unspeakable crimes. She should have laughed at him, as Augusta had done. Instead, she longed to take on the burden of his guilt. He despised her all the more. And in the mornings he woke to the seeping guilt of alcoholic remorse. He was doomed, he believed, to destruction, damned. He played on his wife's credulity. We must feel we exist, "even though in pain". Augusta was his subtlest instrument of torture.

They went to stay with her, and, as the evenings wore on, Byron made plain whose company he preferred. If his wife lingered while he drank his brandy he dismissed her like an unwanted chorus girl. He dropped hints and innuendoes about his affairs. Both women, allied in their wretchedness, were in an hysterical state. Then, when the damage had been done, he moved with his wife to London.

Hoping for her support perhaps, or drawn to her own destruction, Annabella invited Augusta to stay. "You are a fool for letting her come to the house," Byron wrote, "and you will find it will make a great difference to *you* in all ways." He was right, for while the Byrons appeared in society as a devoted and even doting couple, Augusta's presence began to unsettle Lady Byron's mind. There were times when she could have plunged a dagger in her ally's heart.

Byron himself kept out of the house as much as he could. The male camaraderie of his publisher's reception rooms offered him the company of Walter Scott. His friend Douglas Kinnaird introduced him to the world of the theatre. Byron began rejecting bad scripts and commissioning plays for Drury Lane. This brought him into contact with Coleridge, and he also developed his friendship with the radical author Leigh Hunt. *Hebrew Melodies*, though receiving some bad reviews, sold well. Byron was still a star in the literary firmament.

THE DESTRUCTION OF SENNACHERIB

"Is there anything beyond? – who knows?"

Byron's knowledge of the Bible, gleaned largely from his early experiences in Scotland, was surprisingly far-reaching. The portions of the Old Testament offered in his *Hebrew Melodies*, however, are essentially technical exercises and perhaps only this—the most famous of them—is an assured poetic success. Throughout his life Byron remained a troubled sceptic in matters of religion.

The Assyrian came down like the wolf on
    the fold,
And his cohorts were gleaming in purple
    and gold;
And the sheen of their spears was like
    stars on the sea,
When the blue wave rolls nightly on deep
    Galilee.

Like the leaves of the forest when Summer
    is green,
That host with their banners at sunset
    were seen:
Like the leaves of the forest when Autumn
    hath blown,
That host on the morrow lay wither'd and
    strown.

For the Angel of Death spread his wings
    on the blast,
And breathed in the face of the foe as he
    pass'd:
And the eyes of the sleepers wax'd deadly
    and chill,
And their hearts but once heaved, and for
    ever grew still!

And there lay the steed with his nostril
    all wide,
But through it there roll'd not the breath
    of his pride;
And the foam of his gasping lay white on
    the turf,
And cold as the spray of the rock-beating
    surf.

And there lay the rider distorted and pale,
With the dew on his brow, and the rust
    on his mail:
And the tents were all silent, the banners
    alone,
The lances unlifted, the trumpet unblown.

And the widows of Ashur are loud in
    their wail,
And the idols are broke in the temple of
    Baal;
And the might of the Gentile, unsmote
    by the sword,
Hath melted like snow in the glance of the
    Lord!

However, despite the crushing burden of his debts, he continued to decline Murray's offers of payment. Hanson, meanwhile, still failed to sell his estates. Byron was near the end of his tether when, early in November 1815, bailiffs moved into his lodgings at 13 Piccadilly Terrace. Hearing about this, Murray immediately sent £1,500 with a promise of more. Once again, the money was politely and firmly declined.

Byron's drinking had increased with his stress and his moods became more erratic and violent than ever. Annabella was afraid, and, in her fear, she came to realize something of the truth about her husband's nature. Two years before, armed with the naivety of untested virtue, it had been her mission to convert him. He had written her shocking letters in which he had talked of sensation and his craving for stimulus. This she had believed she could calm. Now, as she wrote a moving letter to Augusta, echoing the very tone of her husband's words, so she admitted defeat. Byron's misfortune, she wrote "is an habitual *passion for Excitement* which is always found in ardent temperaments, when these pursuits are not in some degree organised. It is the Ennui of a monotonous existence that drives the best-hearted people of this description to the most dangerous paths, and makes them often seem to act from bad motives."

The analysis is telling because it is his. Left to herself, Lady Byron was beginning to have other ideas. True to her nature, she had sought wisdom from books rather than her heart, and in the pages of the *Medical Journal* she had come across "hydrocephalus". It was not human misery her husband was suffering from but a polysyllabic disease. He was not unhappy, he was mad. She began collecting evidence. She found a bottle of laudanum and a novel by de Sade. She noted Byron's gestures and his figures of speech. The high brow and disdainful lip of the Corsair were medical symptoms now. For safety's sake, her old governess and Byron's cousin were asked to stay. Her fear was no longer for herself alone; Lady Byron was pregnant. On 10 December 1815 she gave birth to a baby girl. She claimed that, as her labour began, Byron had wished both she and the child might die. In her misery, she was starting to embroider events. A month after the birth of her daughter, with her mission failed and her life wrecked, Lady Byron finally left her home.

As she went downstairs to the waiting carriage she passed his room. The tragic futility of her enterprise choked her heart and for just a moment she was tempted, tempted to throw herself down on the rug where his dog customarily lay and there to wait, wait grovelling for anything he might care to say. But it was only a moment. She walked on. She walked out, and never saw Byron again.

ANNABELLA MILBANKE

"a very superior woman a little encumbered
with Virtue"

Some of Byron's most acute and graceful letters were written to Lady
Melbourne, the aunt of his future wife. Lady Melbourne was both
shrewd and kind (qualities rarely shown by Byron's mother) and
Byron expressed his gratitude in letters that suggest the brilliant tone
of his conversation. He reveals a mind delighting in its own intuitions,
yet tragically unaware of the emotional dangers that were soon to
overwhelm him.

My dear Lady Mel[bourn]e.—I delivered your
letters—but have only mentioned ye receipt of your *last* to
myself.————Do you know I have great doubts—if
this will be a marriage now.—her disposition is the very
reverse of *our* imaginings—she is overrun with fine
feelings—scruples about herself & *her* disposition (I
suppose in fact she means mine) and to crown all is taken ill
once every 3 days with I know not what—but the day
before and the day after she seems well—looks & eats well
& is cheerful & confiding & in short like any other person
in good health & spirits.—A few days ago she made one
scene—not altogether out of C[aroline]'s style—it was too
long & too trifling in fact for me to transcribe—but it did
me no good——in the article of conversation however she
has improved with a vengeance—but I don't much admire
these same agitations upon slight occasions.—I don't
know—but I think it by no means impossible you will see
me in town soon—I can only interpret these things one
way—& merely wait to be certain to make my obeisances
and "exit singly." I hear of nothing but "feeling" from
morning till night—except from Sir Ralph with whom I go
on to admiration—Ly. M[ilbanke] too is pretty well—but
I am never sure of A[nnabella]—for a moment—the least
word—and you know I rattle on through thick & thin
(always however avoiding anything I think can offend her
favourite notions) if only to prevent me from
yawning — the least word—or alteration of tone—has
some inference drawn from it—sometimes we are too
much alike—& then again too unlike—this comes of
system—& squaring her notions to the Devil knows

what—for my part I have lately had recourse to the eloquence of *action* (which Demosthenes* calls the first part of oratory) & find it succeeds very well & makes her very quiet which gives me some hopes of the efficacy of the "calming process" so renowned in "*our* philosophy."—In fact and entre nous it is really amusing—she is like a child in that respect—and quite *caressable* into kindness and good humour—though I don't think her temper *bad* at any time—but very *self*-tormenting—and anxious—and romantic.————In short—it is impossible to foresee how this will end *now*—anymore than 2 years ago—if there is a break—it shall be *her* doing not mine.—

ever yrs. most truly
B

The truth was, he had asked her to leave, not forever, not in high melodrama, but from simple practical necessity. He could no longer afford to live in Piccadilly and she was to go to her parents' home where he intended to follow her. But the Milbankes clasped their daughter to their bosom and prepared their revenge. Annabella was torn between her love, her fear and her duty. She continued to send tender letters to her husband, but Augusta—now a regular correspondent—sent almost daily reports of her half-brother's conduct. She said he kept a pistol on the mantelpiece and was in terror of being attacked. Her parents insisted that Annabella should not only have a doctor to pronounce Byron insane (a ruse which eventually collapsed) but a lawyer to work for a separation. She was urged to draw up a list of her husband's offences.

While Annabella's mother was hastening to London with this, Byron, unaware of the disaster that was about to befall him, was lounging in Piccadilly suffering an upset liver—the result of heavy drinking. The lawyer prepared a letter proposing a quiet separation, which Annabella's father copied out and put in the post.

Byron saw through the ploy at once. This could not be Annabella's work. Judging by the tone of her recent letters, she was still on friendly terms. He replied immediately, making his own position clear. He also wrote to Annabella: "Will you explain?" She was forbidden to reply. He wrote again. "I loved you, and will not part with you without your express and expressed refusal to return to, or receive me." She could see how hurt he was, how confused. She rolled on the floor in her grief.

When she had pulled herself together, she replied with haughty logic. He was bitterly upset by her response. "Were you then *never* happy with me? did you never at any time or times express yourself so? have no marks of affection, of the warmest and most reciprocal attachment, passed between us? . . . You are much changed within these twenty days, or you would never have thus poisoned your own better feelings—and trampled upon mine." He was in despair. He told Hobhouse that he was ruined, that he would blow his brains out, that he would go abroad, that he still loved her.

A DISASTROUS MARRIAGE

"the late remorse of love"

The brief and tragic marriage of Byron and Annabella Milbanke had its roots in complex and contradictory emotions. He loved her and he despised her. That he also felt great tenderness for her and was deeply hurt by her leaving him is clear in this letter written when Annabella had returned to her parents in 1816. It took all Annabella's haughty coldness to resist Byron's entreaty.

> All I can say seems useless—and all I could say—might be no less unavailing—yet I still cling to the wreck of my hopes—before they sink forever.——Were you then *never* happy with me?—did you never at any time or times express yourself so?—have no marks of affection—of the warmest & most reciprocal attachment passed between us?—or did in fact hardly a day go down without some such on one side and generally on both?—do not mistake me—[two lines crossed out] I have not denied my state of mind—but you know it's causes—& were those deviations from calmness never followed by acknowledgement & repentance?—was not the last which occurred more particularly so?—& had I not—had we not—the days before & on the day when we parted—every reason to believe that we loved each other—that we were to meet again—were not your letters kind?—had I not acknowledged to you all my faults & follies—& assured you that some had not—& would not be repeated?—I do not require these questions to be answered to me—but to your own heart.——The day before I received your father's letter—I had fixed a day for rejoining you—if I did not write lately—Augusta

did—and as you had been my proxy in correspondence with her—so did I imagine—she might be the same for me to you.—Upon your letter to me—this day—I surely may remark—that it's expressions imply a treatment which I am incapable of inflicting—& you of imputing to me—if aware of their latitude—& the extent of the inferences to be drawn from them.—This is not just———but I have no reproaches—nor the wish to find cause for them.———Will you see me?—when & where you please—in whose presence you please:—the interview shall pledge you to nothing—& I will say & do nothing to agitate either—it is torture to correspond thus—& there are things to be settled & said which cannot be written.———You say "it is my disposition to deem what I *have worthless*"—did I deem *you* so?—did I ever so express myself to you—or of you—to others?———You are much changed within these twenty days or you would never have thus poisoned your own better feelings—and trampled upon mine.———

ever yrs. most truly & affectionately

B

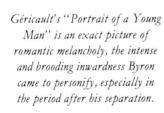

Géricault's "Portrait of a Young Man" is an exact picture of romantic melancholy, the intense and brooding inwardness Byron came to personify, especially in the period after his separation.

Napoleon rides in triumph above corpses massacred in war. The killing fields of early 19th century Europe preoccupied Byron and were one of the major subjects of his poetry. Napoleon himself he regarded with passionate ambiguity. He was at once a man of overweening ambition and a defeated hero with whom the poet identified.

No emotion of Byron's could remain private for long however, and soon loud rumours were flying about London. "I was abused in the public prints, made the common talk of private companies, hissed as I went to the House of Lords, insulted in the streets." He believed, with some justification, that the rumours had been started by Caroline Lamb. He professed to ignore them, but the excommunicating voice of society was rising to a scream. The welfare of a peeress was at stake, and any and every scandal was added to the refrain—affairs with actresses, sodomy—it was all one to the British public as they toppled Childe Harold from his pinnacle and made him the limping demon of Piccadilly.

He wrote, asking a harmless question about the health of his child. Annabella was convinced he wanted custody and at once contacted her lawyer. There was more she must tell him. Dr Lushington realized, of course, that her allegations of Byron's incest with his half-sister—if true—would not be easy to use. His client could not testify against her husband, and the charge, though it might have substance, would be impossible to prove. All in all, it was probably best ignored. Things were, he thought, getting a little out of hand. He advised Lady Byron to cease communication with Augusta. She refused. Through Augusta she could show her husband that it was she herself who was taking the initiative now. It was she who was the avenging angel.

The rumours of incest would not go away. Hobhouse was deeply concerned. In his diary he recorded that he drew up a memorandum in which Lady Byron would deny "cruelty, systematic unremitted neglect, gross & repeated infidelities—incest & ———." The dash stood for sodomy. It was a word Hobhouse could never bring himself to write in his diary.

Dr Lushington examined Hobhouse's paper. He had hoped for a quiet separation, but he now realized that his discreet attempts to involve Lord Holland as an intermediary could be of no avail among people like these. He set about a careful redrafting of Hobhouse's memorandum. Lady Byron would deny that she and her family had spread such rumours, of course. But Lushington would not commit her to saying they were untrue. Who knew what time would show? Meanwhile, the preliminary agreement for the separation was drawn up. Byron signed it and then wrote a poem expressing his feelings of bitterness and confusion over the affair.

Murray showed the poem to Caroline Lamb. Thrilled at a possible reinvolvement, she wrote to Byron promising she would lie for him and deny all the terrible rumours that were circulating. That she thought this gesture could be of use shows the confusion in her mind. Perhaps it also suggests she was instrumental in circulating the rumours in the first place. Byron had certainly told her things he was now beginning bitterly to regret and it is hard to see who else would have found satisfaction in raising the mob. Byron, however, ignored her letter.

If she could not save him, she would help destroy him. Caroline opened a correspondence with her loathed rival. She hinted darkly to Lady Byron that she could tell her things about the poet the very mention of which would make him tremble. Annabella agreed to meet her on 27 March 1816. She made careful notes of the interview.

With great cunning, Lady Caroline began by saying that all she knew she had been told in confidence. She could not break that confidence, but . . . What ought she to do? Annabella at once declared that for the sake of Byron's child, Lady Caroline should realize she was free from all her previous obligations. Lady Caroline, having won her point, began to drip venom. She knew for a fact that Byron had been sleeping with his half-sister since at least 1813, she said. At first he had merely dropped hints about it, later he had boasted of his conquest. But there was worse—other unnatural crimes. Byron had made love to at least three other boys at school. He had even sodomized Rushton, his page. But in Turkey, in Turkey he had done such things "unrestrictedly".

Dr Lushington congratulated his client. None of it amounted to legal proof, of course, but if it could be presented convincingly in court then Byron would not stand a chance. The man Lady Byron had once tried to save she now made the most notorious rake in England. Three weeks later, he signed the final deed of separation.

Partly to divert his bitter mind and feelings, Byron had entered on an affair with another of his admirers. She was quite a pretty little 17-year-old with intelligent eyes and advanced views on women and marriage. Byron himself, "having no very high opinion of the sex" and certain he would soon be out of his hated homeland, was amused and sometimes mildly annoyed by her persistence. Certainly, he underestimated her; for "Clare", "Claire" or "Clara" as she variously called herself (her real name was Mary Jane) had grown up in the home of her stepfather, the radical philosopher William Godwin, and had accompanied his daughter Mary when she eloped to Switzerland with a little-known poet called Percy Shelley. She now rather wanted a poet of her own, particularly one as notorious as Byron. But time was running out. Byron was hurrying into exile. She wrote to him saying she didn't expect him to love her and that she was quite unworthy anyway. Then she baited the hook. "Have you . . . any objection to the following plan?" she asked. "On Thursday Evening we may go out of town together by some stage or mail about the distance of ten or twelve miles. There we shall be free and unknown; we can return early the following morning." He went, of course, and was to regret it bitterly.

But during the following weeks his mind was most deeply engaged with flight and the masochistic sweets of exile. England had betrayed him, he thought, but there was a world elsewhere. Eventually, accompanied by a little group of friends and servants, Byron made his way to Dover. So notorious was he still that his inn was besieged by fashionable ladies, many of them disguised as chambermaids, who had come for a last look at the legendary fiend. Limping on Hobhouse's arm, Byron made his way through the crowd to the waiting ship. As it sailed, Hobhouse ran to the end of the wooden pier. Byron, cap in hand, waved to the receding figure of his most loyal friend. He would never see England again.

Claire Clairmont, meanwhile, was carrying his child.

FARE THEE WELL

"I am convinced I shall never get over it"

Byron's bitterness and confusion at his separation
from his wife mingle harshly in this poem. During
his lifetime, it was one of the most notorious that
he wrote. Murray showed it to Lady Caroline Lamb,
who thought it offered the hope of renewing their
affair. When Byron rebuffed her advances, Lady
Caroline sided with Annabella to help destroy
the poet and drive him into exile.

Fare thee well! and if for ever—
   Still for ever, fare *thee well*—
Even though unforgiving, never
   'Gainst thee shall my heart rebel.—
Would that breast were bared before thee
   Where thy head so oft hath lain,
While that placid sleep came o'er thee
   Which thou ne'er can'st know again:
Would that breast by thee glanc'd over,
   Every inmost thought could show!
Then, thou wouldst at last discover
   'Twas not well to spurn it so—
Though the world for this commend thee—
   Though it smile upon the blow,
Even its praises must offend thee,
   Founded on another's woe—
Though my many faults defaced me,
   Could no other arm be found
Than the one which once embraced me,
   To inflict a cureless wound!
Yet—oh, yet—thyself deceive not—
   Love may sink by slow decay,
But by sudden wrench, believe not,
   Hearts can thus be torn away;
Still thine own its life retaineth—
   Still must mine—though bleeding—beat,
And the undying thought which paineth
   Is—that we no more may meet.—
These are words of deeper sorrow
   Than the wail above the dead,

Both shall live—but every morrow
   Wake us from a widowed bed.—
And when thou wouldst solace gather—
   When our child's first accents flow
Wilt thou teach her to say—'Father!'
   Though his care she must forgo?
When her little hands shall press thee—
   When her lip to thine is prest—
Think of him whose prayer shall bless thee—
   Think of him thy love had bless'd.
Should her lineaments resemble
   Those thou never more may'st see—
Then thy heart will softly tremble
   With a pulse yet true to me.—
All my faults—perchance thou knowest—
   All my madness—none can know;
All my hopes—where'er thou goest—
   Wither—yet with *thee* they go.—
Every feeling hath been shaken,
   Pride—which not a world could bow—
Bows to thee—by thee forsaken
   Even my soul forsakes me now.—
But 'tis done—all words are idle—
   Words from me are vainer still;
But the thoughts we cannot bridle
   Force their way without the will.—
Fare thee well!— thus disunited—
   Torn from every nearer tie—
Seared in Heart—and lone—and blighted—
   More than this, I scarce can die.

"I learned to love despair"

Byron planned to travel through Switzerland and Italy and thence to the remembered joys of Greece and the Levant. Baxters of London had made him a huge, leather-bound travelling coach for the journey. Modelled on Napoleon's, it was fitted out with a daybed, a library and a plate-chest. Now, drawn by four horses and accompanied by an outrider, Byron made his way across a Europe which the defeat of Napoleon had profoundly changed. Behind him lay England seething with political discontent and held in check by the iron administration of the Tory cabinet. Before him lay countries coming to terms with the defeat at Waterloo.

On the site of the battle itself, Byron and Polidori—a young and tiresome doctor he had admitted into his entourage and whom Murray had given £500 for an account of the journey—rode across the battlefield in imitation of a cavalry charge. Byron was deeply stirred by his thoughts of the historic struggle and, as always, he needed to express his feelings in verse. He turned again to the Spenserian stanza. A newly bitter Childe Harold, defiant and sorrowful, began to emerge. He was that archetypal romantic figure, the wronged and suffering genius. As he tells us of his pain and fate, separates himself from the common herd of men and hints at unspeakable woes and crimes, so he also becomes a commentator on the sorrows of Europe, the spokesman of liberty, and the poet whose natural home is among the snow-capped mountains. His words are like lightning.

NAPOLEON

"All Evil Spirit as thou art ... It is enough to grieve the heart ... To see thine own unstrung"

Byron's evocation of Napoleon in stanzas 36–45 of the third canto of *Childe Harold's Pilgrimage* reflects his ambiguous feelings about his hero. He both admired Napoleon as the greatest spirit of the age and detested him for his cruelty. In these respects, Napoleon is a supreme example of the Byronic hero—a man vast in his energies and criminal in many of his passions, a giant of conflicting and tumultuous emotions which drive him to the edges of the world.

There sunk the greatest, nor the worst of men,
Whose spirit antithetically mixt
One moment of the mightiest, and again
On little objects with like firmness fixt,
Extreme in all things! hadst thou been betwixt,
Thy throne had still been thine, or never been;
For daring made thy rise as fall: thou seek'st
Even now to re-assume the imperial mien,
And shake again the world, the Thunderer of the scene!

Conqueror and captive of the earth art thou!
She trembles at thee still, and thy wild name
Was ne'er more bruited in men's minds than now
That thou art nothing, save the jest of Fame,
Who wooed thee once, thy vassal, and became
The flatterer of thy fierceness, till thou wert
A god unto thyself; nor less the same
To the astounded kingdoms all inert,
Who deem'd thee for a time whate'er thou didst assert.

*Cruikshank's cartoon shows a fat and
dissolute Byron fleeing England after
his notorious separation. Lady Byron and
their child stand on the shore. This is
the public condemnation of a rake.*

Oh, more or less than man—in high or low,
Battling with nations, flying from the field;
Now making monarchs' necks thy footstool, now
More than thy meanest soldier taught to yield;
An empire thou couldst crush, command, rebuild,
But govern not thy pettiest passion, nor,
However deeply in men's spirits skill'd,
Look through thine own, nor curb the lust of war,
Nor learn that tempted Fate will leave the loftiest star.

Yet well thy soul hath brook'd the turning tide
With that untaught innate philosophy,
Which, be it wisdom, coldness, or deep pride,
Is gall and wormwood to an enemy.
When the whole host of hatred stood hard by,
To watch and mock thee shrinking, thou hast smiled
With a sedate and all-enduring eye;—
When Fortune fled her spoil'd and favourite child,
He stood unbowed beneath the ills upon him piled.

The image of Napoleon imagined by the French painter David is in many ways comparable to Byron's meditation on his hero in the third canto of "Childe Harold's Pilgrimage".

Sager than in thy fortunes; for in them
Ambition steel'd thee on too far to show
That just habitual scorn which could contemn
Men and their thoughts; 'twas wise to feel, not so
To wear it ever on thy lip and brow,
And spurn the instruments thou wert to use
Till they were turn'd unto thine overthrow;
'Tis but a worthless world to win or lose;
So hath it proved to thee, and all such lot who choose.

If, like a tower upon a headlong rock,
Thou hadst been made to stand or fall alone,
Such scorn of man had help'd to brave the shock;
But men's thoughts were the steps which paved thy throne.
Their admiration thy best weapon shone;
The part of Philip's son was thine, not then*
(Unless aside thy purple had been thrown)
Like stern Diogenes to mock at men;
For sceptred cynics earth were far too wide a den.

But quiet to quick bosoms is a hell,
And *there* hath been thy bane; there is a fire
And motion of the soul which will not dwell
In its own narrow being, but aspire
Beyond the fitting medium of desire;
And, but once kindled, quenchless evermore,
Preys upon high adventure, nor can tire
Of aught but rest; a fever at the core,
Fatal to him who bears, to all who ever bore.

This makes the madmen who have made men mad
By their contagion; Conquerors and Kings,
Founders of sects and systems, to whom add
Sophists, Bards, Statesmen, all unquiet things
Which stir too strongly the soul's secret springs,
And are themselves the fools to those they fool;
Envied, yet how unenviable! what stings
Are theirs! One breast laid open were a school
Which would unteach mankind the lust to shine or rule:

Their breath is agitation, and their life
A storm whereon they ride, to sink at last,
And yet so nurs'd and bigotted to strife,
That should their days, surviving perils past,
Melt to calm twilight, they feel overcast
With sorrow and supineness, and so die;
Even as a flame unfed, which runs to waste
With its own flickering, or a sword laid by
Which eats into itself, and rusts ingloriously.

He who ascends to mountain-tops, shall find
The loftiest peaks most wrapt in clouds and snow;
He who surpasses or subdues mankind,
Must look down on the hate of those below.
Though high *above* the sun of glory glow,
And far *beneath* the earth and ocean spread,
Round him are icy rocks, and loudly blow
Contending tempests on his naked head,
And thus reward the toils which to those summits led.

Like Byron in the third canto of "Childe Harold", Carus's lonely, romantic pilgrim searches for his spiritual home across a deserted landscape.

THE FIELD OF WATERLOO

"I detest the cause and the victors"

Byron's meditation on the battle of Waterloo in the third canto of *Childe Harold's Pilgrimage* is one of his most famous passages. He expresses his bitterness at the slaughter, a bitterness increased by the fact that it seemed to him to have left Europe less free than ever. As in all his best work Byron employs strong contrasts: he creates the brilliance of the ball on the eve of the battle and then juxtaposes this to the morning's slaughter.

Stop!—for thy tread is on an Empire's dust!
An Earthquake's spoil is sepulchred below!
Is the spot mark'd with no colossal bust?
Nor column trophied for triumphal show?
None; but the moral's truth tells simpler so,
As the ground was before, thus let it be;—
How that red rain hath made the harvest grow!
And is this all world has gained by thee,
Thou first and last of fields! king-making Victory?*

And Harold stands upon this place of skulls,
The grace of France, the deadly Waterloo!
How in an hour the power which gave annuls
Its gifts, transferring fame as fleeting too!
In 'pride of place' here last the eagle flew,*
Then tore with bloody talon the rent plain,
Pierced by the shaft of banded nations through;
Ambition's life and labours all were vain;
He wears the shattered links of the world's broken chain.

Fit retribution! Gaul may champ the bit
And foam in fetters;—but is Earth more free?
Did nations combat to make *One* submit;*
Or league to teach all kings true sovereignty?
What! shall reviving Thraldom again be
The patched-up idol of enlightened days?
Shall we, who struck the Lion down, shall we
Pay the Wolf homage? proffering lowly gaze
And servile knees to thrones? No; *prove* before ye praise!

If not, o'er one fallen despot boast no more!
In vain fair cheeks were furrowed with hot tears
For Europe's flowers long rooted up before
The trampler of her vineyards; in vain years
Of death, depopulation, bondage, fears,
Have all been borne, and broken by the accord
Of roused-up millions: all that most endears
Glory, is when the myrtle wreathes a sword
Such as Harmodius drew on Athens' tyrant lord.*

*Polidori—here portrayed at his most
Byronic—galloped across the site of
the battle of Waterloo with Byron.
He later died by his own hand.*

There was a sound of revelry by night,
And Belgium's capital had gathered then
Her Beauty and her Chivalry, and bright
The lamps shone o'er fair women and brave men;
A thousand hearts beat happily; and when
Music arose with its voluptuous swell,
Soft eyes look'd love to eyes which spake again,
And all went merry as a marriage-bell;
But hush! hark! a deep sound strikes like a rising knell!

Did ye not hear it?—No; 'twas but the wind,
Or the car rattling o'er the stony street;
On with the dance! let joy be unconfined;
No sleep till morn, when Youth and Pleasure meet
To chase the glowing Hours with flying feet—
But, hark!—that heavy sound breaks in once more,
As if the clouds its echo would repeat;
And nearer, clearer, deadlier than before!
Arm! Arm! and out—it is—the cannon's opening roar!

*Turner was the English artist most
influenced by Byron, and his watercolour
of the Drachenfels suggests the romantic
scenery of Byron's Germanic period which
culminated in "Manfred".*

Within a windowed niche of that high hall
Sate Brunswick's fated chieftain, he did hear*
That sound the first amidst the festival,
And caught its tone with Death's prophetic ear;
And when they smiled because he deem'd it near,
His heart more truly knew that peal too well
Which stretch'd his father on a bloody bier,
And roused the vengence blood alone could quell:
He rush'd into the field, and, foremost fighting, fell.

Ah! then and there was hurrying to and fro,
And gathering tears, and tremblings of distress,
And cheeks all pale, which but an hour ago
Blush'd at the praise of their own loveliness;
And there were sudden partings, such as press
The life from out young hearts, and choking sighs
Which ne'er might be repeated; who could guess
If ever more should meet those mutual eyes,
Since upon nights so sweet such awful morn could rise?

And there was mounting in hot haste: the steed,
The mustering squadron, and the clattering car,
Went pouring forward in impetuous speed,
And swiftly forming in the ranks of war;
And the deep thunder peal on peal afar;
And near, the beat of the alarming drum
Roused up the soldier ere the morning star;
While throng'd the citizens with terror dumb,
Or whispering, with white lips—'The foe! They come! they come!'

And wild and high the 'Cameron's gathering' rose!
The war-note of Lochiel, which Albyn's hills*
Have heard, and heard, too, have her Saxon foes:—
How in the noon of night that pibroch thrills,
Savage and shrill! But with the breath which fills
Their mountain-pipe, so fill the mountaineers
With the fierce native daring which instils
The stirring memory of a thousand years,
And Evan's, Donald's fame rings in each clansman's ears!*

And Ardennes waves above them her green leaves,
Dewy with nature's tear-drops, as they pass,
Grieving, if aught inanimate e'er grieves,
Over the unreturning brave,—alas!
Ere evening to be trodden like the grass
Which now beneath them, but above shall grow
In its next verdure, when this fiery mass
Of living valour, rolling on the foe
And burning with high hope, shall moulder cold and low.

Last noon beheld them full of lusty life,
Last eve in Beauty's circle proudly gay,
The midnight brought the signal-sound of strife,
The morn the marshalling in arms,—the day
Battle's magnificently-stern array!
The thunder-clouds close o'er it, which when rent
The earth is covered thick with other clay,
Which her own clay shall cover, heaped and pent,
Rider and horse,—friend, foe,—in one red burial blent!

Thomas Cole's "Scene from Manfred" suggests the sublimity and horror of nature, the energy and desolation, which Byron tried to capture in his melodrama.

To such a man as this, the defeat at Waterloo marked not just the destruction of Napoleon but of the whole liberal enterprise. One mighty emperor had been replaced by a host of petty tyrants. In Portugal, Spain, Italy, France and Russia the reins of power had been taken up by the old hands and with the old harshness. For all the posturing, and despite the often borrowed and sometimes badly-expressed egotism, there is a real force in these political passages of the third canto of *Childe Harold's Pilgrimage*, an indication of enthusiasms to come. Further, that great insight into his own character Byron had expressed in a letter to his wife when he told her of his constant craving for stimulus is now given public form in the image of the artist.

The romantic genius, as Byron shows him to us, is wrought in "a whirling gulf of phantasy and flame" and emerges from the ashes of his despair. He becomes the creature of his own fevered imaginings, the restless spirit, wild-eyed, alienated and young. Though Byron was to create subtler images, none was more potent. The Childe Harold of Canto Three bestrides the art of Europe's romantic age. He is the alter ego of Berlioz, the companion of Turner, and the idol of Géricault's youthful painter as he leans his world-weary head on his boyish hand.

While Byron gave literary form to the restless fevers of his imagination, Lady Byron had embarked on yet another rescue mission. The Evangelicals were at work, and cold winds of righteousness were blowing in from their Clapham headquarters. Inexorably, Lady Byron was blown towards Augusta. She had sinned, and Annabella and her friend Mrs Villiers were the instruments of God's wrath. While Lady Caroline vented her love and spite in the tedious pages of her novel *Glenarvon*, Lady Byron seized on Augusta and began to tear at her heart. In the intervals of torture, Mrs Villiers sent gladdening reports of her pain and repentance. The two women found it necessary to proceed "step by step", but eventually they discovered a vein of simple piety in Augusta and, working on this, they reduced her to tearful contrition. Byron, meanwhile, was sending her some of his most tender lyrics. Her soft heart, he declared, had refused to lay bare "the faults which so many could find", and the "Stanzas to Augusta" reflect his gratitude. "I think them beautiful," she wrote.

Turner's watercolour illustrates the Château of
Chillon which Byron visited with Shelley.

Mary Shelley responded deeply to Byron's attraction, and the hero of her novel Frankenstein *not only owes much to him but was conceived while the Shelleys were staying with Byron in Switzerland.*

THE ARTIST AS HERO

"A whirling gulf of phantasy and flame"

The third canto of *Childe Harold's Pilgrimage* deepens the themes of the two preceding ones through Byron's picture of his intense disillusion and suffering after his separation from his wife and half-sister. Only in his imagination can he find the energy by which to live, and stanzas 5–7 provide an important image of the romantic artist creating works out of his own anguish.

He, who grown aged in this world of woe,
In deeds, not years, piercing the depths of life,
So that no wonder waits him; nor below
Can love, or sorrow, fame, ambition, strife,
Cut to his heart again with the keen knife
Of silent, sharp endurance he can tell
Why thought seeks refuge in lone caves, yet rife
With airy images, and shapes which dwell
Still unimpair'd, though old, in the soul's haunted cell.

'Tis to create, and in creating live
A being more intense, that we endow
With form our fancy, gaining as we give
The life we imagine, even as I do now.
What am I? Nothing; but not so art thou,
Soul of my thought! with whom I traverse earth,
Invisible but gazing, as I glow
Mix'd with thy spirit, blended with thy birth,
And feeling still with thee in my crush'd feelings' dearth.

Yet must I think less wildly:—I *have* thought
Too long and darkly, till my brain became,
In its own eddy boiling and o'erwrought,
A whirling gulf of phantasy and flame:
And thus, untaught in youth my heart to tame,
My springs of life were poison'd. 'Tis too late!
Yet am I chang'd; though still enough the same
In strength to bear what time can not abate,
And feed on bitter fruits without accusing Fate.

STANZAS FOR MUSIC

"thine be the gladness and mine be the guilt"

This poem reflects Byron's feelings for his half-sister, and he conveys all the
tenderness and gratitude he felt for the emotional warmth and freedom she had offered him.
The tremulous rhythm of the poem reflects the delicate ambiguity of his emotions.

I speak not—I trace not—I breathe not thy name,
There is grief in the sound—there were guilt in the fame;
But the tear which now burns on my cheek may impart
The deep thought that dwells in that silence of heart.

Too brief for our passion, too long for our peace,
Were those hours, can their joy or their bitterness cease?
We repent—we abjure—we will break from our chain;
We must part—we must fly to—unite it again.

Oh! thine be the gladness and mine be the guilt,
Forgive me adored one—forsake if thou wilt;
But the heart which I bear shall expire undebased,
And man shall not break it—whatever thou may'st.

And stern to the haughty, but humble to thee,
My soul in its bitterest blackness shall be;
And our days seem as swift—and our moments more sweet,
With thee by my side—than the world at our feet.

One sigh of thy sorrow—one look of thy love,
Shall turn me or fix, shall reward or reprove;
And the heartless may wonder at all we resign,
Thy lip shall reply not to them—but to mine.

*Byron was not daunted by the formidable
intellect of his Swiss neighbour Madame
de Staël, and her popularization of
German literature was to have a deep
influence on him.*

Byron's "Napoleonic" coach lumbered on its slow progress along
the Rhine. The party visited Cologne, passed the Drachenfels and, after
a quarrel between Byron and Polidori, crossed into Switzerland at
Basle. The drama of the landscape continued to fuse with Byron's
agony of mind as he worked on the third canto of *Childe Harold*. He
wrote later: "I was half mad during the time of its composition,
between metaphysics, mountains, lakes, love unextinguishable,
thoughts unutterable, and the nightmare of my own delinquencies. I
should, many a good day, have blown my brains out, but for the recollection that it would have given pleasure to my mother-in-law".

Another group of English travellers, also making for Geneva, were similarly impressed by the wild landscape. "The trees . . . stand in scattered clumps in the white wilderness," wrote Mary Shelley. "Never was scene more awfully desolate as that which we passed in one evening of our last day's journey." Eventually the party arrived at their destination and put up at Monsieur Dejan's Hotel d'Angleterre. When Byron, ignorant of their presence, booked in ten days later, Claire, who had persuaded the Shelleys to let her accompany them, knew of his presence within half an hour. She had already sent him a letter hinting of her pregancy and now she sent him another note. He immediately went off to Geneva. He wanted nothing to do with England.

But on his return, the Shelleys spotted him rowing on the lake with Polidori. The skiff was brought to shore and the shy, resentful Byron limped up the beach to greet Shelley and his female entourage. Byron, though flustered, found the grace to invite the poet to dine with him that evening. The women were not asked.

The dinner was a success and there began one of the most famous of English literary friendships. It was not an easy one. Both men were too intelligent, too radical and too eccentric not to be wary of each other. However, Shelley, in particular, was keen to establish a friendship with the most famous poet of his day, and he courted Byron with all the brilliance of his intellect.

Shelley urged on him the importance of considering the merits of the great English romantic poet Wordsworth, and he "dosed" Byron with readings from *The Excursion*. It was a curious interest for them both since Wordsworth, the apostate radical, had written *The Excursion* as his testament of hearth-and-home Toryism and reliance on inner virtue. But the power of Wordsworth's vision of man's unity with nature could not be denied by any young poet. Wordsworth must be reckoned with. Byron, much to Wordsworth's annoyance, wove the theme of nature's restorative power into his third canto of *Childe Harold's Pilgrimage*. The critics declared he had surpassed his teacher.

For his part, Shelley was more critical of the idea. He had already discussed the notion in *Alastor* where his visionary and youthful hero, driven by his passion for nature, rejects the kindly influences of human love and so dies a broken and exiled wraith. For Shelley, hypersensitivity to nature often induced a state of visionary terror, and in the English circle's evening talks at the Villa Diodati where Byron now lodged, the brilliant conversation turned on the themes of madness, corpses and the perils of thwarted passion. Outside, the rain beat on the shutters. Thunder boomed round the Jura, and lightning flashed across the dark bosom of the lake. It was a gothic gathering in the candlelight and it was to produce a masterpiece.

Surrounded by geniuses, "Polly Dolly" had written a play. Everyone admitted it was something of a disappointment, and to make up for it they agreed to regale each other with ghost stories of their own devising. Shelley's (which has not survived) was the first told, but when Byron recited the lines from Coleridge's *Christabel* in which an evil demon visits her victim, Shelley ran shrieking from the room, one hand pulling at his long hair, the other clutching a guttering candle. He had been looking at Mary as Byron recited, and she had merged into a nightmare image of a woman whose nipples were eyes. Polidori calmed Shelley down and then used the incident in his own gothic novel *The Vampyre*, much of the rest of which he stole from Byron.

A few nights later, and while these matters were still weighing on their minds, Mary Shelley had a nightmare. She also, she came to realize, had the plot for her story. This was no longer a matter for an evening's entertainment, however. Throughout the summer she worked on *Frankenstein*, her novel about a scientist so obsessed with his attempts to create a living being artificially that he postpones the offer of love and happiness. Pursued by his creation (whose own chances of sexual happiness he wilfully destroys) Frankenstein is visited by the creature on his wedding night. Helpless, he watches it throttle his bride. The melodrama is superbly grand and subtly resonant. Maker and monster have destroyed each other's chances of joy, and so live as pariahs, the victims of a ghastly and mutual pursuit. In its skilful handling of obsession and the terrors of thwarted sexuality, *Frankenstein* is the permanent record of the evenings at the Villa Diodati.

On 23 June—perhaps to refresh themselves after so much hysteria —Byron and Shelley decided to take a leisurely tour on Lake Leman. A squall blew up. The rudder broke, and the boat was nearly swamped. Shelley, to his chagrin, could not swim. The danger they were in has been greatly exaggerated, however. Byron knew perfectly well he could make for the rocks if necessary. Shelley—already aware that his own genius was dimmed when Byron was near—was further humiliated by the thought that Byron could easily save him.

Of more lasting importance to them both was the fact that they were literary pilgrims in the countryside of Rousseau. Shelley was reading *La Nouvelle Héloïse*. Byron, who already knew the novel well, had worked suggestions from it into the landscape passages of the third canto of *Childe Harold's Pilgrimage*. The idea that nature is a rejuvenating force, especially for the bitter exile, derives in part from Wordsworth and in part from the great French philosopher, in particular his *Rêveries d'un Promeneur Solitaire*. Here Rousseau tells how, when listening to the gentle wash of the waves of Lake Leman, he had intuitions of the divinity of nature more powerful than anything produced by thought alone. Though Voltaire, true to his Enlightenment rationality, was to mock him mercilessly for this—never, he said, had so much intelligence been used to convince us to be stupid—Rousseau's experience was one of the great fertilizing perceptions of his age. Virtually no Romantic artist was unaffected by this most articulate rewording of the old cry: "Back to nature!". Byron was still adding stanzas to his poem, and his invocation to "Clear, placid Leman!" is shot through with grateful reminiscences of this most complex of the Enlightenment giants.

Indeed, during this period, Byron was beginning avidly to explore aspects of himself by borrowing from the great men of the previous age. This need cause no surprise. Writers create as much by absorbing and reacting to each other's books as they do by charting their own experience. And Rousseau was a natural choice. He was a man who, like Byron himself, was capable of the greatest extremes of cruelty and gentleness, an exile passionately involved in politics, who believed that the old order of society must be destroyed so that men and women could be reborn and live under a new and fairer social contract.

Claire Clairmont, the mother of Byron's illegitimate daughter, was a victim of the poet's callous disregard. She pursued Byron across Europe, was rebuffed, and ended her days in poverty.

NATURE

"Are not the mountains, waves, and skies, a part
Of me and of my soul?"

The influence of both Rousseau and Wordsworth is clear in these stanzas from the third canto of *Childe Harold's Pilgrimage.*
Here nature is shown in her power to heal the wounded human spirit by making it at one with her own benign forces.
Wordsworth himself was considerably annoyed at Byron's reworking of his ideas and the praise this won from critics.

Lake Leman woos me with its crystal face,*
The mirror where the stars and mountains view
The stillness of their aspect in each trace
Its clear depth yields of their far height and hue:
There is too much of man here, to look through
With a fit mind the might which I behold;
But soon in me shall Loneliness renew
Thoughts hid, but not less cherish'd than of old,
Ere mingling with the herd had penn'd me in their fold.

To fly from, need not be to hate, mankind;
All are not fit with them to stir and toil,
Nor is it discontent to keep the mind
Deep in its fountain, lest it overboil
In the hot throng, where we become the spoil
Of our infection, till too late and long
We may deplore and struggle with the coil,
In wretched interchange of wrong for wrong
'Midst a contentious world, striving where none are strong.

There, in a moment, we may plunge our years
In fatal penitence, and in the blight
Of our own soul, turn all our blood to tears,
And colour things to come with hues of Night;
The race of life becomes a hopeless flight
To those that walk in darkness: on the sea,
The boldest steer but where their ports invite,
But there are wanderers o'er Eternity
Whose bark drives on and on, and anchored ne'er shall be.

*Shelley "dosed" Byron with passages from
Wordsworth, who was greatly annoyed when
critics declared Byron's reworking of
his ideas in the third canto of
"Childe Harold's Pilgrimage" surpassed
his master's.*

Is it not better, then, to be alone,
And love Earth only for its earthly sake?
By the blue rushing of the arrowy Rhone,
Or the pure bosom of its nursing lake,
Which feeds it as a mother who doth make
A fair but froward infant her own care,
Kissing its cries away as these awake;—
Is it not better thus our lives to wear,
Than join the crushing crowd, doom'd to inflict or bear?

I live not in myself, but I become
Portion of that around me; and to me,
High mountains are a feeling, but the hum
Of human cities torture: I can see
Nothing to loathe in nature, save to be
A link reluctant in a fleshly chain,
Class'd among creatures, when the soul can flee,
And with the sky, the peak, the heaving plain
Of ocean, or the stars, mingle, and not in vain.

And thus I am absorb'd and this is life:
I look upon the peopled desert past,
As on a place of agony and strife,
Where, for some sin, to Sorrow I was cast,
To act and suffer, but remount at last
With a fresh pinion; which I feel to spring,
Though young, yet waxing vigorous, as the blast
Which it would cope with, on delighted wing,
Spurning the clay-cold bonds which round our being cling.

And when, at length, the mind shall be all free
From what it hates in this degraded form,
Reft of its carnal life, save what shall be
Existent happier in the fly and worm,—
When elements to elements conform,
And dust is as it should be, shall I not
Feel all I see, less dazzling, but more warm?
The bodiless thought? the Spirit of each spot?
Of which, even now, I share at times the immortal lot?

Are not the mountains, waves, and skies, a part
Of me and of my soul, as I of them?
Is not the love of these deep in my heart
With a pure passion? should I not contemn
All objects, if compared with these? and stem
A tide of suffering, rather than forgo
Such feelings for the hard and worldly phlegm
Of those whose eyes are only turn'd below,
Gazing upon the ground, with thoughts which dare not glow?

*Joseph Wright of Derby's picture
illustrates a scene from Sterne's*
Sentimental Journey. *The image was to
influence Byron who recalls its pathos
in "The Prisoner of Chillon".*

With such thoughts as these in mind, the two pilgrims visited the nearby château of Chillon. "I never," Shelley wrote, "saw a monument more terrible of that cold and inhuman tyranny, which it has been the delight of man to exercise over man."

The guide told them the story of François Bonivard, a 16th century rebel against authority who had languished in manacles there. Byron was moved, and two days later, when they were detained at Ouchy by the weather, he dashed off the 14 stanzas of *The Prisoner of Chillon*. This time he was not cheated by his own facility. The poem is by far the best of Byron's non-satiric works: vivid, well-organized, and untroubled by crudely melodramatic attitudes. *The Prisoner of Chillon* charts the appalling progress of a man who, stripped of all that makes life worth living, loses his sanity and recovers only to recognize, when freedom comes, that darkness is his natural state. He faces the blunt and dreadful irony of his life: long suffering has leached him of a capacity for joy—"I learned to love despair". The prisoner of Chillon is not just François Bonivard, nor a projection of Byron himself, he is Everyman trapped and defeated in the dungeons of the spirit.

Byron and Shelley returned home from their trip. Claire, grateful now for any attention Byron might show her, was given the task of making the fair copy of his latest work. But the poet, grown tired of her pleading, was glad when she left with the Shelleys for a tour of Chamouni and Mont Blanc.

THE PRISONER OF CHILLON

*"went over the Castle of Chillon again – on our
return met an English party in a carriage – a lady
in it fast asleep!"*

Of all Byron's non-satirical narratives, *The Prisoner of Chillon*
is the most deservedly famous. Written after a visit to the castle
with Shelley, the poem expresses not just a loathing of
tyranny, but an awareness of that most subtle of evils whereby
a victim of oppression comes to love the very chains that
bind him down. Not all English tourists, however, seem
to have responded in quite the same way!

My hair is grey, but not with years,
    Nor grew it white
    In a single night,
As men's have grown from sudden fears:
My limbs are bowed, though not with toil,
    But rusted with a vile repose,
For they have been a dungeon's spoil,
    And mine has been the fate of those
To whom the goodly earth and air
Are bann'd, and barr'd—forbidden fare;
But this was for my father's faith

I suffered chains and courted death;
That father perish'd at the stake
For tenets he would not forsake;
And for the same his lineal race
In darkness found a dwelling-place;
We were seven—who now are one,
    Six in youth, and one in age,
Finish'd as they had begun,
    Proud of Persecution's rage;
One in fire, and two in field,
Their belief with blood have seal'd;

Dying as their father died,
For the God their foes denied;
Three were in a dungeon cast,
Of whom this wreck is left the last.

2

There are seven pillars of gothic mold,
In Chillon's dungeons deep and old,
There are seven columns, massy and grey,
Dim with a dull imprisoned ray,
A sunbeam which hath lost its way,
And through the crevice and the cleft
Of the thick wall is fallen and left;
Creeping o'er the floor so damp,
Like a marsh's meteor lamp:
And in each pillar there is a ring,
And in each ring there is a chain;
That iron is a cankering thing,
For in these limbs its teeth remain,
With marks that will not wear away,
Till I have done with this new day,
Which now is painful to these eyes
Which have not seen the sun so rise
For years—I cannot count them o'er,
I lost their long and heavy score,
When my last brother droop'd and died,
And I lay living by his side.

3

They chain'd us each to a column stone,
And we were three—yet, each alone,
We could not move a single pace,
We could not see each other's face,
But with that pale and livid light
That made us strangers in our sight;
And thus together—yet apart,
Fettered in hand, but pined in heart;
'Twas still some solace in the dearth
Of the pure elements of earth,
To hearken to each other's speech,
And each turn comforter to each,

With some new hope, or legend old,
Or song heroically bold;
But even these at length grew cold.
Our voices took a dreary tone,
An echo of the dungeon-stone,
    A grating sound—not full and free
    As they of yore were wont to be:
    It might be fancy—but to me
They never sounded like our own.

4

I was the eldest of the three,
And to uphold and cheer the rest
I ought to do—and did my best—
And each did well in his degree.
The youngest, whom my father loved,
Because our mother's brow was given
To him—with eyes as blue as heaven,
For him my soul was sorely moved;
And truly might it be distrest
To see such bird in such a nest;
For he was beautiful as day—
(When day was beautiful to me
As to young eagles, being free)—
A polar day, which will not see
A sunset till its summer's gone,
Its sleepless summer of long light,
The snow-clad offspring of the sun:
And thus he was as pure and bright,
And in his natural spirit gay,
With tears for nought but others' ills,
And then they flowed like mountain rills,
Unless he could assuage the woe
Which he abhorr'd to view below.

5

The other was as pure of mind,
But formed to combat with his kind;
Strong in his frame, and of a mood
Which 'gainst the world in war had stood,
And perish'd in the foremost rank

With joy:—but not in chains to pine:
His spirit withered with their clank,
   I saw it silently decline—
   And so perchance in sooth did mine;
But yet I forced it on to cheer
Those relics of a home so dear.
He was a hunter of the hills,
   Had followed there the deer and wolf;
   To him this dungeon was a gulf,
And fettered feet the worst of ills.

6

   Lake Leman lies by Chillon's walls:
A thousand feet in depth below
Its massy waters meet and flow;
Thus much the fathom-line was sent
From Chillon's snow-white battlement,
   Which round about the wave enthralls:
A double dungeon wall and wave
Have made—and like a living grave.
Below the surface of the lake
The dark vault lies wherein we lay,
We heard it ripple night and day;
   Sounding o'er our heads it knock'd;
And I have felt the winter's spray
Wash through the bars when winds were high
And wanton in the happy sky;
   And then the very rock hath rock'd,
   And I have felt it shake, unshock'd,
Because I could have smiled to see
The death that would have set me free.

7

I said my nearer brother pined,
I said his mighty heart declined,
He loath'd and put away his food;
It was not that 'twas coarse and rude,
For we were used to hunter's fare,
And for the like had little care:
The milk drawn from the mountain goat
Was changed for water from the moat,

Our bread was such as captive's tears
Have moisten'd many a thousand years,
Since man first pent his fellow men
Like brutes within an iron den:
But what were these to us or him?
These wasted not his heart or limb;
My brother's soul was of that mould
Which in a palace had grown cold,
Had his free breathing been denied
The range of the steep mountain's side;
But why delay the truth?—he died.
I saw, and could not hold his head,
Nor reach his dying hand—nor dead,
Though hard I strove, but strove in vain,
To rend and gnash my bonds in twain.
He died—and they unlocked his chain,

Caspar David Friedrich's wanderer above the snows
is one of the great images of European romanticism
and bears an uncanny likeness to Byron's self-
portrait in "Childe Harold", Canto Three.

And scoop'd for him a shallow grave
Even from the cold earth of our cave.
I begg'd them, as a boon, to lay
His corse in dust whereon the day
Might shine—it was a foolish thought,
But then within my brain it wrought,
That even in death his freeborn breast
In such a dungeon could not rest.
I might have spared my idle prayer—
They coldly laugh'd—and laid him there:
The flat and turfless earth above
The being we so much did love;
His empty chain above it leant,
Such murder's fitting monument!

8

But he, the favorite and the flower,
Most cherish'd since his natal hour,
His mother's image in fair face,
The infant love of all his race,
His martyred father's dearest thought,
My latest care, for whom I sought
To hoard my life, that his might be
Less wretched now, and one day free;
He, too, who yet had held untired
A spirit natural or inspired—
He, too, was struck, and day by day
Was withered on the stalk away.
Oh God! it is a fearful thing
To see the human soul take wing
In any shape, in any mood:—
I've seen it rushing forth in blood,
I've seen it on the breaking ocean
Strive with a swoln convulsive motion,
I've seen the sick and ghastly bed
Of Sin delirious with its dread:
But these were horrors—this was woe
Unmix'd with such—but sure and slow:
He faded, and so calm and meek,
So softly worn, so sweetly weak,
So tearless, yet so tender—kind,
And grieved for those he left behind;

With all the while a cheek whose bloom
Was as a mockery of the tomb,
Whose tints as gently sunk away
As a departing rainbow's ray—
An eye of most transparent light,
That almost made the dungeon bright,
And not a word of murmur—not
A groan o'er his untimely lot,—
A little talk of better days,
A little hope my own to raise,
For I was sunk in silence—lost
In this last loss, of all the most;
And then the sighs he would suppress
Of fainting nature's feebleness,
More slowly drawn, grew less and less:

Ford Madox Brown was the Victorian painter who
responded most fruitfully to Byron, and his
illustration of Manfred on the Jungfrau, showing
the moment when the hero is saved from death,
captures much of the play's melodramatic concern
with isolation, fear, and suicide.

I listened, but I could not hear—
I called, for I was wild with fear;
I knew 'twas hopeless, but my dread
Would not be thus admonished;
I called, and thought I heard a sound—
I burst my chain with one strong bound,
And rush'd to him:—I found him not,
I only stirr'd in this black spot,
I only lived—*I* only drew
The accursed breath of dungeon-dew;
The last—the sole—the dearest link
Between me and the eternal brink,
Which bound me to my failing race,
Was broken in this fatal place.
One on the earth, and one beneath—
My brothers—both had ceased to breathe:
I took that hand which lay so still,
Alas! my own was full as chill;
I had not strength to stir, or strive,
But felt that I was still alive—
A frantic feeling, when we know
That what we love shall ne'er be so.
     I know not why
     I could not die,
I had no earthly hope—but faith,
And that forbade a selfish death.

9

What next befell me then and there
I know not well—I never knew—
First came the loss of light, and air,
And then of darkness too:
I had no thought, no feeling—none—
Among the stones I stood a stone,
And was, scarce conscious what I wist,
As shrubless crags within the mist;
For all was blank, and bleak, and grey,
It was not night—it was not day,
It was not even the dungeon-light,
So hateful to my heavy sight,
But vacancy absorbing space,
And fixedness—without a place;

There were no stars—no earth—no time—
No check—no change—no good—no crime—
But silence, and a stirless breath
Which neither was of life nor death;
A sea of stagnant idleness,
Blind, boundless, mute, and motionless!

10

A light broke in upon my brain,—
   It was the carol of a bird;
It ceased, and then it came again,
   The sweetest song ear ever heard,
And mine was thankful till my eyes
Ran over with the glad surprise,
And they that moment could not see
I was the mate of misery;
But then by dull degrees came back
My senses to their wonted track,
I saw the dungeon walls and floor
Close slowly round me as before,
I saw the glimmer of the sun
Creeping as it before had done,
But through the crevice where it came
That bird was perch'd, as fond and tame,
   And tamer than upon the tree;
A lovely bird, with azure wings,
And song that said a thousand things,
   And seem'd to say them all for me!
I never saw its like before,
I ne'er shall see its likeness more:
It seem'd like me to want a mate,
But was not half so desolate,
And it was come to love me when
None lived to love me so again,
And cheering from my dungeon's brink,
Had brought me back to feel and think.
I know not if it late were free,
   Or broke its cage to perch on mine,
But knowing well captivity,
   Sweet bird! I could not wish for thine!
Or if it were, in winged guise,
A visitant from Paradise;

For—Heaven forgive that thought! the while
Which made me both to weep and smile;
I sometimes deemed that it might be
My brother's soul come down to me;
But than at last away it flew,
And then 'twas mortal—well I knew,
For he would never thus have flown,
And left me twice so doubly lone,—
Lone—as the corse within its shroud,
Lone—as a solitary cloud,
    A single cloud on a sunny day,
While all the rest of heaven is clear,
A frown upon the atmosphere,
That hath no business to appear
    When skies are blue, and earth is gay.

11

A kind of change came in my fate,
My keepers grew compassionate,
I know not what had made them so,
They were inured to sights of woe,
But so it was:—my broken chain
With links unfasten'd did remain,
And it was liberty to stride
Along my cell from side to side,
And up and down, and then athwart,
And tread it over every part;
And round the pillars one by one,
Returning where my walk begun,
Avoiding only, as I trod,
My brothers' graves without a sod;
For if I thought with heedless tread
My step profaned their lowly bed,
My breath came gaspingly and thick,
And my crush'd heart fell blind and sick.

12

I made a footing in the wall,
    It was not therefrom to escape,
For I had buried one and all,
    Who loved me in a human shape;

And the whole earth would henceforth be
A wider prison unto me:
No child—no sire—no kin had I,
No partner in my misery;
I thought of this, and I was glad,
For thought of them had made me mad;
But I was curious to ascend
To my barr'd windows, and to bend
Once more, upon the mountains high,
The quiet of a loving eye.

13

I saw them—and they were the same,
They were not changed like me in frame;
I saw their thousand years of snow
On high—their wide long lake below,
And the blue Rhone in fullest flow;
I heard the torrents leap and gush
O'er channell'd rock and broken bush;
I saw the white-wall'd distant town,
And whiter sails go skimming down;
And then there was a little isle,
Which in my very face did smile,
    The only one in view;
A small green isle, it seem'd no more,
Scarce broader than my dungeon floor,
But in it there were three tall trees,
And o'er it blew the mountain breeze,
And by it there were waters flowing,
And on it there were young flowers growing,
    Of gentle breath and hue.
The fish swam by the castle wall,
And they seemed joyous each and all;
The eagle rode the rising blast,
Methought he never flew so fast
As then to me he seemed to fly,
And then new tears came in my eye,
And I felt troubled—and would fain
I had not left my recent chain;
And when I did descend again,
The darkness of my dim abode
Fell on me as a heavy load;

It was as is a new-dug grave,
Closing o'er one we sought to save,
And yet my glance, too much opprest,
Had almost need of such a rest.

14

It might be months, or years, or days,
    I kept no count—I took no note,
I had no hope my eyes to raise,
    And clear them of their dreary mote;
At last men came to set me free,
    I ask'd not why, and reck'd not where,
It was at length the same to me,
Fettered or fetterless to be,
    I learn'd to love despair.
And thus when they appear'd at last,
And all my bonds aside were cast,

These heavy walls to me had grown
A hermitage—and all my own!
And half I felt as they were come
To tear me from a second home:
With spiders I had friendship made,
And watch'd them in their sullen trade,
Had seen the mice by moonlight play,
And why should I feel less than they?
We were all inmates of one place,
And I, the monarch of each race,
Had power to kill—yet, strange to tell!
In quiet we had learn'd to dwell,
Nor slew I of my subjects one,
What Sovereign hath so little done?
My very chains and I grew friends,
So much a long communion tends
To make us what we are:—even I
Regain'd my freedom with a sigh.

While they were away, Byron visited the nearby villa of Madame de Staël, whose account of German romantic literature in *De l'Allemagne* was soon to be of great importance to him. When the Shelleys returned it was obvious to everyone that something had to be decided about Claire. It fell to Shelley himself to open negotiations. Byron had at first wanted Augusta to look after the expected child. They finally agreed that Byron would bring it up in Europe, but that it should be born in England. Shelley nobly offered to support the mother until the child joined Byron.

With the heartless wit that came so easily to the period, Byron had written of Claire: "I was not in love with her nor have any love left for any, but I could not exactly play the Stoic with a woman who had scrambled eight hundred miles to unphilosophise me". This, however, is merely the defence of a rake, and when Hobhouse and the raffish Scrope Beardmore Davies arrived in August, the Shelleys realized it was time for them to go. Byron would not even bid Claire farewell. In future, he would only communicate with her through Shelley.

Byron also dismissed the tiresome Polidori and then set out with Hobhouse for a tour of the Bernese Alps. He kept a journal of the trip for Augusta, and the intense excitement he felt in the mountains is clear in every sentence. So, too, is its relation to his more troubled feelings. "Passed *whole woods of withered pines, all withered*; trunks stripped and barkless, branches lifeless; done by a single winter,—their appearance reminded me of me and my family." Out of such gloom, and further stimulated by memories of *De l'Allemagne* and the passages of Goethe's *Faust*, which the gothic horror writer "Monk" Lewis had translated for him during a recent visit, there emerged a new version of the Byronic hero.

Like the pirates and brigands of the *Oriental Tales*, Manfred was popular and extremely influential in his day; but like them again, he emerges now as a rather embarrassing disappointment: an adolescent superman, vain, posturing and confused with self-pity.

THE PAINS OF EXILE

"she—or rather—the Separation—has broken my heart"

During his journey through the Alps after his separation, Byron kept a journal for his half-sister, Augusta. In this passage he evokes his sense of personal desolation amid a wild and beautiful landscape. This theme was to be powerfully developed in the third canto of *Childe Harold's Pilgrimage* and in *Manfred*.

I was disposed to be pleased—I am a lover of
Nature—and an Admirer of Beauty—I can bear
fatigue—& welcome privation—and have seen some of
the noblest views in the world.—But in all this—the
recollections of bitterness—& more especially of recent &
more home desolation—which must accompany me
through life—have preyed upon me here—and neither the
music of the Shepherd—the crashing of the
Avalanche—nor the torrent—the mountain—the
Glacier—the Forest—nor the Cloud—have for one
moment—lightened the weight upon my heart—nor
enabled me to lose my own wretched identity in the
majesty & the power and the Glory—around—above—&
beneath me.—I am past reproaches—and there is a time
for all things—I am past the wish of vengeance—and I
know of none like for what I have suffered—but the hour
will come—when what I feel must be felt—& the
——but enough.——To you—dearest Augusta—I
send—and *for* you—I have kept this record of what I have
seen & felt.—Love me as you are beloved by me.——

The text is conceived as a play for the theatre of the imagination, although many of its effects recall the elaborate devices of the Regency stage. So, too, as Manfred soliloquizes on his suffering for inexpiable crime and, against a confused supernatural scenario, rejects the comforts of nature and faith only to learn from his beloved Astarte that he will soon die, we can glimpse something of the great melodramatic performances of Kean and his kind. But the fact is, Byron had no real aptitude for metaphysical melodrama. This last attempt to claim a philosophic value for the Byronic hero merely shows that there is none, and that T.S. Eliot was right when he declared that it is impossible to make anything coherent out of Byron's "diabolism". Wholly new aspects of the Byron myth were needed.

MANFRED

"The translations have been very frequent of several of the works—and Goethe made a comparison between Faust and Manfred"

Manfred is an attempt to explore some of the philosophical implications of the Byronic hero, and is best read as an autobiographical work. Byron uses the fashionable interest in Germanic literature as a vehicle for expressing his own guilt and despair after the break-up of his marriage and his separation from Augusta. The play was widely influential, especially for its expression of the *weltschmerz*, or "world sorrow", of the romantic imagination.

> Look on me! there is an order
> Of mortals on the earth, who do become
> Old in their youth, and die ere middle age,
> Without the violence of warlike death;
> Some perishing of pleasure—some of study—
> Some worn with toil—some of mere weariness—
> Some of disease—and some insanity—
> And some of withered, or of broken hearts;
> For this last is a malady which slays
> More than are numbered in the lists of Fate,
> Taking all shapes, and bearing many names.
> Look upon me! for even of all these things
> Have I partaken; and of all these things,
> One were enough; then wonder not that I
> Am what I am, but that I ever was,
> Or, having been, that I am still on earth.

Don Juan in Italy

Italy provided Byron with fresh inspiration and, in showing him
the true nature of his genius, she recreated him with all the
warmth and laughter of her ancient benevolence. The process,
being a natural one at first, was slow.

He arrived at Venice in the teeming rain. Huddled under the black
covering of their gondola, Byron and Hobhouse could for a while see
nothing. Then, as they turned under the Rialto, lights from the palaces
threw jagged reflections on the water of the Grand Canal. They
glimpsed the fading pinks of crumbling walls, gothic arches, the gilt
and painted silks of their magnificent hotel. Next to Greece, Venice
was the "greenest island" of his imagination. Later, in the narrow *calle*
of the Frezzeria, near the domes and columns of San Marco, he rented
an apartment and fell in "fathomless love" with Marianna Segati, the
black-eyed wife of his landlord. His recuperation was beginning.

He went to the *conversazioni* or literary gatherings of the Countess
Albrizzi and chatted about poetry with the Italian writer Foscolo.
News reached him of the huge success of the third canto of *Childe
Harold* and *The Prisoner of Chillon*; but he felt, for the moment, that he
had written himself out. Besides, poetry, he increasingly believed, was
not his true vocation. He yearned for a life of action. Looking for
something on which to exercise his intelligence, he began to study
Armenian in the library of San Lazzaro and helped Padre Aucher with
his Armenian dictionary. He regularly made love to Marianna, and by
January the Carnival was on its way. He had finished now with the
lonely posturings of *Manfred*. He put the completed manuscript aside,
and went down among the masked, excited revellers thronging the
squares in their gaiety. Here he exhausted himself with pleasure, and
expressed his feelings in one of his most delicate lyrics:

SO WE'LL GO NO MORE A ROVING

So, we'll go no more a roving
  So late into the night,
Though the heart be still as loving,
  And the moon be still as bright.

For the sword outwears its sheath,
  And the soul wears out the breast,
And the heart must pause to breathe,
  And love itself have rest.

Though the night was made for loving,
   And the day returns too soon,
Yet we'll go no more a roving
   By the light of the moon.

Spring came to Venice, and winds from the Adriatic blew in to warm the ancient stones. The preoccupations of winter began to dull, and Marianna gave him permission to follow Hobhouse to Rome for a while. Travel, as always, stimulated his senses, and a new Childe Harold was ripening in the Italian spring. By the end of April Byron was in Rome and excited by its grandeur. Hobhouse, ever indefatigable, acted as his *cicerone*.

But there were other English people in Rome and Byron's notoriety was still rife. Lady Liddell observed the poet among the baroque extravagances of St Peter's. Fortunately, he did not see her as she turned terrified to her daughter and begged her not to look at him. "He is dangerous to look at," she hissed. The myth was still very strong.

Back in England itself, Claire had now given birth to his daughter. "I am a little puzzled how to dispose of this new production," Byron wrote to Augusta, "but shall probably send for and place it in a Venetian convent, to become a good Catholic, and (it may be) a *Nun*." The callous wit does not hide deeper feelings. The illegitimate child of a peer was simply a nuisance to be dealt with quietly. A month later, Byron was back in the arms of Marianna Segati.

To escape from the fierce Venetian summer, Byron rented the Villa Foscarini on the dusty road to Padua. Here, once again, he began to write, working up his Italian travels between visits from Marianna who, conveniently, had friends nearby. He wrote with his old energy, drafting the fourth canto of *Childe Harold's Pilgrimage* at the rate of nearly 60 lines a day.

Once again, the haste shows. There is a fault even in the famous opening lines:

I stood in Venice on the Bridge of Sighs:
A palace and a prison on each hand:
I saw from out the wave her structures rise
As from the stroke of the enchanter's wand:
A thousand years their cloudy wings expand
Around me, and a dying Glory smiles
O'er the far times, when many a subject land
Look'd to the winged Lion's marble piles,
Where Venice sate in state, thron'd on her hundred isles!

He meant that on the one hand there was a palace and on the other a prison, but he seems to have been unable to get the truth to scan. That he begins with a city and with symbols of power and suffering is suggestive, however, since the fourth canto of *Childe Harold's Pilgrimage* is a meditation on the fall of civilizations and the sufferings of its great men. Byron's own woes merge with these, but he now sees that true artists are finally justified by their immortality.

In the central stanzas on his own sufferings, writing.at the fevered height of his rhetoric, Byron indeed achieves something of lasting significance. In fact, the lines on his memorial stone in Westminster Abbey are taken from here. In the very force of his passion to forgive his enemies, he heaps live coals on their heads, revealing the bitter irony of a satirist at work.

IMMORTALITY

"the remembered tone of a mute lyre"

In the fourth canto of *Childe Harold's Pilgrimage*, Byron meditates not just on his own suffering but on how, by forgiving his enemies, he will heap coals of fire on their heads. He also suggests that the poetry he has created out of his anguish will make his name eternal. Lines from the last stanza printed here adorn his memorial stone in Westminster Abbey.

And if my voice break forth, 'tis not that now
I shrink from what is suffered: let him speak
Who hath beheld decline upon my brow,
Or seen my mind's convulsion leave it weak;
But in this page a record will I seek.
Not in the air shall these my words disperse,
Though I be ashes; a far hour shall wreak
The deep prophetic fullness of this verse,
And pile on human heads the mountain of my curse!

That curse shall be Forgiveness.—Have I not—
Hear me, my mother Earth! behold it, Heaven!—
Have I not had to wrestle with my lot?
Have I not suffered things to be forgiven?
Have I not had my brain seared, my heart riven,
Hopes sapp'd, name blighted, Life's life lied away?
And only not to desperation driven,
Because not altogether of such clay
As rots into the souls of those whom I survey.

From mighty wrongs to petty perfidy
Have I not seen what human things could do?
From the loud roar of foaming calumny
To the small whisper of the as paltry few,
And subtler venom of the reptile crew,
The Janus glance of whose significant eye,*
Learning to lie with silence, would *seem* true,
And without utterance, save the shrug or sigh,
Deal round to happy fools its speechless obloquy.

But I have lived, and have not lived in vain:
My mind may lose its force, my blood its fire,
And my frame perish even in conquering pain,
But there is that within me which shall tire
Torture and Time, and breathe when I expire;
Something unearthly, which they deem not of,
Like the remembered tone of a mute lyre,
Shall on their softened spirits sink, and move
In hearts all rocky now the late remorse of love.

But the Childe Harold mode had worn itself out. There were other matters to attend to and visitors at the Villa Foscarini. In September, Douglas Kinnaird and his brother brought news and books. A month earlier, Hobhouse had called.

Byron was able to keep horses at his villa, and as he and Hobhouse rode through the cicada-ticking heat of an Italian August they met a couple of earthy peasant girls. Byron's was tall, black-eyed and 22. In her Venetian dialect she told him with rousing frankness that she had no objection to having sex with him since she was a married woman and every married woman had her *cavalier servente*. He should be wary of her baker husband though, who was a jealous man. Matters were soon arranged, and Margarita Cogni, delighting Byron with her sharp tongue and pungent sexuality, defied her rival in comic-opera style. Byron was hugely amused. Staring straight into Marianna's eyes, Margarita declared: "*You* are *not* his *wife*; *I* am *not* his *wife*: *you* are his *Donna*, and *I* am his *Donna*: *your* husband is a cuckold, and *mine* is another. For the rest, what *right* have you to reproach me? if he prefers what is mine to what is yours, is it my fault?'

Signor Segati, meanwhile, was visiting his own *inamorata* nearby and brought Byron gossip from Venice. He had rather taken to his wife's lover, and he told Byron of a local woman who, believing she had lost her husband at sea, took a *cavalier servente*. After some years a Turk appeared at her house and eventually revealed himself as her husband. He had now told her that she must either quit her *amoroso* and return to him, stay with her lover, or take an annuity and live alone. To date, the lady had not made up her mind. Margarita declared she would not leave her lover for the sake of a mere husband, and smiled at Byron. The English Hobhouse was deeply shocked.

Byron was delighted. Here was the very substance of his Venetian freedom. But how could the gloomy poet of *Manfred* and *The Corsair* put it into verse?

He found the answer among the books Douglas Kinnaird had brought him. *Whistlecraft*, by John Hookham Frere, was a minor satire in the witty, carefree, wandering manner of the 15th century Italian poet Luigi Pulci. Its laughter at once freed Byron from his *Manfred* mode. Translated back into the shimmering Venice of Guardi and Casanova, and expressed in the light *ottava rima* of Pulci and Frere, Signor Segati's tale became *Beppo*, the first comic masterpiece of the English romantic movement. In the brightness of an Italian summer, Byron had found his true voice. Wit, tenderness and worldly-wise comedy mingle in a poem whose construction is always carefree but never careless. Its staggering virtuosity, sudden and inexplicable, shows that Byron's long apprenticeship was at last over.

In November he moved back to Venice, and in the following month learned that Newstead had finally been sold. Very soon, he hoped, his £30,000 burden of debt would be cleared. When Hobhouse had departed, Byron threw himself into the January revels of the carnival, finding in its vibrant life, perhaps, some compensation for the wilting of his affair with Marianna. By February, he had contracted a venereal disease.

BEPPO

*"I have settled into regular Serventismo –
and find it the happiest state of all"*

Beppo is Byron's first comic masterpiece.
With this poem he suddenly found his
artistic freedom and his truest voice. The
subject is the Italian convention that a
married woman may take a lover, or *cavalier
servente*. This was deeply shocking to
conventional English morality, but in his
opening stanzas Byron creates an irresistible
picture of the careless gaiety of
18th century Venice.

'Tis known, at least it should be, that throughout
    All countries of the Catholic persuasion,
Some weeks before Shrove Tuesday comes about,
    The people take their fill of recreation,
And buy repentance, ere they grow devout,
    However high their rank, or low their station,
With fiddling, feasting, dancing, drinking, masquing,
And other things which may be had for asking.

The moment night with dusky mantle covers
    The skies (and the more duskily the better),
The time less liked by husbands than by lovers
    Begins, and prudery flings aside her fetter;
And gaiety on restless tiptoe hovers,
    Giggling with all the gallants who beset her;
And there are songs and quavers, roaring, humming,
Guitars, and every other sort of strumming.

And there are dresses splendid, but fantastical,
    Masks of all times and nations, Turks and Jews,
And harlequins and clowns, with feats gymnastical,
    Greeks, Romans, Yankee-doodles, and Hindoos;
All kinds of dress, except the ecclesiastical,
    All people, as their fancies hit, may choose,
But no one in these parts may quiz the clergy,
Therefore take heed, ye Freethinkers! I charge ye.

Byron creates a lighthearted sketch
of the *cavalier servente*, but when obliged
to play this role himself with the
Contessa Teresa Guiccioli – the deepest
love of his life – he found it both
irksome and humiliating.

And then he was a count, and then he knew
    Music, and dancing, fiddling, French and Tuscan;
The last not easy, be it known to you,
    For few Italians speak the right Etruscan.
He was a critic upon operas, too,
    And knew all niceties of the sock and buskin;
And no Venetian audience could endure a
Song, scene, or air, when he cried 'seccatura.'*

His 'bravo' was decisive, for that sound
    Hushed 'academie' sighed in silent awe;
The fiddlers trembled as he looked around,
    For fear of some false note's detected flaw.
The 'prima donna's' tuneful heart would bound,
    Dreading the deep damnation of his 'bah!'
Soprano, basso, even the contra-alto,
Wished him five fathom under the Rialto.

He patroniz'd the Improvisatori,*
    Nay, could himself extemporize some stanzas,
Wrote rhymes, sang songs, could also tell a story,
    Sold pictures, and was skilful in the dance as
Italians can be, though in this their glory
    Must surely yield the palm to that which France has;
In short, he was a perfect cavaliero,
And to his very valet seem'd a hero.

Then he was faithful, too, as well as amorous,
    So that no sort of female could complain,
Although they're now and then a little clamorous,
    He never put the pretty souls in pain;
His heart was one of those which most enamour us,
    Wax to receive, and marble to retain.
He was a lover of the good old school,
Who still become more constant as they cool.

No wonder such accomplishments should turn
    A female head, however sage and steady—
With scarce a hope that Beppo could return,
    In law he was almost as good as dead, he
Nor sent, nor wrote, nor show'd the least concern,
    And she had waited several years already;
And really if a man won't let us know
That he's alive, he's *dead*, or should be so.

Besides, within the Alps, to every woman
(Although, God knows, it is a grievous sin)
'Tis, I may say, permitted to have *two* men;
    I can't tell who first brought the custom in,
But 'Cavalier Serventes' are quite common,
    And no one notices, nor cares a pin;
And we may call this (not to say the worst)
A *second* marriage which corrupts the *first*.

The word was formerly a 'Cicisbeo,'
    But *that* is now grown vulgar and indecent;
The Spaniards call the person a '*Cortejo*,'
    For the same mode subsists in Spain, though recent;
In short it reaches from the Po to Teio,
    And may perhaps at last be o'er the sea sent.
But Heaven preserve Old England from such courses!
Or what becomes of damage and divorces?

However, I still think, with all due deference
    To the fair *single* part of the Creation,
That married ladies should preserve the preference
    In *tête-à-tête* or general conversation—
And this I say without peculiar reference
    To England, France, or any other nation—
Because they know the world, and are at ease,
And being natural, naturally please.

Thomas Moore was one of Byron's favoured
correspondents for whom he wrote his
exquisite lyric describing the Venetian
carnival, "So we'll go no more a roving".

'Tis true, your budding Miss is very charming,
　　But shy and awkward at first coming out,
So much alarmed, that she is quite alarming,
　　All Giggle, Blush;—half Pertness, and half Pout;
And glancing at *Mamma*, for fear there's harm in
　　What you, she, it, or they, may be about,
The Nursery still lisps out in all they utter—
Besides, they always smell of bread and butter.

But 'Cavalier Servente' is the phrase
　　Used in politest circles to express
This supernumerary slave, who stays
　　Close to the lady as a part of dress,
Her word the only law which he obeys.
　　His is no sinecure, as you may guess;
Coach, servants, gondola, he goes to call,
And carries fan, and tippet, gloves, and shawl.

Guardi's drawing of a ridotto *or masked
Venetian ball suggests the amoral 18th
century Venice of Casanova which Byron
recreated in "Beppo"—the first great comic
masterpiece of his Italian period.*

Satirical digression is the hallmark of
Byron's mature style. In these lines from
Beppo he contrasts the laxity of Italian morals
with the rigid hypocrisy of contemporary
England. The attack is all the more
powerful for the narrator's laughing ease.

'England! with all thy faults I love thee still,'
　　I said at Calais, and have not forgot it;
I like to speak and lucubrate my fill;
　　I like the government (but that is not it);
I like the freedom of the press and quill;
　　I like the Habeas Corpus (when we've got it);*
I like a parliamentary debate,
Particularly when 'tis not too late;

I like the taxes, when they're not too many;
　　I like a seacoal fire, when not too dear;
I like a beef-steak, too, as well as any;
　　Have no objection to a pot of beer;
I like the weather, when it is not rainy,
　　That is, I like two months of every year.
And so God save the Regent, Church, and King!
Which means that I like all and every thing.

Our standing army, and disbanded seamen,
　Poor's rate, Reform, my own, the nation's debt,
Our little riots just to show we are free men,
　Our trifling bankruptcies in the Gazette,
Our cloudy climate, and our chilly women,
　All these I can forgive, and those forget,
And greatly venerate our recent glories,
And wish they were not owing to the Tories.

　Byron's description of Laura at the
　　ball reveals his genius for close
　observation and satire. In these lines he
　　creates a scene which rivals the
　　delicacy of his admired Pope in
　　　The Rape of the Lock.

Now Laura moves along the joyous crowd,
　Smiles in her eyes, and simpers on her lips;
To some she whispers, others speaks aloud;
　To some she curtsies, and to some she dips,
Complains of warmth, and this complaint avow'd,
　Her lover brings the lemonade, she sips;
She then surveys, condemns, but pities still
Her dearest friends for being drest so ill.

One has false curls, another too much paint,
　A third—where did she buy that frightful turban?
A fourth's so pale she fears she's going to faint,
　A fifth's look's vulgar, dowdyish, and suburban,
A sixth's white silk has got a yellow taint,
　A seventh's thin muslin surely will be her bane,
And lo! an eighth appears,—'I'll see no more!'
For fear, like Banquo's kings, they reach a score.

Mean time, while she was thus at others gazing,
　Others were levelling their looks at her;
She heard the men's half-whispered mode of praising,
　And, till 'twas done, determined not to stir;
The women only thought it quite amazing
　That at her time of life so many were
Admirers still,—but men are so debased,
Those brazen creatures always suit their taste.

The conclusion to *Beppo* reveals Byron as a
master of verse narrative. Gone is the strained
melodrama of the *Oriental Tales*, and in its
place is a lightness of touch—the warm
ironic tolerance of the man of the world who
was soon to start on that masterpiece of
worldly wisdom, *Don Juan*.

The Count and Laura found their boat at last,
　　And homeward floated o'er the silent tide,
Discussing all the dances gone and past;
　　The dancers and their dresses, too, beside;
Some little scandals eke: but all aghast
　　(As to their palace stairs the rowers glide)
Sate Laura by the side of her Adorer,
When lo! the Mussulman was there before her.

'Sir,' said the Count, with brow exceeding grave,
　　'Your unexpected presence here will make
It necessary for myself to crave
　　Its import? But perhaps 'tis a mistake;
I hope it is so; and at once to wave
　　All compliment, I hope so for *your* sake;
You understand my meaning, or you *shall*.'
'Sir,' (quoth the Turk) ''tis no mistake at all.

'That lady is *my wife!*' Much wonder paints
　　The lady's changing cheek, as well it might;
But where an Englishwoman sometimes faints,
　　Italian females don't do so outright;
They only call a little on their saints,
　　And then come to themselves, almost or quite;
Which saves much hartshorn, salts, and sprinkling faces,
And cutting stays, as usual in such cases.

She said,—what could she say? Why not a word:
　　But the Count courteously invited in
The stranger, much appeased by what he heard:
　　'Such things perhaps, we'd best discuss within,'
Said he, 'don't let us make ourselves absurd
　　In public, by a scene, nor raise a din,
For then the chief and only satisfaction
Will be much quizzing on the whole transaction.'

They entered, and for coffee called,—it came,
　A beverage for Turks and Christians both,
Although the way they make it's not the same.
　Now Laura, much recovered, or less loth
To speak, cries 'Beppo! what's your pagan name?
　Bless me! your beard is of amazing growth!
And how came you to keep away so long?
Are you not sensible 'twas very wrong?

'And are you *really*, *truly*, now a Turk?
　With any other women did you wive?
Is't true they use their fingers for a fork?
　Well, that's the prettiest shawl—as I'm alive!
You'll give it me? They say you eat no pork.
　And how so many years did you contrive
To—Bless me! did I ever? No, I never
Saw a man grown so yellow! How's your liver?

'Beppo! that beard of yours becomes you not;
　It shall be shaved before you're a day older;
Why do you wear it? Oh! I had forgot—
　Pray don't you think the weather here is colder?
How do I look? You shan't stir from this spot
　In that queer dress, for fear that some beholder
Should find you out, and make the story known.
How short your hair is! Lord! how grey it's grown!'

What answer Beppo made to these demands,
　Is more than I know. He was cast away
About where Troy stood once, and nothing stands;
　Became a slave of course, and for his pay
Had bread and bastinadoes, till some bands
　Of pirates landing in a neighbouring bay,
He joined the rogues and prospered, and became
A renegado of indifferent fame.

But he grew rich, and with his riches grew so
　Keen the desire to see his home again,
He thought himself in duty bound to do so,
　And not be always thieving on the main;
Lonely he felt, at times, as Robin Crusoe,
　And so he hired a vessel come from Spain,
Bound for Corfu; she was a fine polacca,
Manned with twelve hands, and laden with tobacco.

Byron was to suggest the passionate servitude
of his numerous Venetian amours *in his poem*
"Mazeppa". Like many of his themes, it was to
be widely popular among the romantics, as
Horace Vernet's picture suggests.

Himself, and much (heaven knows how gotten) cash,
    He then embarked, with risk of life and limb,
And got clear off, although the attempt was rash;
    He said that *Providence* protected him—
For my part, I say nothing, lest we clash
    In our opinions:—well, the ship was trim,
Set sail, and kept her reckoning fairly on,
Except three days of calm when off Cape Bonn.

They reached the island, he transferred his lading,
    And self and live-stock, to another bottom,
And pass'd for a true Turkey-merchant, trading
    With goods of various names, but I've forgot 'em.
However, he got off by this evading,
    Or else the people would perhaps have shot him;
And thus at Venice landed to reclaim
His wife, religion, house, and Christian name.

His wife received, the patriarch re-baptized him,
    (He made the church a present by the way);
He then threw off the garments which disguised him,
    And borrowed the Count's small-clothes for a day:
His friends the more for his long absence prized him,
    Finding he'd wherewithal to make them gay,
With dinners, where he oft became the laugh of them,
For stories,—but *I* don't believe the half of them.

Whate'er his youth had suffered, his old age
    With wealth and talking made him some amends;
Though Laura sometimes put him in a rage,
    I've heard the Count and he were always friends.
My pen is at the bottom of a page,
    Which being finished, here the story ends;
'Tis to be wished it had been sooner done,
But stories somehow lengthen when begun.

*This picture of Byron in the Palazzo
Moncenigo suggests the sumptuous
lassitude of his Venetian indulgences.
This was also the period of Byron's most
fruitful poetic activity when he became
a master of comedy and satire.*

And now he had to honour his promise to Claire and Shelley. They arrived in Milan with Byron's daughter Allegra in early April. He wrote, asking them to send the child with its nurse to Venice. Shelley replied, begging that Claire herself be allowed to see the father. Claire's own letters suggested that she was still in love with him however, and Byron replied merely that she would be allowed to see the child again if she so wished.

*The "cult of the south" was one of the great enriching forces in
English romantic poetry and painting. It can be felt in the works of
Keats and Shelley as well as in the fourth canto of "Childe Harold's
Pilgrimage". It stood for spontaneity and pleasure as against the
self-doubt of much of the German romantic movement. Turner's "Childe
Harold in Italy" suggests an innocent and natural joyousness found
amid the pleasing melancholy of classical ruins.*

Partly to have space for the little girl and, more importantly, to get
away from Marianna, Byron now moved out of the crowded Frezzeria
and into the magnificent 17th century spaciousness of the Palazzo
Mocenigo on the Grand Canal, a short distance from the Piazza San
Marco. Here Margarita Cogni, the baker's wife, held brief but passionate sway, halving the expenses, bullying the 14 servants, and raising
her strident voice above a menagerie of birds, mastiffs and monkeys.
But, alas, transported to the palace, Margarita grew above herself. She
wanted hats and fine feathers, while Byron liked the common girls of
the streets in their simple, sensuous dresses. In a brilliant letter to
Murray, Byron described the turbulent end of the affair with Margarita.
The letter is a masterpiece of narrative, a brilliantly mocking self-
portrait, and a vivid picture of Byron's Venetian life.

Even the tolerant Venetians found Byron *stravagante*, while English tourists—with a prurient desire to see Venice's most notorious spectacle—bribed his servants for a view inside the palace. With malicious glee, one reported back to Lady Byron that her husband was now "extremely fat . . bloated and heavy". His carefree life was rapidly taking its toll.

Another major painter to be influenced by Byron was Delacroix, and this preparatory sketch for his "Shipwreck of Don Juan" suggests how influential was Byron's diversity of subject matter. In this scene of tragic turmoil, Delacroix has depicted the moment when the survivors draw lots to see which of their company they will eat first.

MARGARITA COGNI

"fit to breed gladiators from"

This is the masterpiece among Byron's many brilliant letters. It was written to John Murray, his publisher, to be passed around his English friends. None of them could have failed to be amused by the shrewd and lively humour, but as a self-portrait of a man revelling in the most bizarre circumstances, the letter is also one of the great prose passages in English romantic literature.

Longhi's genre scene "The Masked Party" suggests the world of leisured and sophisticated Venetian life which Byron recreated in "Beppo". The mask itself, of course, was a convenient disguise for the cavalier servente *and his* amica.

. . . and then I have effeminated and enervated myself with love and the summer in these last two months . . . You have bought Harlow's drawings of Margarita and me rather dear methinks—but since you desire the story of Margarita Cogni—you shall be told it—though it may be lengthy.——Her face is of the fine Venetian cast of the old Time—and her figure though perhaps too tall not less fine—taken altogether in the national dress.——In the summer of 1817, Hobhouse and myself were sauntering on horseback along the Brenta one evening—when amongst a group of peasants we remarked two girls as the prettiest we had seen for some time.—About this period there had been great distress in the country—and I had a little relieved some of the people.—Generosity makes a great figure at very little cost in Venetian livres—and mine had probably been exaggerated—as an Englishman's——Whether they remarked us looking at them or no—I know not—but one of them called out to me in Venetian—"Why do not you who relieve others—think of us also?"—I turned round and answered her—"Cara—tu sei troppo bella e giovane per aver' bisogno del' soccorso mio"*—she answered—["]if you saw my hut and my food—you would not say so["]—All this passed half jestingly—and I saw no more of her for some days—A few evenings after—we met with these two girls again—and they addressed us more seriously—assuring us of the truth of their statement.—They were cousins—Margarita married—the other single.—As I doubted still of the circumstances—I took the business up in a different light—and made an appointment with them for the next evening.—Hobhouse had taken a fancy to the single lady—who was much shorter—in stature—but a very pretty girl also.——They came attended by a third woman—who was cursedly in the way—and Hobhouse's charmer took fright (I don't mean at Hobhouse but at not being married—for here no woman will do anything under adultery), and flew off—and mine made some bother—at the propositions—and wished to consider of them.—I told her "if you really are in want I will relieve you without any conditions whatever—and you may make love with me or no just as you please—*that* shall make no difference—but if you are not in absolute necessity—this is naturally a rendezvous—and I presumed that you understood this—when you made the appointment".——(She said that she had no objection to make love with me—as she was married—and all married women did it—but that her husband (a baker) was somewhat ferocious—and would do her a mischief.—In short—in a few evenings we arranged our affairs—and for two years—in the course of which I had < almost two > more women than I can count or recount—she was the only one who preserved over me an ascendancy—which was often disputed & never impaired.—As she herself used to say publicly—"It don't matter—he may have five hundred—but he will always come back to me".——The reasons of this were firstly—her person—very dark—tall—the Venetian face—very fine black eyes—and certain other qualities which need not be mentioned.—She was two & twenty years old—and never having had children—had not spoilt her figure—nor *anything else*—which is I assure you—a great desideratum in a hot climate where they grow relaxed and doughy and *flumpity* in a short time after breeding.——She was besides a thorough Venetian in her dialect—in her thoughts—in her countenance—in every thing—with all their naïveté and Pantaloon humour.—Besides she could neither read nor write—and could not plague me with letters—except twice that she paid sixpence to a public scribe under the piazza—to make a letter for her—upon some occasion when I was ill and could not see her.——In other respects she was somewhat fierce and "prepotente" that is—overbearing—and used to walk in whenever it suited her—with no very great regard to time, place, nor persons—and if she found any women in her way she knocked them down.—When I first knew her I was in "relazione" (liaison) with la Signora Segati—who was silly enough one evening at Dolo—accompanied by some of her female friends—to threaten her—for the Gossips of the Villeggiatura—had

Byron's treatment of his illegitimate daughter Allegra is one of the more distasteful episodes in his career and is only partly to be excused by the conventional reactions of a Regency peer to his bastard offspring.

already found out by the neighing of my horse one
evening—that I used to "ride late in the night" to meet the
Fornarina.——Margarita threw back her veil (fazziolo)
and replied in very explicit Venetian—"*You* are *not* his *wife:*
I am *not* his *wife*—*you* are his Donna—and *I* am his
donna—*your* husband is a cuckold—and mine is
another;—for the rest, what *right* have you to reproach
me?—if he prefers what is mine—to what is yours—is it
my fault? if you wish to secure him—tie him to your
petticoat-string—but do not think to speak to me without
a reply because you happen to be richer than I
am."——Having delivered this pretty piece of eloquence
(which I translate as it was related to me by a byestander)
she went on her way—leaving a numerous audience with
Madame Segati—to ponder at her leisure on the dialogue
between them.—When I came to Venice for the Winter she
followed:—I never had any regular *liaison* with her—but
whenever she came I never allowed any other connection
to interfere with her—and as she found herself out to be a
favourite she came pretty often.—But She had inordinate
Self-love—and was not tolerant of other women—except
of the Segati—who was as she said my regular
"Amica"—so that I being at that time somewhat
promiscuous—there was great confusion—and demolition
of head dresses and handkerchiefs—and sometimes my
servants in "redding the fray" between her and other
feminine persons—received more knocks than
acknowledgements for their peaceful endeavours.——At
the "Cavalchina" the masqued ball on the last night of the
Carnival—where all the World goes—she snatched off the
mask of Madame Contarini—a lady noble by birth—and
decent in conduct—for no other reason but because she
happened to be leaning on my arm. —You may suppose
what a cursed noise this made—but this is only one of her
pranks. —At last she quarrelled with her husband—and
one evening ran away to my house—I told her this would
not do—she said she would lie in the street but not go
back to him—that he beat her (the gentle tigress) spent her
money— and scandalously neglected his Oven. As it was
Midnight—I let her stay—and next day there was no
moving her at all.——Her husband came roaring &
crying—& entreating her to come back, *not* She!—He
then applied to the Police—and they applied to me—I told

them and her husband to *take* her—I did not want
her—she had come and I could not fling her out of the
window—but they might conduct her through that or the
door if they chose it——She went before the
Commissary—but was obliged to return with that "becco
Ettico" (consumptive cuckold), as she called the *poor* man
who had a Ptisick.—In a few days she ran away
again.—After a precious piece of work she fixed herself in
my house—really & truly without my consent—but
owing to my indolence—and not being able to keep my
countenance—for if I began in a rage she always finished
by making me laugh with some Venetian pantaloonery or
other—and the Gipsy knew this well enough—as well as
her other powers of persuasion—and exerted them with
the usual tact and success of all She-things—high and
low—they are all alike for that.—Madame Benzone also
took her under her protection—and then her head
turned.—She was always in extremes either crying or
laughing—and so fierce when angered that she was the
terror of men women and children—for she had the
strength of an Amazon with the temper of Medea. She was
a fine animal—but quite untameable. *I* was the only person
that could at all keep her in any order—and when she saw
me really angry—(which they tell me is rather a savage
sight), she subsided.—But she had a thousand
fooleries—in her fazziolo—the dress of the lower
orders—she looked beautiful—but alas! she longed for a
hat and feathers and all I could say or do (and I said much)
could not prevent this travestie.—I put the first into the
fire—but I got tired of burning them before she did of
buying them—so that she made herself a figure—for they
did not at all become her.—Then she would have her
gowns with a *tail*—like a lady forsooth—nothing would
serve her—but "l'abito colla *coua*", or *cua*, (that is the
Venetian for "*la Coda*" the tail or train) and as her cursed
pronunciation of the word made me laugh—there was an
end of all controversy—and she dragged this diabolical tail
after her every where.——In the mean time she beat the
women—and stopped my letters.—I found her one day
pondering over one—she used to try to find out by their
shape whether they were feminine or no—and she used to
lament her ignorance—and actually studied her
Alphabet—on purpose (as she declared) to open all letters

Margarita Cogni's earthy passion excited Byron, but her demands and pretensions finally wearied him. If she did not directly inspire any poetry, she is the subject of the finest of Byron's many fine letters —a masterpiece of romantic prose.

addressed to me and read their contents.——I must not omit to do justice to her housekeeping qualities—after she came into my house as "donna di governo" the expences were reduced to less than half—and every body did their duty better—the apartments were kept in order and every thing and every body else except herself.——That she had a sufficient regard for me in her wild way I had many reasons to believe—I will mention one.——In the autumn one day going to the Lido with my Gondoliers—we were overtaken by a heavy Squall and the Gondola put in peril—hats blown away—boat filling—oar lost—tumbling sea—thunder—rain in torrents—night coming—& wind increasing.—On our return—after a tight struggle: I found her on the open steps of the Mocenigo palace on the Grand Canal—with her great black eyes flashing through her tears and the long dark hair which was streaming drenched with rain over her brows & breast;—she was perfectly exposed to the storm—and the wind blowing her hair & dress about her tall thin figure—and the lightning flashing round her—with the waves rolling at her feet—made her look like Medea alighted from her chariot—or the Sibyl of the tempest that was rolling around her—the only living thing within hail at that moment except ourselves.—On seeing me safe—she did not wait to greet me as might be expected—but calling out to me—"Ah! Can' della Madonna xe esto il tempo per andar' al' Lido?" (ah! Dog of the Virgin!—is this a time to go to Lido?) ran into the house—and solaced herself with scolding the boatmen for not foreseeing the "temporale".*—I was told by the servants that she had only been prevented from coming in a boat to look after me—by the refusal of all the Gondoliers of the Canal to put out into the harbour in such a moment and that then she sate down in the steps in all the thickest of the Squall—and would neither be removed nor comforted. Her joy at seeing me again—was moderately mixed with ferocity—and gave me the idea of a tigress over her recovered Cubs.——But her reign drew near a close.—She became quite ungovernable some months after—and a concurrence of complaints some true and many false—"a favourite has no friend"—determined me to part with her.—I told her quietly that she must return home—(she had acquired a sufficient provision for herself and mother, &c. in my service,) and She refused to quit the house.—I was firm—and she went—threatening knives and revenge.—I told her—that I had seen knives drawn before her time—and that if she chose to begin—there was a knife—and fork also at her service on the table and that intimidation would not do.—The next day while I was at dinner—she walked in, (having broke open a glass door that led from the hall below to the staircase by way of prologue) and advancing strait up to the table snatched the knife from my hand—cutting me slightly in the thumb in the operation—Whether she meant to use this against herself or me I know not—probably against neither—but Fletcher seized her by the arms— and disarmed her.—I then called my boatmen—and desired them to get the Gondola ready and conduct her to her own house again—seeing carefully that she did herself no mischief by the way.—She seemed quite quiet and walked down stairs.—I resumed my dinner.—We heard a great noise—I went out—and met them on the staircase—carrying her up stairs.—She had thrown herself into the Canal.—That she intended to destroy herself I do not believe—but when we consider the fear women and men who can't swim have of deep or even of shallow water—(and the Venetians in particular though they live on the waves) and that it was also night—and dark—& very cold—it shows that she had a devilish spirit of some sort within her.—They had got her out without much difficulty or damage except the salt water she had swallowed and the wetting she had undergone.—I foresaw her intention to refix herself, and sent for a Surgeon—enquiring how many hours it would require to restore her from her agitation, and he named the time.—I then said—"I give you that time—and more if you require it—but at the expiration of the prescribed period—if *She* does not leave the house—*I* will".——All my people were consternated—they had always been frightened at her—and were now paralyzed—they wanted me to apply to the police—to guard myself—&c. &c.— like a pack of sniveling servile boobies as they were——I did nothing of the kind—thinking that I might as well end that way as another—besides—I had been used to savage women and knew their ways.—I had her sent home quietly after her recovery—and never saw her since except twice at the opera—at a distance amongst the audience.—She made

Byron's letters were designed for the camaraderie of his publisher's reception rooms. This illustration of 50 Albemarle Street shows Byron, in the left corner, talking to Sir Walter Scott.

many attempts to return—but no more violent ones. And this is the story of Margharita Cogni—as far as it belongs to me.—I forgot to mention that she was very devout —and would cross herself if she heard the prayer-time strike—sometimes—when that ceremony did not appear to be much in unison with what she was then about.—She was quick in reply—as for instance;—one day when she made me very angry with beating somebody or other—I called her a *Cow* (*Cow* in Italian is a sad affront and tantamount to the feminine of dog in English) I called her "Vacca" she turned round—curtsied—and answered "Vacca *tua*—'Celenza" (i.e. Eccelenza) *your* Cow—please your Excellency.—In short—she was—as I said before—a very fine Animal— of considerable beauty and energy—with many good & several amusing qualities—but wild as a witch—and fierce as a demon.—She used to boast publicly of her ascendancy over me—contrasting it with that of other women—and assigning for it sundry reasons physical and moral which did more credit to her person than her modesty.——True it was that they all tried to get her away—and no one succeeded—till her own absurdity helped them.—Whenever there was a competition, and sometimes—one would be shut in one room and one in another—to prevent battle—she had generally the preference.——

yrs. very truly and affectly
B

Clearly, the Palazzo Mocenigo was no place to raise the pretty, petulant Allegra, and therefore, early in August arrangements were made for the child to move in with the family of Hoppner, the British Consul, who was a friend of Byron's. When Claire heard about this from the nurse, she was so upset that she persuaded Shelley to leave at once with her for Venice. They visited the Hoppners and then, at three in the afternoon, Shelley went on his own to see Byron. He judged the poet would have risen by that time and any compromising guests would have gone.

Byron greeted him affably and was told by Shelley that Claire was not in Venice. Byron at once agreed that she should see her daughter, and could even look after her, though he did not think this was in the child's best interests. Having then offered them all the use of a house for the summer, Byron took Shelley in his gondola across to the Lido where they went for an afternoon ride. This, and the subjects of the excited talk that went on until five the following morning, form the substance of Shelley's poem *Julian and Maddalo*.

Shelley was now both fascinated and appalled by Byron—an ambiguity which seemed to cement their friendship—and in the preface to his poem he gives an interesting portrait of the genius of the Grand Canal: "Count Maddalo . . . is a person of the most consummate genius, and capable, if he would direct his energies to such an end, of becoming the redeemer of his degraded country. But it is his weakness to be proud: he derives from a comparison of his own extraordinary mind with the dwarfish intellects that surround him, an intense apprehension of the nothingness of human life . . . but . . . in social life no human being can be more gentle, patient, and unassuming than Maddalo. He is cheerful, frank, and witty. His more serious conversation is a sort of intoxication; men are held by it as by a spell." Shelley clearly was.

It was not only Byron's weakness to be proud, however; the pace of his neurotic quest for women and stimulation was now destroying his health. At 30, his hair was greying and his teeth were loosening, yet still he pursued excitement, boasting of his conquests over a couple of hundred women. Indeed, the record of his sex life is exhausting: countesses and cobblers' wives, mothers and daughters, daughters and sisters, "the Tarantella, the Da Mosti, the Spineda, the Lotti, the Rizzato, the Eleanora, the Carlotta, the Giulietta, the Alvisi, the Zambieri, the Eleanora de Bezzi . . ." Like the hero of his poem *Mazeppa*, Byron seemed bound to the wild forces of passion.

But he was also busy on other fronts. In the full torrent of his manhood, and with his desires both endlessly distracted and voluptuously satisfied, his creative powers were at their peak. He wrote best, he declared, "when a C--t is tied close to my Inkstand". And certainly his labours at both were sustained. In a whirl of stimulation, the Don Juan of the Grand Canal was creating his literary alter ego. On 19 September 1819 he told Tom Moore, "I have finished the first canto (a long one, of about 180 octaves) of a poem in the style and manner of *Beppo*, encouraged by the good success of the same. It is called *Don Juan*. But I doubt whether it is not . . too free for these very modest days."

He was probably being ironic, but he had touched on an important issue. Social, political and moral changes in England after 1815 ensured that a poem so laughingly and radiantly concerned with sexuality as the first Canto of *Don Juan*, so wittily directed against the censorious, and so clearly equating personal liberty with political freedom, inevitably appeared dangerously radical. As Byron himself declared, could it have been written by a man "who has not lived in the world?—and tooled in a poste-chaise? in a hackney coach? in a Gondola? Against a wall? in a court carriage?—in a vis a vis?—on a table?—and under it?" The narrator reflects this abundant life with humour, and a pathos that gives his self-portrait real psychological depth.

MAZEPPA

"a strong passion of some kind . . . is the poetry of life"

Byron discovered the story of Mazeppa, the Polish page who was punished for adultery by being tied to the back of a wild horse, in Voltaire's *Histoire de Charles XII*. As an image of a man trapped and punished by the forces of desire, the story made a deep appeal to many romantic poets and painters. Sections 11 and 12 of the poem, in particular, convey the excitement of the story.

'Away, away, my steed and I,
    Upon the pinions of the wind,*
    All human dwellings left behind;
We sped like meteors through the sky,
When with its crackling sound the night
Is chequer'd with the northern light:
Town—village—none were on our track,
    But a wild plain of far extent,
And bounded by a forest black;
    And, save the scarce seen battlement
On distant heights of some strong hold,
Against the Tartars built of old,
No trace of man. The year before
A Turkish army had march'd o'er;
And where the Spahi's hoof hath trod,*
The verdure flies the bloody sod:—
The sky was dull, and dim, and gray,
    And a low breeze crept moaning by—
    I could have answer'd with a sigh—
But fast we fled, away, away—
And I could neither sigh nor pray;
And my cold sweat-drops fell like rain
Upon the courser's bristling mane;
But, snorting still with rage and fear,
He flew upon his far career:
At times I almost thought, indeed,

He must have slacken'd in his speed;
But no—my bound and slender frame
    Was nothing to his angry might,
And merely like a spur became:
Each motion which I made to free
My swoln limbs from their agony
    Increased his fury and affright:
I tried my voice,—'twas faint and low,
But yet he swerved as from a blow;
And, starting to each accent, sprang
As from a sudden trumpet's clang:
Meantime my cords were wet with gore,
Which, oozing through my limbs, ran o'er;
And in my tongue the thirst became
A something fierier far than flame.

12

'We near'd the wild wood—'twas so wide,
I saw no bounds on either side;
'Twas studded with old sturdy trees,
That bent not to the roughest breeze
Which howls down from Siberia's waste,
And strips the forest in its haste,—
But these were few, and far between
Set thick with shrubs more young and green,

Luxuriant with their annual leaves,
Ere strown by those autumnal eves
That nip the forest's foliage dead,
Discolour'd with a lifeless red,
Which stands thereon like stiffen'd gore
Upon the slain when battle's o'er,
And some long winter's night hath shed
Its frost o'er every tombless head,
So cold and stark the raven's beak
May peck unpierced each frozen cheek:
'Twas a wild waste of underwood,
And here and there a chestnut stood,
The strong oak, and the hardy pine;
   But far apart—and well it were,
Or else a different lot were mine—
   The boughs gave way, and did not tear
   My limbs; and I found strength to bear
My wounds, already scarr'd with cold—
My bonds forbade to loose my hold.
We rustled through the leaves like wind,
Left shrubs, and trees, and wolves behind;
By night I heard them on the track,
Their troop came hard upon our back,
With their long gallop, which can tire
The hound's deep hate, and hunter's fire:

Where'er we flew they follow'd on,
Nor left us with the morning sun;
Behind I saw them, scarce a rood,
At day-break winding through the wood,
And through the night had heard their feet
Their stealing, rustling step repeat.
Oh! how I wish'd for spear or sword,
At least to die amidst the horde,
And perish—if it must be so—
At bay, destroying many a foe.
When first my courser's race begun,
I wish'd the goal already won;
But now I doubted strength and speed.
Vain doubt! his swift and savage breed
Had nerved him like the mountain-roe;
Nor faster falls the blinding snow
Which whelms the peasant near the door
Whose threshold he shall cross no more,
Bewilder'd with the dazzling blast,
Than through the forest-paths he past—
Untired, untamed, and worse than wild;
All furious as a favour'd child
Balk'd of its wish; or fiercer still—
A woman piqued—who has her will.

AUGUSTA

"For thee – my own sweet Sister – in thy heart
I know myself secure – as thou in mine"

Of all Byron's love letters, this to his half-sister is perhaps the most moving. Writing in 1819 amid his dissolute life in Venice, Byron recalls their illicit relationship as a tie of great emotional strength and purity.

   My dearest Love—I have been negligent in not writing, but what can I say[.] Three years absence— & the total change of scene and habit make such a difference—that we have now nothing in common but our affections & our relationship.—
   But I have never ceased nor can cease to feel for a

moment that perfect & boundless attachment which bound
& binds me to you—which renders me utterly incapable of
real love for any other human being—what could they be
to me after *you*? My own XXXX [Short word crossed out]
we may have been very wrong—but I repent of nothing
except that cursed marriage—& your refusing to continue
to love me as you had loved me—I can neither forget nor
quite forgive you for that precious piece of
reformation.—but I can never be other than I have
been—and whenever I love anything it is because it
reminds me in some way or other of yourself—for instance
I not long ago attached myself to a Venetian for no earthly
reason (although a pretty woman) but because she was
called XXXX [short word crossed out] and she often
remarked (without knowing the reason) how fond I was of
the name.—It is heart-breaking to think of our long
Separation—and I am sure more than punishment enough
for all our sins—Dante is more humane in his "Hell" for
he places his unfortunate lovers (Francesca of Rimini &
Paolo whose case fell a good deal short of *ours*—though
sufficiently naughty) in company—and though they
suffer—it is at least together.—If ever I return to
England—it will be to see you—and recollect that in all
time—& place—and feelings—I have never ceased to be
the same to you in heart—Circumstances may have ruffled
my manner—& hardened my spirit—you may have seen
me harsh & exasperated with all things around me; grieved
& tortured with *your new resolution*,—& the soon after
persecution of that infamous fiend who drove me from my
Country & conspired against my life—by endeavouring to
deprive me of all that could render it precious—but
remember that even then *you* were the sole object that cost
me a tear? and *what tears!* do you remember *our* parting? I
have not spirits now to write to you upon other
subjects—I am well in health—and have no cause of grief
but the reflection that we are not together—When you
write to me speak to me of yourself—& say that you love
me—never mind common-place people & topics—which
can be in no degree interesting—to me who see nothing in
England but the country which holds *you*—or around it
but the sea which divides us.—They say absence destroys
weak passions—& confirms strong ones—Alas! *mine* for
you is the union of all passions & of all affections—Has

strengthened itself but will destroy me—I do not speak of
physical destruction—for I have endured & can endure
much—but of the annihilation of all thoughts feelings or
hopes—which have not more or less a reference to you &
to *our recollections*—

Ever dearest
[Signature erased]

When Byron went on to satirize Robert Southey, the Liberal poet turned Tory, who was rewarded with the poet laureateship, he hoped to ridicule the official voice of the English establishment and suggest, in contrast to himself, not only its political corruption, but its emotional emasculation. This purpose was reinforced by the adolescent trials and triumphs of his innocent and very sexy young hero. The Don Juan of the first Canto has a charm that can only be criticized by a prig. But when Byron attacked the prudish and ridiculous in the figure of Donna Inez, his hero's mother, he was not merely satirizing his own wife, but that whole self-righteous half-existence that was soon to be enshrined in Victorian values. The age of hypocrisy was not far off.

Byron's correspondent Tom Moore was keenly aware of this. "The natural tendency of the excesses of the French Revolution," he wrote in his life of the playwright Sheridan, "was to produce in the higher classes of England an increased reserve of manner, and, of course, a proportionate restraint on all within their circle, which have been fatal to conviviality and humour, and not very propitious to wit, subduing both manners and conversation to a sort of polished level, to rise above which is often thought almost as vulgar as to sink below it." *Don Juan* is the work of a Regency radical and an exile. It was written for an England narrowing with change.

Important changes were also taking place in Byron's own life. The tardy Hanson eventually arrived with the papers concerning the sale of Newstead. They were signed (one of Hanson's party noticed how Byron's knuckles were sunk in the fat of his hands), and Kinnaird then invested two thirds of the £94,000 and began settling Byron's debts with the rest. This left a deficiency of nearly £6,000. Henceforth, however, Byron would be able to live comfortably in Italy on the £3,300 earned from his capital, plus the annual marriage settlement of £200, and the fees from his writing. These last he now accepted with alacrity.

The significance of this transformation in his financial affairs was soon to be matched by yet another change—he was to fall very deeply in love.

DON JUAN

"is it not life, is it not the thing?"

Byron's comic genius is nowhere more apparent than in these stanzas from the first canto of *Don Juan*. His naive and ardent young hero is in bed with Julia, the almost equally innocent wife of the aging Don Alfonso. The jealous husband arrives, and Byron lavishes on the inevitable farce all the energy of his humour and dazzling technical expertise. The choice of words and rhythms is masterly in its apparent casualness. The long outburst of Donna Julia, especially, has great comic brilliance. The whole episode, indeed, shows a virtuosity unrivalled in English comic literature save by Chaucer and Shakespeare.

By this time Don Alfonso was arrived,
    With torches, friends, and servants in great number;
The major part of them had long been wived,
    And therefore paused not to disturb the slumber
Of any wicked woman, who contrived
    By stealth her husband's temples to encumber:
Examples of this kind are so contagious,
Were *one* not punish'd, *all* would be outrageous.

I can't tell how, or why, or what suspicion
    Could enter into Don Alfonso's head;
But for a cavalier of his condition
    It surely was exceedingly ill-bred,
Without a word of previous admonition,
    To hold a levee round his lady's bed,
And summon lackeys, arm'd with fire and sword,
To prove himself the thing he most abhorr'd.

Poor Donna Julia! starting as from sleep,
    (Mind—that I do not say—she had not slept)
Began at once to scream, and yawn, and weep;
    Her maid Antonia, who was an adept,
Contrived to fling the bed-clothes in a heap,
    As if she had just now from out them crept:
I can't tell why she should take all this trouble
To prove her mistress had been sleeping double.

Byron's loathing of Castlereagh surpassed even his contempt for Wellington. He viewed him as cold, calculating and cruel, damning him in a memorable epithet as "that intellectual eunuch Castlereagh".

But Julia mistress, and Antonia maid,
　Appear'd like two poor harmless women, who
Of goblins, but still more of men afraid,
　Had thought one man might be deterr'd by two,
And therefore side by side were gently laid,
　Until the hours of absence should run through,
And truant husband should return, and say,
'My dear, I was the first who came away.'

Now Julia found at length a voice, and cried,
　'In heaven's name, Don Alfonso, what d'ye mean?
Has madness seized you? would that I had died
　Ere such a monster's victim I had been!
What may this midnight violence betide,
　A sudden fit of drunkenness or spleen?
Dare you suspect me, whom the thought would kill?
Search, then, the room!'—Alfonso said, 'I will.'

He search'd, *they* search'd, and rummaged every where,
　Closet and clothes'-press, chest and window-seat.
And found much linen, lace, and several pair
　Of stockings, slippers, brushes, combs, complete,
With other articles of ladies fair,
　To keep them beautiful, or leave them neat:
Arras they prick'd and curtains with their swords,
And wounded several shutters and some boards.

Under the bed they search'd, and there they found—
　No matter what—it was not that they sought;
They open'd windows, gazing if the ground
　Had signs or footmarks, but the earth said nought;
And then they stared each other's faces round:
　'Tis odd, not one of all these seekers thought,
And seems to me almost a sort of blunder,
Of looking *in* the bed as well as under.

During this inquisition Julia's tongue
　Was not asleep—'Yes, search and search,' she cried,
'Insult on insult heap, and wrong on wrong!
　It was for this that I became a bride!
For this in silence I have suffer'd long
　A husband like Alfonso at my side;
But now I'll bear no more, nor here remain,
If there be law, or lawyers, in all Spain.

John Murray, Byron's Scots publisher,
was one of the most successful figures
in the profession of his day, a man with
a nose for best sellers who carefully
cultivated his authors and introduced
innovatory sales techniques.

'Yes, Don Alfonso! husband now no more,
     If ever you indeed deserved the name,
Is't worthy of your years?—you have threescore,
     Fifty, or sixty—it is all the same—
Is't wise or fitting causeless to explore
     For facts against a virtuous woman's fame?
Ungrateful, perjured, barbarous Don Alfonso,
How dare you think your lady would go on so?

'Is it for this I have disdain'd to hold
     The common privileges of my sex?
That I have chosen a confessor so old
     And deaf, but any other it would vex,
And never once he has had cause to scold,
     But found my very innocence perplex
So much, he always doubted I was married
How sorry you will be when I've miscarried'.

'Was it for this that no Cortejo ere*
     I yet have chosen from out the youth of Seville?
Is it for this I scarce went any where,
     Except to bull-fights, mass, play, rout, and revel?
Is it for this, whate'er my suitors were,
     I favour'd none—nay, was almost uncivil?
Is it for this that General Count O'Reilly,
Who took Algiers, declares I used him vilely?

'Did not the Italian Musico Cazzani
     Sing at my heart six months at least in vain?
Did not his countryman, Count Corniani,
     Call me the only virtuous wife in Spain?
Were there not also Russians, English, many?
     The Count Strongstroganoff I put in pain,
And Lord Mount Coffeehouse, the Irish peer,
Who kill'd himself for love (with wine) last year.

'Have I not had two bishops at my feet?
     The Duke of Ichar, and Don Fernan Nunez,
And is it thus a faithful wife you treat?
     I wonder in what quarter now the moon is:
I praise your vast forbearance not to beat
     Me also, since the time so opportune is—
Oh, valiant man! with sword drawn and cock'd trigger,
Now, tell me, don't you cut a pretty figure?

This is the official image of the Prince Regent after he had become George IV. It belies his lubricity and corpulence. Byron satirized him for his disgraceful treatment of his wife Queen Caroline.

'Was it for this you took your sudden journey,
    Under pretence of business indispensible
With that sublime of rascals your attorney,
    Whom I see standing there, and looking sensible
Of having play'd the fool? though both I spurn, he
    Deserves the worst, his conduct's less defensible,
Because, no doubt, 'twas for his dirty fee,
And not from any love to you nor me.

'If he comes here to take a deposition,
    By all means let the gentleman proceed;
You've made the apartment in a fit condition:—
    There's pen and ink for you, sir, when you need—
Let every thing be noted with precision,
    I would not you for nothing should be fee'd—
But, as my maid's undrest, pray turn your spies out.'
'Oh!' sobb'd Antonia, 'I could tear their eyes out.'

'There is the closet, there the toilet, there
    The ante-chamber—search them under, over:
There is the sofa, there the great arm-chair,
    The chimney—which would really hold a lover.
I wish to sleep, and beg you will take care
    And make no further noise, till you discover
The secret cavern of this lurking treasure—
And when 'tis found, let me, too, have the pleasure.

'And now, Hidalgo! now that you have thrown*
    Doubt upon me, confusion over all,
Pray have the courtesy to make it known
    Who is the man you search for? how d'ye call
Him? what's his lineage? let him but be shown—
    I hope he's young and handsome—is he tall?
Tell me—and be assured, that since you stain
My honour thus, it shall not be in vain.

'At least, perhaps, he has not sixty years,
    At that age he would be too old for slaughter,
Or for so young a husband's jealous fears—
    (Antonia! let me have a glass of water)
I am ashamed of having shed these tears,
    They are unworthy of my father's daughter;
My mother dream'd not in my natal hour
That I should fall into a monster's power.

Cartoonists saw the Byron of the Italian
period as inspired by the devil. This is
a clear reference to Southey's slighting
description of the poet as the leader of a
"satanic" school of writers. A copy of "The
Vision of Judgment" lies at Byron's feet.

Géricault's "The Raft of the Medusa" was produced almost contemporaneously with Byron's shipwreck scene in the second canto of "Don Juan". This sketch for the figures on Géricault's raft suggests the heroic despair of the finished work.

'Perhaps 'tis of Antonia you are jealous,
    You saw that she was sleeping by my side
When you broke in upon us with your fellows:
    Look where you please—we've nothing, sir, to hide;
Only another time, I trust, you'll tell us,
    Or for the sake of decency abide
A moment at the door, that we may be
Drest to receive so much good company.

'And now, sir, I have done, and say no more;
    The little I have said may serve to show
The guileless heart in silence may grieve o'er
    The wrongs to whose exposure it is slow:—
I leave you to your conscience as before,
    'Twill one day ask you *why* you used me so?
God grant you feel not then the bitterest grief!
Antonia! Where's my pocket-handkerchief?'

She ceased, and turn'd upon her pillow; pale
    She lay, her dark eyes flashing through their tears,
Like skies that rain and lighten; as a veil,
    Waved and o'ershading her wan cheek, appears
Her streaming hair; the black curls strive, but fail,
    To hide the glossy shoulder, which uprears
Its snow through all;—her soft lips lie apart,
And louder than her breathing beats her heart.

JULIA'S LETTER

"Man's love is of his life a thing apart . . . 'Tis woman's whole existence"

Donna Julia's letter to her young lover as she faces her own disgrace and a life without Juan, reveals Byron as a master of pathos. Set amid so much satire and comedy, Julia's letter exemplifies the mercurial changes of mood which are the essence of the poem's achievement.

'They tell me 'tis decided; you depart:
    'Tis wise—'tis well, but not the less a pain;
I have no further claim on your young heart,
    Mine was the victim, and would be again;
To love too much has been the only art
    I used;—I write in haste, and if a stain
Be on this sheet, 'tis not what it appears,
My eyeballs burn and throb, but have no tears.

'I loved, I love you, for that love have lost
   State, station, heaven, mankind's, my own esteem,
And yet can not regret what it hath cost,
   So dear is still the memory of that dream;
Yet, if I name my guilt, 'tis not to boast,
   None can deem harshlier of me than I deem:
I trace this scrawl because I cannot rest—
I've nothing to reproach, nor to request.

'Man's love is of his life a thing apart,
   'Tis woman's whole existence; man may range
The court, camp, church, the vessel, and the mart,
   Sword, gown, gain, glory, offer in exchange
Pride, fame, ambition, to fill up his heart,
   And few there are whom these can not estrange;
Man has all these resources, we but one,
To love again, and be again undone.

'My breast has been all weakness, is so yet;
   I struggle, but cannot collect my mind;
My blood still rushes where my spirit's set,
   As roll the waves before the settled wind;
My brain is feminine, nor can forget—
   To all, except your image, madly blind;
As turns the needle trembling to the pole
It ne'er can reach, so turns to you, my soul.

*Francesco Guardi's study of a gondola on
the Venetian lagoon suggests the
melancholy sometimes felt in this great
city. The gondola plays an important
part in "Beppo" and figured in numerous
of Byron's Venetian amours.*

'You will proceed in beauty, and in pride,
   Beloved and loving many; all is o'er
For me on earth, except some years to hide
   My shame and sorrow deep in my heart's core;
These I could bear, but cannot cast aside
   The passion which still rends it as before,
And so farewell—forgive me, love me—No,
That word is idle now—but let it go.

'I have no more to say, but linger still,
   And dare not set my seal upon this sheet,
And yet I may as well the task fulfil,
   My misery can scarce be more complete:
I had not lived till now, could sorrow kill;
   Death flies the wretch who fain the blow would meet,
And I must even survive this last adieu,
And bear with life, to love and pray for you!'

"*Fair as sunrise, and warm as noon*"

The Contessa Teresa Guiccioli was 19. She had rich auburn curls, a full figure, beautiful soft eyes, and a husband of 58. She was his third wife. Early in April 1819, the Conte was in Venice on business and, somewhat reluctantly, she went with him to a *conversazione*. She was feeling, she later remembered, rather tired.

For many romantics, Tasso's persecution and madness was a symbol of the artist's plight in general. Delacroix's picture expresses this, as does Byron's "Lament of Tasso", which is in part a self-portrait.

Despite his protestations (Byron was growing weary of his numerous affairs) his hostess introduced him as "a peer of England and its greatest poet". Byron and the Contessa talked, and the melodiousness of his voice at once delighted her. Byron discovered she came from Ravenna and said—perhaps to impress—that he had always wished to visit the tomb of Dante there. To his surprise, she responded with an enthusiastic knowledge of the great Italian poet. The Contessa Guiccioli had received a fine education. Byron's interest was kindled. They continued to talk, and he was touched by her breeding and warmed by her vitality. He was also intrigued by her mind. She was very different to the women he had recently known. When Conte Guiccioli came to fetch Teresa at the end of the evening, she and Byron had arranged to meet the next day.

He waited for her in his gondola and took her to an establishment he kept for such purposes. "I was strong enough to resist at that first encounter," she recalled, "but was so imprudent as to repeat it the next day, when my strength gave way—for B. was not a man to confine himself to sentiment." Nor, as a woman, was she. For ten days, with the contrivance of her confidante and giving the excuse of studying French, she slipped away. Together, the *cavalier servente* and his *amica* watched the golden sunsets melting over Venice.

Byron was more involved than his strangely stilted letters might suggest, and the discreet conventions of Venetian adultery did not altogether suit either of them. Contessa Guiccioli, told by her husband of their imminent departure from the city, at once rushed to the Fenice Theatre, entered Byron's box, and there, in full view of the audience, told him of her grief.

He attempted to laugh off his feelings in letters to Hobhouse, who shrewdly guessed how serious the matter had become. During April and May Byron experimented with other affairs, but his troubled feelings poured out in his "Stanzas to the Po". He knew from Pope, his favourite poet, that love can draw one with a single hair, and by the first of June he realized that it was futile to resist. Byron's "Napoleonic" coach arrived in Ravenna ten days later, and he put up at the wretched Albergo Imperiale. It was close to the tomb of Dante which, he had told her, he had always wanted to see.

He was at once informed that Teresa was seriously ill. He went, at her husband's invitation, to see her the next day. She immediately began to revive. In the stuffiness and frustration of his hotel room, meanwhile, Byron considered the possibilities of an elopement. Shrewdly, she declined—she wanted him for longer than that. With the help of her maid, her blackamoor and her priest, Teresa smuggled "mio Byron" into the sombre magnificence of the Palazzo Guiccioli. There they passed afternoons of thrilling danger, the risk intensifying their pleasure. "*She* manages very well," Byron wrote to Hoppner, "though the locale is inconvenient—(no *bolts* and be d———d to them) . . . and *no* place but the great Saloon of his own palace—so that if I come away with a Stiletto in my gizzard some fine afternoon I shall not be astonished."

Pleasure revived them both. She, though her health was still a matter for concern, returned to the radiance of young womanhood; he found a new capacity for love. By July, Byron had decided to leave Venice entirely. The townspeople of Ravenna sang in the streets about their cuckolded count.

Guiccioli himself, clever, cultured, endlessly addicted to intrigue, played an impenetrable game. He allowed Byron to accompany him and his wife to Bologna, and while he went out to the theatre, they made love in the beautiful Palazzo Savioli, or strolled through the gardens in the scented night. The Austrian secret police, meanwhile, noted that Byron had rooms in the nearby Palazzo Merendoni.

Perversely, Byron felt trapped in this provincial paradise. Every particle of his being belonged to La Guiccioli and he began to long for freedom. For the moment, however, he followed her to Ravenna, where the Conte agreed to rent Byron the ground floor of his palazzo.

TO THE PO, JUNE 2ND 1819

"Farewell, my dearest Evil – farewell, my torment"

This is Byron's meditation on his growing love for Teresa Guiccioli. The intensity and surprising rebirth of passion is mingled with regret that love itself has returned to torment the poet.

River! that rollest by the antient walls
  Where dwells the Lady of my Love, when she
Walks by thy brink and there perchance recalls
  A faint and fleeting memory of me,
What if thy deep and ample stream should be
  A mirror of my heart, where she may read
The thousand thoughts I now betray to thee
  Wild as thy wave and headlong as thy speed?
What do I say? 'a mirror of my heart'?
  Are not thy waters sweeping, dark, and strong,
Such as my feelings were and are, thou art,
  And such as thou art were my passions long.
Time may have somewhat tamed them, not forever
  Thou overflow'st thy banks, and not for aye
The bosom overboils, congenial River!
  Thy floods subside, and mine have sunk away,
But left long wrecks behind us, yet again
  Borne on our old career unchanged we move,
Thou tendest wildly to the wilder main
  And I to loving one I should not love.
The current I behold will sweep beneath
  Her palace walls, and murmur at her feet,
Her eyes will look on thee, when she shall breathe
  The twilight air unchained from Summer's heat.
She will look on thee,—I have looked on thee
  Full of that thought, and from this moment ne'er

Thy waters could I name, hear named, or see
  Without the inseparable Sigh for her.
Her bright eyes will be imaged in thy Stream—
  Yes, they will meet the wave I gaze on now,
But mine can not even witness in a dream
  That happy wave repass me in its flow.
The wave that bears my tear returns no more
  Will She return by whom that wave shall sweep?
Both tread thy bank, both wander by thy shore,
  I near thy source, and She by the blue deep.
But that which keepeth us apart, is not
  Distance, nor depth of wave, nor space of earth,
But the distractions of a various lot,
  Ah! various as the climates of our birth!
A Stranger loves a lady of the land,
  Born far beyond the Mountains, but his blood
Is all meridian, as if never fanned
  By the bleak wind that chills the Polar flood.
My heart is all meridian, were it not
  I had not suffered now, nor should I be—
Despite of tortures ne'er to be forgot—
  The Slave again, Oh Love! at least of thee!
'Tis vain to struggle, I have struggled long
  To love again no more as once I loved.
Oh! Time! why leave this earliest Passion strong?
  To tear a heart which pants to be unmoved?

Conte Guiccioli allowed himself to be cuckolded in his own house. His price, though he was a wealthy man, was a large loan. It seems as if he were determined to tie Byron down by pleasure and debt. Byron refused to lend him the money, however, and Guiccioli turned on his wife instead. Teresa had an immediate relapse. She discovered she needed the attentions of Dr Aglietti and had Byron take her to Venice. Two days after her arrival, she was installed in the Palazzo Mocenigo.

They spent that summer in Byron's villa near Padua. He grew his whiskers and began to wear his hair long. It was almost as if he were settling to the life of a married man. The comfort of his existence, however, with its lack of action, seemed to be a reproach. His irremediable Calvinism began to assert itself, and he thought constantly of the countries of Europe and South America where the battle for freedom was being fought. "I am not tired of Italy," he wrote to Hobhouse, "but a man must be . . . a Singer in duets, and a connoisseur of Operas—or nothing—here. I have made some progress in all these accomplishments, but I can't say that I don't feel the degradation. Better be an unskilful Planter, an awkward settler,—better be a hunter, or anything, than a flatterer of fiddlers, and fan carrier of a woman. I like women— God he knows—but the more their system here developes [sic] upon me, the worse it seems, after Turkey too; here the *polygamy* is all on the female side. I have been an intriguer, a husband, a whoremonger, and now I am a Cavalier Servente—by the holy! it is a strange sensation." It was a humiliating one, too. He even thought of returning to England. The need for action, for new stimulation, gnawed at him constantly, but for the moment he settled to writing his Memoirs. They were intended for posthumous publication, for although only in his early 30s, Byron was becoming increasingly aware of advancing age.

Byron's affair with Teresa Guiccioli was the warmest and most sustaining of his life. Her passion for him was absolute, defying all conventions, and to the end of her days she was proud of the association.

MIDDLE AGE

*"I always looked to about thirty as the barrier
of any real or fierce delight in the passions"*

Byron's consideration of his advancing years is a common
enough theme in poetry, but few poets have so wholly
refashioned it in their own style, creating a mixture of
humour and pathos that is both new and permanently
valid. Byron juxtaposes petty details such as his thoughts of
buying a wig against the most musical lines of lament for
lost youth. He expresses tender, ironic regret and then
contrasts this with an image of his future as a cartoonlike,
miserly old man. Once again, the rapid alterations of
mood, and Byron's mastery of an aristocratic colloquial
style make this passage emotionally rich and credible.

But now at thirty years my hair is gray—
  (I wonder what it will be like at forty?
I thought of a peruke the other day)*
    My heart is not much greener; and, in short, I
Have squander'd my whole summer while 'twas May,
    And feel no more the spirit to retort; I
Have spent my life, both interest and principal,
And deem not, what I deem'd, my soul invincible.

No more—no more—Oh! never more on me
  The freshness of the heart can fall like dew,
Which out of all the lovely things we see
    Extracts emotions beautiful and new,
Hived in our bosoms like the bag o' the bee:
    Think'st thou the honey with those objects grew?
Alas! 'twas not in them, but in thy power
To double even the sweetness of a flower.

No more—no more—Oh! never more, my heart,
  Canst thou be my sole world, my universe!
Once all in all, but now a thing apart,
    Thou canst not be my blessing or my curse:
The illusion's gone for ever, and thou art
    Insensible, I trust, but none the worse,
And in thy stead I've got a deal of judgement,
Though heaven knows how it ever found a lodgement.

My days of love are over, me no more
   The charms of maid, wife, and still less of widow,
Can make the fool of which they made before,
   In short, I must not lead the life I did do;
The credulous hope of mutual minds is o'er,
   The copious use of claret is forbid too,
So for a good old-gentlemanly vice,
I think I must take up with avarice.

Ambition was my idol, which was broken
   Before the shrines of Sorrow and of Pleasure;
And the two last have left me many a token
   O'er which reflection may be made at leisure:
Now, like Friar Bacon's brazen head, I've spoken,*
   'Time is, Time was, Time's past, a chymic treasure*
Is glittering youth, which I have spent betimes—
My heart in passion, and my head on rhymes.

What is the end of fame? 'tis but to fill
   A certain portion of uncertain paper:
Some liken it to climbing up a hill,
   Whose summit, like all hills', is lost in vapour;
For this men write, speak, preach, and heroes kill,
   And bards burn what they call their 'midnight taper'.
To have, when the original is dust,
A name, a wretched picture, and worse bust.

What are the hopes of man? old Eygpt's King
   Cheops erected the first pyramid
And largest, thinking it was just the thing
   To keep his memory whole, and mummy hid;
But somebody or other rummaging,
   Burglariously broke his coffin's lid:
Let not a monument give you or me hopes,
Since not a pinch of dust remains of Cheops.

But I being fond of true philosophy,
   Say very often to myself, 'Alas!
All things that have been born were born to die,
   And flesh (which Death mows down to hay) is grass;
You've pass'd your youth not so unpleasantly,
   And if you had it o'er again—'twould pass—
So thank your stars that matters are no worse,
And read your Bible, sir, and mind your purse.'

But for all this, he was now at the height of his literary powers. In particular, he had finished the second canto of *Don Juan*. It is among his finest achievements, and one of the greatest sustained passages of English romantic poetry.

In its never excessive length, the second canto juxtaposes comedy, satire, adventure and a visionary evocation of pure and natural love, and it does so with unique assurance. The shipwreck scene, for example, is factual and thrilling, disgusting and moving by turns—the deaths, especially, are handled with a unique blend of irony and pathos —but when Juan, the sole survivor, is restored to life by the exotic Haidee, Byron discovers a poetry of innocence unmatched elsewhere in his work. These stanzas are perhaps his supreme claim to a place among the English poets, and, despite carping comments—some critics could not appreciate the mercurial changes of mood—Byron was well aware of his new poem's qualities. "It may be profligate but is it not *life*, is it not *the thing*?" he asked Douglas Kinnaird.

JUAN AND HAIDEE

"I do detest everything which is not perfectly mutual."

The love of Juan and Haidee is the most unexpected, and perhaps the finest of Byron's achievements. It is a picture of love that is pure, innocent, and rapturous. The narrator's irony is present, as always, but it is contrasted with a delicacy and refinement of desire that manages to be both intensely physical and poetically evocative.

Ford Madox Brown's study of Haidee finding Juan combines the exotic, the innocent, and the sexual.

It was the cooling hour, just when the rounded
    Red sun sinks down behind the azure hill,
Which then seems as if the whole earth is bounded,
    Circling all nature, hush'd, and dim, and still,
With the far mountain-crescent half surrounded
    On one side, and the deep sea calm and chill
Upon the other, and the rosy sky,
With one star sparkling through it like an eye.

And thus they wander'd forth, and hand in hand,
    Over the shining pebbles and the shells,
Glided along the smooth and harden'd sand,
    And in the worn and wild receptacles
Work'd by the storms, yet work'd as it were plann'd,
    In hollow halls, with sparry roofs and cells,
They turn'd to rest; and, each clasp'd by an arm,
Yielded to the deep twilight's purple charm.

They look'd up to the sky, whose floating glow
   Spread like a rosy ocean, vast and bright;
They gazed upon the glittering sea below,
   Whence the broad moon rose circling into sight;
They heard the wave's splash, and the wind so low,
   And saw each other's dark eyes darting light
Into each other—and, beholding this,
Their lips drew near, and clung into a kiss;

A long, long kiss, a kiss of youth, and love,
   And beauty, all concentrating like rays
Into one focus, kindled from above;
   Such kisses as belong to early days,
Where heart, and soul, and sense, in concert move,
   And the blood's lava, and the pulse a blaze,
Each kiss a heart-quake,—for a kiss's strength,
I think, it must be reckon'd by its length.

By length I mean duration; theirs endured
   Heaven knows how long—no doubt they never reckon'd;
And if they had, they could not have secured
   The sum of their sensations to a second:
They had not spoken; but they felt allured,
   As if their souls and lips each other beckon'd,
Which, being join'd, like swarming bees they clung—
Their hearts the flowers from whence the honey sprung.

They were alone, but not alone as they
   Who shut in chambers think it loneliness;
The silent ocean, and the starlight bay,
   The twilight glow, which momently grew less,
The voiceless sands, and dropping caves, that lay
   Around them, made them to each other press,
As if there were no life beneath the sky
Save theirs, and that their life could never die.

They fear'd no eyes nor ears on that lone beach,
   They felt no terrors from the night, they were
All in all to each other: though their speech
   Was broken words, they *thought* a language there,—
And all the burning tongues the passions teach
   Found in one sigh the best interpreter
Of nature's oracle—first love,—that all
Which Eve has left her daughters since her fall.

Count d'Orsay's pencil sketch of Byron, drawn in 1823, shows the poet advancing towards premature middle age. The walking stick he carries was not just a fashionable accessory. Byron's lame foot made him walk with a limp.

Hobhouse's political ambitions resulted in his becoming the radical Member of Parliament for Westminster. Here he is seen canvassing. He was later imprisoned for breach of parliamentary privilege. His career ended in the House of Lords.

Haidee spoke not of scruples, ask'd no vows,
    Nor offer'd any; she had never heard
Of plight and promises to be a spouse,
    Or perils by a loving maid incurr'd;
She was all which pure ignorance allows,
    And flew to her young mate like a young bird;
And, never having dreamt of falsehood, she
Had not one word to say of constancy.

She loved, and was beloved—she adored,
    And she was worshipp'd; after nature's fashion,
Their intense souls, into each other pour'd,
    If souls could die, had perish'd in that passion,—
But by degrees their senses were restored,
    Again to be o'ercome, again to dash on;
And, beating 'gainst *his* bosom, Haidee's heart
Felt as if never more to beat apart.

Alas! they were so young, so beautiful,
    So lonely, loving, helpless, and the hour
Was that in which the heart is always full
    And, having o'er itself no further power,
Prompts deeds eternity can not annul,
    But pays off moments in an endless shower
Of hell-fire—all prepared for people giving
Pleasure or pain to one another living.

Alas! for Juan and Haidee! they were
    So loving and so lovely—till then never,
Excepting our first parents, such a pair
    Had run the risk of being damn'd for ever;
And Haidee, being devout as well as fair,
    Had, doubtless, heard about the Stygian river,
And hell and purgatory—but forgot
Just in the very crisis she should not.

They look upon each other, and their eyes
    Gleam in the moonlight; and her white arm clasps
Round Juan's head, and his around her lies
    Half buried in the tresses which it grasps;
She sits upon his knee, and drinks his sighs,
    He hers, until they end in broken gasps;
And thus they form a group that's quite antique,
Half naked, loving, natural, and Greek.

And when those deep and burning moments pass'd,
    And Juan sunk to sleep within her arms,
She slept not, but all tenderly, though fast,
    Sustain'd his head upon her bosom's charms;
And now and then her eye to heaven is cast,
    And then on the pale cheek her breast now warms,
Pillow'd on her o'erflowing heart, which pants
With all it granted, and with all it grants.

An infant when it gazes on a light,
    A child the moment when it drains the breast,
A devotee when soars the Host in sight,
    An Arab with a stranger for a guest,
A sailor when the prize has struck in fight,
    A miser filling his most hoarded chest,
Feel rapture; but not such true joy are reaping
As they who watch o'er what they love while sleeping.

For there it lies so tranquil, so beloved,
    All that it hath of life with us is living;
So gentle, stirless, helpless, and unmoved,
    And all unconscious of the joy 'tis giving;
And it hath felt, inflicted, pass'd, and proved,
    Hush'd into depths beyond the watcher's diving;
There lies the thing we love with all its errors
And all its charms, like death without its terrors.

The lady watch'd her lover—and that hour
    Of Love's, and Night's, and Ocean's solitude,
O'erflow'd her soul with their united power;
    Amidst the barren sand and rocks so rude
She and her wave-worn love had made their bower,
    Where nought upon their passion could intrude,
And all the stars that crowded the blue space
Saw nothing happier than her glowing face.

Alas! the love of women! it is known
    To be a lovely and a fearful thing;
For all of theirs upon that die is thrown,
    And if 'tis lost, life hath no more to bring
To them but mockeries of the past alone,
    And their revenge is as the tiger's spring,
Deadly, and quick, and crushing; yet, as real
Torture is theirs, what they inflict they feel.

Of all Byron's literary friendships, Shelley's was by far the most fruitful. A radical intellectual, he stimulated Byron's thought more powerfully than anyone else.

Delacroix's "The Massacres of Chios" is an evocation of the brutalities that led to the Greek War of Independence—a scene of hopelessness and cruelty, of defeat played out before an almost limitless vista.

They are right; for man, to man so oft unjust,
　　Is always so to women; one sole bond
Awaits them, treachery is all their trust;
　　Taught to conceal, their bursting hearts despond
Over their idol, till some wealthier lust
　　Buys them in marriage—and what rests beyond?
A thankless husband, next a faithless lover,
Then dressing, nursing, praying, and all's over.

Some take a lover, some take drams or prayers,
　　Some mind their household, others dissipation,
Some run away, and but exchange their cares,
　　Losing the advantage of a virtuous station;
Few changes e'er can better their affairs,
　　Theirs being an unnatural situation,
From the dull palace to the dirty hovel:
Some play the devil, and then write a novel.*

Haidee was Nature's bride, and knew not this;
　　Haidee was Passion's child, born where the sun
Showers triple light, and scorches even the kiss
　　Of his gazelle-eyed daughters; she was one
Made but to love, to feel that she was his
　　Who was her chosen: what was said or done
Elsewhere was nothing—She had nought to fear,
Hope, care, nor love beyond, her heart beat *here*.

And oh! that quickening of the heart, that beat!
　　How much it costs us! yet each rising throb
Is in its cause as its effect so sweet,
　　That Wisdom, ever on the watch to rob
Joy of its alchymy, and to repeat
　　Fine truths: even Conscience, too, has a tough job
To make us understand each good old maxim,
So good—I wonder Castlereagh don't tax 'em.

And now 'twas done—on the lone shore were plighted
　　Their hearts; the stars, their nuptial torches, shed
Beauty upon the beautiful they lighted:
　　Ocean their witness, and the cave their bed,
By their own feelings hallow'd and united,
　　Their priest was Solitude, and they were wed:
And they were happy, for to their young eyes
Each was an angel, and earth paradise.

THE SHIPWRECK SCENE

"But I hate things all fiction . . . there should
always be some foundation of fact"

The shipwreck scene in the second canto of *Don Juan* once again
reveals Byron's mastery of dramatic and ironic contrasts. He draws
on the memoirs of his ancestor "Foul-Weather" Byron for many
details but brings to the scene his own responses. The situation itself
is appalling. Juan, his tutor, and a few of the passengers on the boat he
took from Spain are now adrift and starving. Having eaten Juan's dog,
they draw lots to see who will be their first human victim. The lot falls
to Juan's tutor. Pathos and grotesque humour combine with physical
suffering, but these are juxtaposed to real tragedy when children start
dying in their parents' arms. This is a deeply disturbing passage of great
technical assurance, which reveals the nature of Byron's mature art.

The lots were made, and mark'd, and mix'd, and handed,
   In silent horror, and their distribution
Lull'd even the savage hunger which demanded,
   Like the Promethean vulture, this pollution;*
None in particular had sought or plann'd it,
   'Twas nature gnaw'd them to this resolution,
By which none were permitted to be neuter—
And the lot fell on Juan's luckless tutor.

He but requested to be bled to death:
   The surgeon had his instruments, and bled
Pedrillo, and so gently ebb'd his breath,
   You hardly could perceive when he was dead.
He died as born, a Catholic in faith,
   Like most in the belief in which they're bred,
And first a little crucifix he kiss'd,
And then held out his jugular and wrist.

The surgeon, as there was no other fee,
   Had his first choice of morsels for his pains;
But being thirstiest at the moment, he
   Preferr'd a draught from the fast-flowing veins:
Part was divided, part thrown in the sea,
   And such things as the entrails and the brains
Regaled two sharks, who follow'd o'er the billow—
The sailors ate the rest of poor Pedrillo.

Fournier's picture "The Funeral of
Shelley" recreates with an attempt at
historical accuracy one of the most
bizarre scenes in English romantic
literature. Byron is the figure on the
right of the standing group.

*At the end of his Italian period
Byron was increasingly preoccupied
with Greek independence. Delacroix's
figure of an awakening Greece
(often mistitled "Greece expiring on the
Ruins of Missolonghi') expresses similar hopes.*

The sailors ate him, all save three or four,
    Who were not quite so fond of animal food;
To these were added Juan, who, before
    Refusing his own spaniel, hardly could
Feel now his appetite increased much more;
    'Twas not to be expected that he should,
Even in extremity of their disaster,
Dine with them on his pastor and his master.

'Twas better that he did not; for, in fact,
    The consequence was awful in the extreme;
For they, who were most ravenous in the act,
    Went raging mad—Lord! how they did blaspheme!
And foam and roll, with strange convulsions rack'd,
    Drinking salt-water like a mountain-stream,
Tearing and grinning, howling, screeching, swearing,
And, with hyaena laughter, died despairing.

Their numbers were much thinn'd by this infliction,
    And all the rest were thin enough, heaven knows;
And some of them had lost their recollection,
    Happier than they who still perceived their woes;
But others ponder'd on a new dissection,
    As if not warn'd sufficiently by those
Who had already perish'd suffering madly,
For having used their appetites so sadly.

And next they thought upon the master's mate,
    As fattest; but he saved himself, because,
Besides being much averse from such a fate,
    There were some other reasons; the first was,
He had been rather indisposed of late,
    And that which chiefly proved his saving clause,
Was a small present made to him at Cadiz,
By general subscription of the ladies.

Of poor Pedrillo something still remain'd,
    But was used sparingly,—some were afraid,
And others still their appetites constrain'd,
    Or but at times a little supper made;
All except Juan, who throughout abstain'd,
    Chewing a piece of bamboo, and some lead:
At length they caught two boobies, and a noddy,
And then they left off eating the dead body.

And if Pedrillo's fate should shocking be,
    Remember Ugolino condescends*
To eat the head of his arch-enemy
    The moment after he politely ends
His tale; if foes be food in hell, at sea
    'Tis surely fair to dine upon our friends,
When shipwreck's short allowance grows too scanty,
Without being much more horrible than Dante.

And the same night there fell a shower of rain,
    For which their mouths gaped, like the cracks of earth
When dried to summer dust; till taught by pain,
    Men really know not what good water's worth;
If you had been in Turkey or in Spain,
    Or with a famish'd boat's-crew had your berth,
Or in the desert heard the camel's bell,
You'd wish yourself where Truth is—in a well.

It pour'd down torrents, but they were no richer
    Until they found a ragged piece of sheet,
Which served them as a sort of spongy pitcher,
    And when they deem'd its moisture was complete,
They wrung it out, and though a thirsty ditcher
    Might not have thought the scanty draught so sweet
As a full pot of porter, to their thinking
They ne'er till now had known the joys of drinking.

And their baked lips, with many a bloody crack,
    Suck'd in the moisture, which like nectar stream'd;
Their throats were ovens, their swoln tongues were black,
    As the rich man's in hell, who vainly scream'd
To beg the beggar, who could not rain back
    A drop of dew, when every drop had seem'd
To taste of heaven—If this be true, indeed,
Some Christians have a comfortable creed.

There were two fathers in this ghastly crew,
    And with them their two sons, of whom the one
Was more robust and hardy to the view,
    But he died early; and when he was gone,
His nearest messmate told his sire, who threw
    One glance on him, and said 'Heaven's will be done!
I can do nothing,' and he saw him thrown
Into the deep without a tear or groan.

Théodore Gudin's picture of a shipwreck captures with melodramatic romantic flair something of the terror Byron describes in a similar scene from the second canto of "Don Juan".

Of all the figures drawn to Byron's Pisan circle, the confidence-trickster Trelawny— who claimed to model himself on Byron's Corsair—was the most exotic and also the most critical of Byron himself.

The other father had a weaklier child,
    Of a soft cheek, and aspect delicate;
But the boy bore up long, and with a mild
    And patient spirit held aloof his fate;
Little he said, and now and then he smiled,
    As if to win a part from off the weight
He saw increasing on his father's heart,
With the deep deadly thought, that they must part.

And o'er him bent his sire, and never raised
    His eyes from off his face, but wiped the foam
From his pale lips, and ever on him gazed,
    And when the wish'd-for shower at length was come,
And the boy's eyes, which the dull film half glazed,
    Brighten'd, and for a moment seem'd to roam,
He squeezed from out a rag some drops of rain
Into his dying child's mouth—but in vain.

The boy expired—the father held the clay,
    And look'd upon it long, and when at last
Death left no doubt, and the dead burthen lay
    Stiff on his heart, and pulse and hope were past,
He watch'd it wistfully, until away
    'Twas borne by the rude wave wherein 'twas cast;
Then he himself sunk down all dumb and shivering,
And gave no sign of life, save his limbs quivering.

It is indeed—although even Byron's closest friends, realizing how the opening cantos would offend the smug sensibilities of his countrymen, voiced their anxiety. Hobhouse and Kinnaird urged cuts; Byron argued vehemently against them. He would not, he declared, have his poem castrated. Nevertheless, he was worried by the doubts of his friends. "The outcry has frightened me," he declared. "I had such projects for the Don, but Cant is [so] much stronger than C--t now-a-days, that the benefit of experience in a man who has well weighed the worth of both monosyllables, must be lost to a despairing posterity."

In October, Byron and La Guiccioli returned to Venice. The Conte, unaccountably roused from his complaisant inertia, arrived at the Palazzo Mocenigo with an ultimatum: Teresa must make up her mind, it was Byron or him. For Teresa, there was no choice, but for Byron himself matters were more complex. The conventions of the *cavalier servente* increasingly irked him. He still had unformed but persistent dreams of freedom, of serving liberty rather than his mistress. Now he was offered the chance of decently cutting himself free. Eventually, after much difficulty, he persuaded Teresa to go back to Ravenna, "not absolutely denying that I might come there again; else she refused to go".

She left, and Byron procrastinated. He was not entirely ready for freedom yet. While he idled, Teresa's father, the Conte Gamba, wrote to inform him of his daughter's prostrate grief. Still Byron delayed. He could not finally part from Teresa, but he dared not return. Nor, in the end, could he do nothing. On Christmas Eve, the "Napoleonic" coach, rather battered now, arrived in Ravenna, and the following day Teresa paraded her poet at a ball in the Palazzo Guiccioli.

He moved back into the palace and chafed under the reins of her guidance. There were rows and misunderstandings, but in the end, and for the moment, he did as he was told. Their passion died down to warm and convenient habits of intimacy. Conte Gamba, meanwhile, introduced Byron to those radical Italian circles for whom freedom from the tyranny of Austrian rule was an imperative.

Byron was still seeking his true political role, but for the moment his energies were directed towards the Gambas' radical friends and the theatre of his imagination. He began work on *Marino Faliero*, a drama of Venetian politics in which a liberal aristocrat sides with the popular cause against tyranny. Though tedious in its attempts at classical correctness, the nature of the play's hero and his sympathies are a pointer to Byron's own.

England, to which he had had vague thoughts of returning, was in a state of deepening reactionary crisis. Increased government repression, the writings of the radical Cobbett and the demagogy of Henry Hunt, stirred many ordinary people to revolt against high food prices, the exploitation of their labour, and inadequate representation in Parliament. In 1816, at a great open air meeting in London, the tricolour of the "British Republic" waved beside a pike crowned with the Liberty Cap of the French Revolutionaries of 1789. A suspension of Habeas Corpus was immediately rushed through Parliament, public meetings were banned, and rebellion was apparently crushed.

Though the shocked Tory government thought it wise to concede to a few Whig demands for reform, in reality the crisis was deepening. In 1819 it reached its climax. On 16 August a great meeting to urge the reform of Parliament was called in Manchester—60,000 working men and women gathered in St Peter's Fields. Henry Hunt arrived. He mounted the rostrum. Silence fell. Hunt began to speak, and the assembled band of cavalrymen, drawing their swords, charged the crowd. Eleven protesters were killed, many hundreds more were wounded.

Amid howls of execration at the "Peterloo massacre", the government rushed through yet more legislation. The Whigs protested, but the radicals now doubted their sincerity. Hobhouse was among them. He wrote a pamphlet denouncing the Whig party, and was summoned before the House of Commons, and then committed to Newgate prison for a breach of parliamentary privilege.

Byron was appalled, neither by the sentence, nor by the fate of his friend, but by what he considered Hobhouse's desertion of the true Whig cause. By making public his sympathies with Cobbett and Hunt, it appeared Hobhouse had sided with the rabble. Byron's political ideas focussed in sharp contempt. The liberty of the people, he considered, could only be maintained by radical aristocrats, such as himself. This was the oldest form of the Whig ideal, but now, in reality, was a mere dream of benevolent power. Five years earlier, Walter Scott, a Tory to the core, had shrewdly observed the real nature of Byron's politics, "at heart, I would have termed Byron a patrician on principle". And Scott, of course, was right.

At the same time, a crisis was brewing in Byron's private life. The climax came when Conte Guiccioli caught the poet in an intimate embrace with his wife. The embarrassment was at once considered a matter between gentlemen. The English peer told the Italian count that he would, of course, honourably withdraw from his house. Teresa, shrewder and braver in hysterical grief, brushed such poses aside. She would keep her poet, although the price might be the loss of her reputation. She begged her father to apply at once for a Papal separation on the grounds that she could no longer live in safety with her husband.

A favourable reply was received on 14 July 1820. Gamba was well pleased. His daughter was at last happy, and in Byron he had an international celebrity whom he was winning to the cause of Italian freedom.

Conte Gamba and Pietro, his delightfully hot-headed son, had already introduced Byron to the *carbonari*—the secret societies who were plotting to free and unify the various and oppressively ruled kingdoms of Italy. Byron himself now joined the *Cacciatore Americani* (the "American Hunters"), and for a time had high hopes of throwing off the Bourbon tyranny in Naples. The combination of intrigue and radical politics, along with the warm, cultured ease of the Gamba family, appealed deeply to his aristocratic sensibilities, and, for a while, also provided a new edge of excitement to his relationship with Teresa.

The secret police suspected Byron of supplying the insurgents with money and were already plotting to remove him from the region; Byron's loyalties, however, were ambiguous. This emerges clearly in a letter to Tom Moore in which Byron describes the one really dramatic incident of the period—the shooting of the local troop commandant Luigi Dal Pinto. Coming on the scene of murder as he was making his evening visit to Teresa, Byron at once insisted "the mob" carry the dying officer's body to his lodgings. But, as Byron stared down at the corpse, he realized both how Dal Pinto had made himself unpopular with "the people"—a suddenly noble epithet—and how he himself had enjoyed the conversation of this well-bred officer. His motives were as muddled as Italian politics themselves.

ITALIAN POLITICS AND A MURDER

"There will be blood shed like water,
and tears like mist; but the peoples
will conquer in the end"

Of all the arts of narrative, vivid
and violent action is the most
difficult to render effectively. In
these hurried, broken phrases Byron
describes an Italian political murder,
achieving a vigour matched only
by the greatest thriller writers.

Dear Murray—I intended to have written to you at some length by this post,—but as the Military Commandant is now lying dead in my house—on Fletcher's bed—I have other things to think of.——He was shot at 8 o Clock this evening about two hundred paces from our door. —I was putting on my great Coat to pay a visit to the Countess G[uiccioli]—when I heard a shot—and on going into the hall—found all my servants on the balcony—exclaiming that "a Man was murdered".——As it is the custom here to let people fight it through—they wanted to hinder me from going out—but I ran down into the Street—Tita the bravest of them followed me—and we made our way to the Commandant who was lying on his back with five wounds—of which three in the body—one in the heart.——There were about him—Diego his Adjutant—crying like a Child—a priest howling—a Surgeon who dared not touch him—two or three confused

& frightened Soldiers—one or two of the boldest of the mob—and the Street dark as pitch—with the people flying in all directions.—As Diego could only cry and wring his hands—and the Priest could only pray—and nobody seemed able or willing to do anything except exclaim shake and stare—I made my Servant & one of the mob take up the body—sent off Diego crying to the Cardinal—the Soldiers for the Guard—& had the Commandant carried up Stairs to my own quarters.—But he was quite gone.—I made the Surgeon examine him & examined him myself.—He had bled inwardly, & very little external blood was apparent.— One of the Slugs had gone quite through—all but the Skin, I felt it myself.—Two more shots in the body—one in a finger—and another in the arm.—His face not at all disfigured—he seems asleep—but is growing livid.—The Assassin has not been taken—but the gun was found—a gun filed down to half the barrel.——

He said nothing—but "O Dio!" and "O Gesu" two or three times. The house was filled at last with Soldiers—officers—police—and military—but they are clearing away—all but the Sentinels—and the [body] is to be removed tomorrow.—It seems [that] if I had not had him taken into my house he might have lain in the Street till morning—for here nobody meddles with such things—for fear of the consequences—either of public suspicion, or private revenge on the part of the Slayers.—They may do as they please—I shall never be deterred from a duty of humanity by all the assassins of Italy—and that is a wide word.——He was a brave officer—but an unpopular man.—The whole town is in confusion.—You may judge better of things here by this detail than by anything which I could add on the Subject—communicate this letter to Hobhouse & Douglas K[innair]d—and believe me.

yrs. truly

B

P.S. The poor Man's wife is not yet aware of his death—they are to break it to her in the morning.—The lieutenant who is watching the body is smoking with the greatest Sangfroid—a strange people.—

The Neapolitan uprising eventually collapsed in confusion, betrayal and recrimination. Byron turned again to his writing. *Don Juan* was continued through its fourth and fifth cantos. In *Cain*, attempting a metaphysical melodrama once again, Byron's vague, but thwarted, hopes of political revolution were expressed in incoherent defiance against what he considered the greatest of all tyrants—the Old Testament Jehovah. In *Sardanapalus*, Byron portrayed himself as that ancient king rendered impotent not simply by self-indulgence, but by his hatred of war and his contempt for worldly ambition.

Events, however, were conspiring to force Byron from his unsatisfactory ease. Pietro was suddenly arrested and cast into perpetual exile for a mild affray in which they had all been involved. Conte Gamba followed him. By the terms of her separation, Teresa was obliged to live under her father's roof, which meant that she too would have to leave Ravenna. Byron, the authorities believed, would follow her without question. In addition, his own servant Tita had also been sentenced to banishment, which was a slight no decent master could allow. Nonetheless, Byron delayed in Ravenna, perhaps because loneliness was a sort of freedom for him. He was, however, thinking vaguely of taking his friends and servants to Switzerland.

The arrival of Shelley prevented this. The two poets had not met since Shelley's visit to the Palazzo Mocenigo over two years before. Still deeply concerned about Claire and the fate of her child whom Byron had placed in a convent near Ravenna, Shelley persuaded Byron to agree that he would move with Allegra and the Gambas to Pisa, where Shelley himself hoped "to form for ourselves a society of our own class, as much as possible, in intellect or in feelings". His slight qualification is significant, for Shelley was secretly hoping that the radical journalist Leigh Hunt and his wife might join them from London. However, when Mr and Mrs Hunt, who were living in poverty on the dubious fringes of bohemian St John's Wood, eventually came to Italy they were jarringly out of tune with the intellect and feelings of the radical Lord Byron.

Meanwhile, Byron still delayed going to Pisa. Once again, there was the possibility of a break from La Guiccioli. Byron's emotional dependence on her humiliated him and his dreams of personal and political freedom were becoming ever more insistent. He wrote movingly to Moore of his quandary. "It is awful work, this love, and prevents all a man's projects of good or glory. I wanted to go to Greece lately (as everything seems to be up here) . . . . But the tears of a woman who has left her husband for a man, and the weakness of one's own heart, are paramount to these projects, and I can hardly indulge them."

Pacing the floors of a Palazzo Guiccioli emptied of its mistress,

Byron's thoughts revolved his predicament. The endless confusions of Italian politics seemed derisory, yet he had not the courage to go to Greece. In addition, he was infuriated to learn that, although the stanzas satirizing Southey which he had placed at the opening of *Don Juan* had been cut, Southey himself had nonetheless referred obliquely to Byron as a "spirit of pride and audacious impiety", who led a Satanic school of writers. Byron now seized on the ridiculous pieties of the poem Southey had written on the occasion of the death of George III and parodied them mercilessly. *The Vision of Judgment* is the greatest of Byron's short satires. Southey, the grovelling spokesman of a disreputable England, is laughed into an immortality his works could never have earned him. At this point, however, it seemed unlikely that Byron would find a publisher willing to accept so controversial a poem. He was a radical with no clear cause, a satirist with no obvious publisher. There seemed nothing for him to do but join the others in Pisa.

The Pisan spies had watched the arrival of his furniture; now they observed Byron settling in among a brilliant and radical set of English ex-patriots and Italian republicans. In addition to the Gambas and the Shelleys, there were Edward and Jane Williams, the Shelleys' closest friends, and Thomas Medwin who began to make notes of Byron's conversation like a true Boswell. Then, at the beginning of 1822, there arrived in Pisa one of the most extraordinary figures of the period— Edward Trelawny, part adventurer, part fantasist, part con-man, who claimed he slept with *The Corsair* under his pillow, and certainly tried to live up to the poem's pantomime ideals.

With the shrewdness of a confidence trickster, Trelawny later recalled there was already something slightly *passé* about the man he had come to Italy to see. Though, in retrospect, he was to appreciate its range and depth, Byron's conversation was, Trelawny declared, "anything but literary, except when Shelley was near him. The character he most commonly appeared in was of the free and easy sort, such as had been in vogue when he was in London, and George IV was Regent; and his talk was seasoned with anecdotes of the great actors on and off the stage, boxers, gamblers, duellists, drunkards, &c., &c., appropriately garnished with the slang and scandal of that day. Such things had all been in fashion, and were at that time considered accomplishments by gentlemen . . . . His long absence had not effaced the mark John Bull brands his children with; the instant he loomed above the horizon, on foot or horseback, you saw at a glance he was a Britisher."

These are telling observations. It was indeed Shelley who was the sharpest stimulus to Byron's mind, and in their discussions about religion Shelley managed to touch those Calvinistic weaknesses of Byron's that lay so deep in his personality. These Shelley despised.

Trelawny recalls Shelley turning in suprise to his wife during one such discussion and declaring, "I do believe, Mary, that he is little better than a Christian!" Mary herself, however, was clearly in sympathy with a temperament so complementary to her own, and her later novels are full of heroes wrought from her fascination with Byron's personality. Trelawny, in the meantime, encouraged both Byron and Shelley to have boats built for their recreation.

THE VISION OF JUDGMENT

"Southey . . . is . . . the vainest & most intolerant of men – and a rogue besides"

Southey had turned from his early liberal views to high Toryism and been rewarded with the Poet Laureateship. He had also called Byron the leader of a "Satanic" school of poets. Byron's wrath expressed itself in *The Vision of Judgment*, a satire on Southey himself and on his foolish poem mourning the death of George III who had died insane.

In the first year of freedom's second dawn*
  Died George the Third; although no tyrant, one
Who shielded tyrants, till each sense withdrawn
  Left him nor mental nor external sun:
A better farmer ne'er brush'd dew from lawn,
  A weaker king never left a realm undone!
He died—but left his subjects still behind,
One half as mad—and t'other no less blind.

He died!—his death made no great stir on earth;
  His burial made some pomp; there was profusion
Of velvet, gilding, brass, and no great dearth
  Of aught but tears—save those shed by collusion;
For these things may be bought at their true worth:
  Of elegy there was the due infusion—
Bought also; and the torches, cloaks, and banners,
Heralds, and relics of old Gothic manners.

Form'd a sepulchral melo-drame. Of all
  The fools who flock'd to swell or see the show,
Who cared about the corpse? The funeral
  Made the attraction, and the black the woe.
There throbb'd not there a thought which pierced the pall;
  And when the gorgeous coffin was laid low,
It seem'd the mockery of hell to fold
The rottenness of eighty years in gold.*

During his time with Teresa Guiccioli Byron wrote a number of historical and political tragedies. Though modern taste may find them frigid, Delacroix's "Execution of Doge Marino Faliero" suggests Byron's wide influence.

So mix his body with the dust! It might
Return to what it *must* far sooner, were
The natural compound left alone to fight
Its way back into earth, and fire, and air;
But the unnatural balsams merely blight
What nature made him at his birth, as bare
As the mere million's base unmummied clay—
Yet all his spices but prolong decay.

At the conclusion of Byron's poem, Southey is presented as
a hack writer and hypocrite, a man atrociously servile and
woefully prolific, who causes consternation and boredom
when he is summoned to heaven. Southey's poem on the
death of George III is so bad that it appals the angels and
makes the devils flee back to hell. In desperation,
St Peter knocks Southey back down to earth where he
drowns, while the king slips quietly into heaven.

He said—(I only give the heads)—he said,
He meant no harm in scribbling; 'twas his way
Upon all topics; 'twas, besides, his bread,
Of which he butter'd both sides; 'twould delay
Too long the assembly (he was pleased to dread)
And take up rather more time than a day,
To name his works—he would but cite a few—
Wat Tyler—Rhymes on Blenheim—Waterloo.

He had written praises of a regicide;
He had written praises of all kings whatever;
He had written for republics far and wide,
And then against them bitterer than ever;
For pantisocracy he once had cried*
Aloud, a scheme less moral than 'twas clever;
Then grew a hearty antijacobin—
Had turn'd his coat—and would have turn'd his skin.

He had sung against all battles, and again
In their high praise and glory: he had call'd
Reviewing 'the ungentle craft,' and then
Become as base a critic as ere crawl'd—
Fed, paid, and pamper'd by the very men
By whom his muse and morals had been maul'd:
He had written much blank verse, and blanker prose,
And more of both than any body knows.

*Byron's drama "Sardanapalus" discusses
the problems of a sensual man torn between
tenderness and action. It influenced
Delacroix's luxurious recreation
of the ancient king's dilemma.*

He had written Wesley's life:—here, turning round*
    To Satan, 'Sir, I'm ready to write yours,
In two octavo volumes, nicely bound,
    With notes and preface, all that most allures
The pious purchaser; and there's no ground
    For fear, for I can choose my own reviewers:
So let me have the proper documents,
That I may add you to my other saints.'

Satan bow'd, and was silent. 'Well, if you,
    With amiable modesty, decline
My offer, what says Michael? There are few
    Whose memoirs could be render'd more divine.
Mine is a pen of all work; not so new
    As it was once, but I would make you shine
Like your own trumpet; by the way, my own
Has more of brass in it, and is as well blown.

'But talking about trumpets, here's my Vision!
    Now you shall judge, all people; yes, you shall
Judge with my judgment! and by my decision
    Be guided who shall enter heaven or fall!
I settle all these things by intuition,
    Times present, past, to come, heaven, hell, and all,
Like King Alfonso! When I thus see double,*
I save the Deity some worlds of trouble.'

He ceased; and drew forth an MS; and no
    Persuasion on the part of devils, or saints,
Or angels, now could stop the torrent; so
    He read the first three lines of the contents;
But at the fourth, the whole spiritual show
    Had vanish'd with variety of scents,
Ambrosial and sulphureous, as they sprang,
Like lightning, off from his 'melodious twang'.

Those grand heroics acted as a spell:
    The angels stopp'd their ears and plied their pinions;
The devils ran howling, deafen'd, down to hell;
    The ghosts fled, gibbering, for their own dominions—
(For 'tis not yet decided where they dwell,
    And I leave every man to his opinions);
Michael took refuge in his trump—but lo!
His teeth were set on edge, he could not blow!

For the greater part of his career, Byron had a justified loathing of the Poet Laureate Robert Southey whom he regarded as a hypocritical hack. He pilloried both him and the establishment in "The Vision of Judgment".

*The radical Leigh Hunt
and his brother published
Byron's "The Vision of
Judgment", but Byron found
Hunt an abrasive dependent.*

Saint Peter, who has hitherto been known
   For an impetuous saint, upraised his keys,
And at the fifth line knock'd the Poet down;
   Who fell like Phaeton, but more at ease,
Into his lake, for there he did not drown,*
   A different web being by the Destinies
Woven for the Laureate's final wreath, whene'er
Reform shall happen either here or there.

He first sunk to the bottom—like his works,
   But soon rose to the surface—like himself;
For all corrupted things are buoy'd, like corks,*
   By their own rottenness, light as an elf,
Or wisp that flits o'er a morass: he lurks,
   It may be, still, like dull books on a shelf,
In his own den, to scrawl some 'Life' or 'Vision,'
As Wellborn says—'the devil turn'd precisian'.*

As for the rest, to come to the conclusion
   Of this true dream, the telescope is gone
Which kept my optics free from all delusion,
   And show'd me what I in my turn have shown:
All I saw farther in the last confusion,
   Was, that King George slipp'd into heaven for one;
And when the tumult dwindled to a calm,
I left him practising the hundredth psalm.

There were a number of annoyances to upset Byron's calm retreat. Murray was threatened with prosecution for publishing *Cain*, and Byron promised to refund from his fee any expenses this might entail. In addition, Leigh Hunt wrote to Byron asking for money to finance his journey to Italy. His manner was both brazen and fawning, a repellent combination that was to drive Byron to distraction when the Hunt family finally arrived. Byron, nonetheless, felt committed to the radical periodical Hunt was about to launch in London.

The affair with Teresa continued as a warm and placid glow, but Claire was now writing angry letters about Byron's neglect of his daughter. Despite Shelley's requests, Allegra remained with the nuns in the convent at Bagnacavallo; an apparently callous disregard which considerably annoyed Shelley. News then came that the child was ill. Byron was "dreadfully agitated", but when Teresa informed him that the girl had died, "a mortal paleness spread itself over his face . . . . and no consolation which I endeavoured to offer him seemed to reach his ears". Byron wished to have his daughter buried in Harrow churchyard, the scene of his boyhood melancholy, but the vicar objected to raising a tablet in his church for a bastard, and Allegra was eventually buried in an unmarked grave just inside the door. The distraught Claire wrote Byron a savage letter full of grief, bitterness and righteous indignation.

The Pisan authorities were increasingly unhappy about the presence of Byron's radical circle in their city, and took advantage of an embarrassing scuffle between Byron's party, who were returning from a ride, and an Italian soldier who was lightly wounded in the affray. Byron's servant, the magnificently bearded Tita, was arrested and then condemned to exile for the incident. Byron, realizing the persecution was really directed at him, eventually decided to move with the Gambas from Pisa to the Villa Dupuy near Leghorn. The Pisan circle was dissolving: Trelawny was in Genoa; the Shelleys and the Williamses had gone to Lerici where they were soon planning to sail Shelley's boat across the Bay of Spezia.

When he arrived at Leghorn, Byron found the Mediterranean squadron of the United States navy at anchor in the harbour. The Americans had long recognized his genius, and Byron was invited aboard the *Ontario*, where he was shown a New York edition of his poems. Byron, deeply in sympathy with the Americans' republican ideals, declared he would rather have "a nod from an American, than a snuff-box from an Emperor".

Meanwhile, at the beginning of July, Hunt and his family had arrived in Italy. Hunt, who had last met Byron during the poet's years of London fame, was surprised by how stout he had grown. Byron welcomed him, and amid a welter of personal problems—his grief for Allegra, the machinations of the secret police, and the tedious business of completing his move from Pisa—he tried to give the Hunts what help and attention he could. Hunt was, in fact, wholly dependent on Byron for financial assistance and the hoped-for success of his journal. Shelley, realizing this, persuaded Byron to offer *The Vision of Judgment* for publication in the first issue. Byron wrote to Murray asking him to deliver the text to Hunt's brother in London. Shelley, having received Byron's promise that he would help the Hunts all he could, then departed with Williams to sail his boat.

The drowning of Shelley in the Gulf of Spezia is one of the great and tragic episodes in the history of English literature. It shook Byron profoundly. Though relations between the two poets had recently grown strained, Byron showered kindnesses on the poet's widow (she became his copyist) and wrote to Murray declaring that Shelley was "without exception, the *best* and least selfish man I ever knew. I never knew a man who was not a beast in comparison." Byron realized he had lost the one writer who could really challenge his intellect.

The bodies of Shelley, Williams and a member of their crew were washed ashore ten days after their boat sank. Trelawny retrieved Shelley's corpse from the Italian authorities, but since the flesh of the arms and face had been entirely eaten away, Trelawny could only identify it by the vestiges of the clothes it still wore and by the opened copy of Keats's poems he found in one of the pockets. To comply with the quarantine laws, the body was briefly buried in sand and quicklime while Trelawny negotiated to have it removed to Rome, where Shelley would be buried beside his son, William. Permission was also obtained to cremate the body, and for this purpose Trelawny had had a portable iron furnace constructed. When he had lit the fire beneath the corpse he cast oil and spices on the flames while muttering incantations. "I knew you were a Pagan," Byron declared, "not that you were a Pagan priest; you do it very well." The ashes were then sealed in a box, and Byron, Trelawny and Hunt got drunk in order to relieve their feelings. Shelley's heart had not burned, however, and Trelawny kept it as a souvenir. Later he gave it to Hunt, who, rather reluctantly, passed it on to the poet's widow.

Byron was increasingly exasperated by the Hunts. Their unruly children shouted in his house and soiled the walls with their dirty hands. It was also clear that, with the death of Shelley, the proposed journal was doomed. Byron himself could take little interest in it for, once again, the Gambas had been exiled and had now taken up residence in Genoa. Byron would follow them, of course, but he knew in his heart that only escape from Italy would ever really allow him to fulfil himself. The Pisan spies read his mind even better than he did. "Lord Byron," they reported, "has finally decided to leave for Genoa. It is said that he is already sated or tired of his Favourite, the Guiccioli. He has, however, expressed his intention of not remaining in Genoa, but of going on to Athens in order to make himself adored by the Greeks . . . ."

In the meantime, the appearance of *The Vision of Judgment* in the first issue of Leigh Hunt's *The Liberal* had led to considerable friction between Byron and his publisher, John Murray, from whom he now parted. It also led to Hunt's brother, who was the publisher of *The Liberal*, being prosecuted. Byron still felt committed to continue publishing with the Hunts, however, and it was John Hunt who brought out the later cantos of *Don Juan* and much of Byron's subsequent work.

Byron was ever more restless in Genoa and, as the winter drew on, he became depressed. He felt he ought to do more for mankind than just write verses. He was also becoming acutely conscious of advancing age. A few days before his 35th birthday he wrote, "I always looked to about thirty as the barrier of any real or fierce delight in the passions, and determined to work them out in the younger ore and better veins of the mine, and I flatter myself (perhaps) that I have pretty well done so." Teresa's charms, though he was not indifferent to them, had begun to pall. She was no longer allowed to see him whenever she wished, as she had when he was writing *Marino Faliero*. Then she had burst in on him unexpectedly with her fierce, exciting demands. Now she had to wait to be invited. She fitted herself as calmly as she could to her new role, and only when Byron's spirits were too obviously raised by the refined and lively personality of Lady Blessington, an English admirer who arrived in Genoa with her entourage in April 1823, did Teresa show her fierce Italian jealousy. Byron, meanwhile, was thinking more and more of Greece and dared not tell her of his plans.

When a representative of the London Greek Committee called on him, Byron's interest in Greek independence deepened still further. The committee itself, of which both Hobhouse and Douglas Kinnaird were members, had been founded to provide money and support for the Greek patriots in the War of Independence. Here was a glorious, humanitarian aim, and the chance of an escape to action, to stimulus. Hobhouse wrote to congratulate Byron on his election to the committee, but still Byron could not bring himself to tell Teresa of the depth of his involvement. He feared parting from a woman who, though he now only half-loved her, and that with an all but paternal affection, had surrendered to him the whole of her life. It was an agonizing conflict. It seemed, he confessed to Lady Blessington, that there was something in him that doomed both himself and those closest to him to unhappiness. In the end, he persuaded Pietro to tell Teresa of his plans.

When she had recovered from her first torrent of grief, Teresa knew that, despite his promises and despite his insistence that he was only making a brief journey of reconnoitre, she would never see Byron again. He had raised substantial amounts of money, gathered Trelawny and Pietro around him, and chartered the *Hercules* for the voyage. In the last hours she waited, half delirious, for Byron to come to her. Between three and five on the afternoon of 15 July 1823 they said their last farewells. The next day she left for Ravenna with her father. As the carriage rolled away she wrote down her anguished thoughts in a little notebook that had once belonged to her lover, "the pain grows every moment and I feel as though I were dying. Send after me Byron . . .". But she was already writing to her past; between Teresa and her poet there soon stretched the severing waves of the Ionian Sea.

"I dreamed that Greece might still be free"

B yron had won his freedom and found a cause. He was also returning to the land that had made him a poet and determined his political views. With the coming of war there was a real chance that the Greeks might throw off their Turkish oppressors, and their hopes now became Byron's own. Childe Harold had come home.

The Greek War of Independence sprang from a quarrel between Ali Pasha and the Turkish Sultan, who had declared the tyrant of Tepelene an outlaw. With the wrath of Constantinople directed against him, Ali appealed for help to the Greeks, even going as far as drinking a health to the Virgin and making offers of religious liberty and political independence. His overtures were ignored. No one had any reason to trust him. Besides, there was a new confidence among the Greeks. Many of their merchants had enriched themselves by carrying merchandise for the French when, at the end of the Napoleonic Wars, the French themselves no longer dared sail the Mediterranean. Some of this money had gone towards the founding of schools, and, when these were suppressed, outraged Greek patriotism reached revolutionary fervour. Secret societies, such as the *Philike Hetaireia*, organized themselves into armed bands and prepared to govern their homeland in the wake of Ali's apparently inevitable defeat.

The Sultan attempted to crush such hopes by a brutal and arbitrary assertion of his power. Having patched up a peace with Ali, he landed his troops on Chios and massacred or enslaved three quarters of the Greek population there. European opinion was outraged, but for a long time the great powers remained neutral. The Greeks seemed to be on their own. Though they managed to defeat the Turkish forces sent against them, they soon turned from victory to self-destructive bickering. They had neither a fully united form of government nor the machinery for collecting taxes. The rivalries of the Greek princes apparently rendered the former problem insoluble, the latter appeared to be at least temporarily eased by the offices of the London Greek

Committee. To their generous efforts were now added the heavy purse of the English milord who was sailing romantically to their aid, accompanied by a group of friends wearing helmets emblazoned with his family motto "Crede Byron" (Trust Byron).

THE ISLES OF GREECE

"The very poetry of politics"

This is perhaps Byron's most famous lyric, and is sung by a poet
for Juan and Haidee in a scene from the third canto of *Don Juan*.
Its mixture of fervour and self-defeat is typical of the strongly
contrasting moods Byron achieves in his best work.

The isles of Greece, the isles of Greece!
   Where burning Sappho loved and sung,
Where grew the arts of war and peace,—
   Where Delos rose, and Phoebus sprung!
Eternal summer gilds them yet,
But all, except their sun, is set.

The Scian and the Teian muse,*
   The hero's harp, the lover's lute,
Have found the fame your shores refuse;
   Their place of birth alone is mute
To sounds which echo further west
Than your sires' 'Islands of the Blest'.

The mountains look on Marathon—
   And Marathon looks on the sea;
And musing there an hour alone,
   I dream'd that Greece might still be free;
For standing on the Persian's grave,
I could not deem myself a slave.

A king sate on the rocky brow*
   Which looks o'er sea-born Salamis;
And ships, by thousands, lay below,
   And men in nations;—all were his!
He counted them at break of day—
And when the sun set where were they?

And where are they? and where art thou,
   My country? On thy voiceless shore
The heroic lay is tuneless now—
   The heroic bosom beats no more!
And must thy lyre, so long divine,
Degenerate into hands like mine?

'Tis something, in the dearth of fame,
   Though link'd among a fetter'd race,
To feel at least a patriot's shame,
   Even as I sing, suffuse my face;
For what is left the poet here?
For Greeks a blush—for Greece a tear.

Must *we* but weep o'er days more blest?
   Must *we* but blush?—Our fathers bled.
Earth! render back from out thy breast
   A remnant of our Spartan dead!
Of the three hundred grant but three,
To make a new Thermopylae!

What, silent still? and silent all?
   Ah! no, the voices of the dead
Sound like a distant torrent's fall,
   And answer, 'Let one living head,
But one arise,—we come, we come!'
'Tis but the living who are dumb.

In vain—in vain: strike other chords;
    Fill high the cup with Samian wine!
Leave battles to the Turkish hordes,
    And shed the blood of Scio's vine!
Hark! rising to the ignoble call—
How answers each bold bacchanal!

You have the Pyrrhic dance as yet,
    Where is the Pyrrhic phalanx gone?*
Of two such lessons, why forget
    The nobler and the manlier one?
You have the letters Cadmus gave—*
Think ye he meant them for a slave?

Fill high the bowl with Samian wine!
    We will not think of themes like these!
It made Anacreon's song divine:
    He served—but served Polycrates—*
A tyrant; but our masters then
Were still, at least, our countrymen.

The tyrant of the Chersonese
    Was freedom's best and bravest friend;
That tyrant was Miltiades!*
    Oh! that the present hour would lend
Another despot of the kind!
Such chains as his were sure to bind.

Fill high the bowl with Samian wine!
    On Suli's rock, and Parga's shore,
Exists the remnant of a line*
    Such as the Doric mothers bore;
And there, perhaps, some seed is sown,
The Heracleidan blood might own.*

Trust not for freedom to the Franks—*
    They have a king who buys and sells:
In native swords, and native ranks,
    The only hope of courage dwells;
But Turkish force, and Latin fraud,
Would break your shield, however broad.

Fill high the bowl with Samian wine!
    Our virgins dance beneath the shade—
I see their glorious black eyes shine;
    But gazing on each glowing maid,
My own the burning tear-drop laves,
To think such breasts must suckle slaves.

Place me on Sunium's marbled step,
    Where nothing, save the waves and I,
May hear our mutual murmurs sweep;
    There, swan-like, let me sing and die:
A land of slaves shall ne'er be mine—
Dash down yon cup of Samian wine!

When he anchored off Cephalonia, Byron felt the bitterness of the years since his last visit instantly disappear. Remembering the Suliote, or Albanian warriors he had taken into his service during his previous stay, he was now eager to hire a band of them as his bodyguard. These splendid men, mustachioed, wild haired and quarrelsome, were to cause him endless problems; for the moment however, they appealed to his romantic concept of his mission. Meanwhile, as he waited for clear information on the true state of the war, Byron made an expedition to the nearby island of Ithaca.

As the weeks passed, Byron became discouraged by what he learned about the complexities of the Greek leaders' internecine greed, but he refused to be despondent, and the softer, charitable side of his nature, so quickly moved to spontaneous kindness, at once prompted him to set up a fund for the refugees he met on Ithaca. A little while later, unaware of the searing repercussions this would have for him, he also provided a home for the Chalandritsanos family, who were newly destitute, and happened to come to the poet's attention.

However, his constitution, battered by the years of excess and further worn by the strict regimen he was now imposing on himself, began to reveal how frail Byron really was. Though he swam and sailed in the sun, the after-effects of a lavish dinner at Saint Euphemia resulted in a sudden paroxysm. He was eventually persuaded to take some pills prescribed by his physician, Dr Bruno, and appeared to calm down. By the following day he had recovered. His fit, however, was a warning, which he refused to heed.

Byron now settled in a small villa at Metaxa and was at once besieged by requests for money on the one hand and troubled by the unruly behaviour of his Suliote warriors on the other. In what spare hours he had, the pious Dr Kennedy, a local medical officer, tried to convert the "Satanic" lord to Evangelical Christianity. Byron listened to Kennedy with patience, but with no real conversion from a scepticism which Byron himself sometimes questioned. He challenged the truths of Kennedy's faith with a surprising degree of familiarity with the Bible. Then he questioned his own questioning. Byron's rebellious intellect had always chafed against the deep Calvinist influences of his boyhood, and his spiritual problems remained unresolved. Meantime, he yearned for action.

But local politics seemed hopelessly confused. Perhaps from sentiment, perhaps after persuasion by his unruly bodyguard, Byron began to turn his attention away from Cephalonia and towards the struggle in Western Greece. He wrote to the Greek Committee explaining his position and outlining what he had already done; for instance, he had offered to advance a thousand Levantine dollars a month for the relief of Missolonghi. The Provisional Greek Government, however, responded by saying that they wanted to confer with him on the matter. In other words, "they wish me to expend my money in some other direction". Such attitudes began to annoy Byron intensely. He was becoming ever more disillusioned, and at last he came to see that in the confusion of Greek politics he would have to take his own initiatives.

He now wrote to the Provisional Government informing them that he would definitely expend his money and energies on building up the defences of the strategic port of Missolonghi, and hence the cause of the little, bespectacled Prince Mavrocordatos, a scholarly captain chief whom Byron declared to be the George Washington of Greece. The Prince replied eagerly to Byron's letters. "Be assured, My Lord, that it depends only on yourself to succour the destiny of Greece," he wrote.

"I have ordered one of the best ships in our squadron to sail for Cephalonia. . . ."

Byron saw through the flattery, but was resolved to go. Towards six o'clock on the evening of 29 December 1823, having written to the Greek Committee in London, he set sail for Missolonghi. With him went Dr Bruno, Fletcher his valet, and the striking 15-year-old son of the family he had recently rescued, Loukas Chalandritsanos.

GREECE

"I did not come here to join a faction but a nation"

Byron was not seduced by the idealism he brought to the Greek cause. Though his commitment was wholehearted and one of the abiding interests of his life, he was fully aware of the political and personal shortcomings of the oppressed Greeks themselves. These feelings he largely confided to his *Journal in Cephalonia*, a moving record of a political idealist confronting real life.

Missolonghi is forever associated with Byron's death and the War of Greek Independence. Byron found it a small, unattractive and provincial town, wracked by dissension, boredom and hope postponed.

I also transferred to the resident in Ithaca—the sum of two hundred and fifty dollars* for the refugees there—and I had conveyed to Cephalonia—a Moriote family who were in the greatest helplessness—and provided them with a house and decent maintenance under the protection of Messrs. Corgialegno—wealthy merchants of Argostoli—to whom I had been recommended by my Correspondents.——I had caused a letter to be written to Marco Bozzari the acting Commander of a body of troops in Acarnania—for whom I had letters of recommended [sic];—his answer was probably the last he ever signed or dictated—for he was killed in action the very day after it's date—with the character of a good Soldier—and an honourable man—which are not always found together nor indeed separately.——I was also invited by Count Metaxa the Governor of Missolonghi to go over there—but it was necessary in the present state of parties that I should have some communication with the existing Gov[ernmen]t on the subject of their opinion *where* I might be—if not *most* useful—at any rate *least* obnoxious.——

As I did not come here to join a faction but a nation—and to deal with honest men and not with speculators or peculators — (charges bandied about daily by the Greeks of each other) it will require much circumspection < for me > to avoid the character of a partizan — and I perceive it to be the more difficult — as I have already received invitations from more than one of the contending parties — always under the pretext that *they* are the "real Simon Pure"*. —— After all — one should not despair — though all the foreigners that I have hitherto met with from amongst the Greeks — are going or gone back disgusted. —

Whoever goes into Greece at present should do it as Mrs. Fry went into Newgate — not in the expectation of meeting with any especial indication of existing probity — but in the hope that time and better treatment will reclaim the present burglarious and larcenous tendencies which have followed this General Gaol delivery. — When the limbs of the Greeks are a little less stiff from the shackles of four centuries — they will not march so much "as if they had gyves on their legs".* —— At present the Chains are broken indeed — but the links are still clanking — and the Saturnalia is still too recent to have converted the Slave into a sober Citizen. — The worst of them is — that (to use a coarse but the only expression that will not fall short of the truth) they are such d————d liars; — there never was such an incapacity for veracity shown since Eve lived in Paradise. — One of them found fault the other day with the English language — because it had so few shades of a Negative — whereas a Greek can so modify a No — to a yes — and vice versa — by the slippery qualities of his language — that prevarication may be carried to any extent and still leave a loop-hole through which perjury may slip without being perceived.

The Greeks welcomed Byron as a saviour, and Lodovico Lipparini's picture of Byron pledging himself to Greek freedom at the tomb of the hero Botzaris is an attempt to give his cause a heroic dimension.

Missolonghi, the main port for Western Greece and the place so fatefully and romantically attached to the cause of Greek freedom, was actually a small and ugly town. Built on marshes, in days of winter rain and tide it was to become for Byron a mud-sodden hell of boredom and acrimony. Prince Mavrocordatos and his friends however, excited by Byron's mythical status and even more by his Levantine dollars, were looking forward to his arrival "as they would to the coming of a

Messiah". Nonetheless, the local fleet was all but mutinous and, on the day before Byron set sail, having less faith than Mavrocordatos in their saviour's powers, the sailors cut the cables of their ships and left the seas off Missolonghi to the Turks.

On his arrival, having narrowly escaped the Turkish fleet, Byron at once agreed to provide for 500 of the Suliote warriors who were bickering and plotting in the town. He later discovered that this, in fact, meant supplying nearly three times that number since custom demanded he should support the Suliotes' families and livestock as well. By 14 February 1824 Byron was disbursing some 2000 Levantine dollars a week, but at least it seemed he was now close to attaining his new image of himself. "His house," wrote an observer, "was filled with soldiers; his receiving room resembled an arsenal of war, rather than the habitation of a poet. Its walls were decorated with swords, pistols, Turkish sabres, dirks, rifles, guns, blunderbusses, bayonets, helmets, and trumpets . . . and attacks, surprises, charges, ambuscades, battles, sieges, were almost the only topics of his conversation with the different capitani."

He longed for action, for the stimulus and rushing blood of high, heroic deeds. These, however, were denied him. His Suliotes quarrelled among themselves and were reluctant to accept a single leader. They constantly pressed for their arrears of pay. Supplies were delayed and, when they at last arrived, were found to be inadequate. In addition, it rained incessantly. Byron and Mavrocordatos planned to spearhead an attack on Lepanto, but, before they could act, the Turkish fleet blockaded the muddy and dismal little town.

Byron tried to find relief by riding the pathways of the hinterland in the blinding rain. Loukas was a constant companion. He was the last and, Byron was discovering, the coldest of those 15-year-old boys, who seemed to stir something deep in his psyche. To Loukas, however, the friendship of this middle-aged English adventurer was merely a source of cash and prestige. The boy swaggered in his embroidered clothes, played with his gilded pistols, and spent the coins in his purse. Byron, on the eve of his 36th birthday and desperately in need of affection, acknowledged with guilty despair that he could no longer command love where he wished.

And still it rained. Parry, Byron's munitions expert, realized the poet felt forlorn and forsaken, but could not know the full reasons for this. Parry believed Byron's low spirits were sufficiently accounted for by the appalling weather, the fact that although the London Greek Committee had managed to avoid the Turkish fleet, they had sent the wrong type of rockets, and the expense of maintaining the Suliotes. These he now caught deceiving Byron about their true numbers. In addition, the Suliotes even refused to carry what supplies there were to a dry place since it was beneath their dignity to act as porters in the rain. Byron, in a blazing temper, vowed to withdraw his support. The Suliotes realized they had gone too far, but Byron's sudden outburst had seriously weakened his health. On 15 January he suffered another violent convulsion. The following morning, Dr Bruno, relying on his inexpert knowledge, insisted Byron should be bled. This was the Doctor's favourite remedy, and eight leeches were applied to Byron's temples. When they were removed the blood still flowed and Byron fainted. Four days later, however, although weakened and shaken, he calmly put down a threatened mutiny among his Suliotes.

ON THIS DAY I COMPLETE MY THIRTY-SIXTH YEAR

"Reviving passions"

This was probably Byron's last poem. His abiding themes of age, liberty and death centre around his guilty and hopeless love for the Greek boy, Loukas Chalandritsanos.

'Tis time this heart should be unmoved,
  Since others it hath ceased to move:
Yet though I cannot be beloved,
      Still let me love!

My days are in the yellow leaf;
  The flowers and fruits of Love are gone;
The worm—the canker, and the grief
      Are mine alone!

The fire that on my bosom preys
  Is lone as some Volcanic Isle;
No torch is kindled at its blaze
      A funeral pile!

The hope, the fear, the jealous care,
  The exalted portion of the pain
And power of Love I cannot share,
      But wear the chain.

But 'tis not *thus*—and 'tis not *here*
  Such thoughts should shake my Soul, nor *now*
Where Glory decks the hero's bier
      Or binds his brow.

The Sword, the Banner, and the Field,
  Glory and Greece around us see!
The Spartan borne upon his shield*
      Was not more free!

Awake (not Greece—she *is* awake!)
  Awake, my Spirit! think through *whom*
Thy life-blood tracks its parent lake
      And then strike home!

Tread those reviving passions down
  Unworthy Manhood—unto thee
Indifferent should the smile or frown
      Of Beauty be.

If thou regret'st thy Youth, *why live?*
  The land of honourable Death
Is here:—up to the Field, and give
      Away thy Breath!

Seek out—less often sought than found—
  A Soldier's Grave, for thee the best;
Then look around, and choose thy Ground,
      And take thy Rest!

Despite a letter from Hobhouse telling Byron that many of the English considered him a hero, despair and physical decay continued to work their will. The Suliotes were again threatening to desert, Loukas swaggered unlovingly, and still there was no military action. Instead, the rain fell on the muddy streets and across the grey and heaving sea. "Do you suppose I wish for life," Byron confessed. "I have grown heartily sick of it." He was not afraid to die, only of dying in pain or as an idiot. He was also deeply concerned that his fits might return.

Between spells of gloom and intense high spirits, he began to recognize the stark facts of his failure. "A mist fell from Lord Byron's eyes," declared an observer. "He owned that his sagacity was at fault, and he abandoned all hope of being able to guide the Greeks, or to assist them in improving their administration." It was the end. In despair, he wrote what was probably his last poem—a lyric of hopeless love. Then, having dealt ably with yet another outburst of local violence, Byron went for his last ride. He had already caught a fever. Now he returned to die.

Death took many days, approaching slowly, painfully, and with the help of his doctors. For a long time he held out against their insistence that he should be bled. Stubborn commonsense told him their remedies were lethal. Only when they had persuaded him he might go mad if he did not submit did Byron throw out his arm to the rough mercies of their scalpels. The doctors drained a pound of blood. There was no effect, and so they drained another. In the lucid intervals of his delirium, Byron managed to persuade them against taking a third. They plied him with purgatives instead. His hands and feet grew cold. The doctors gave him wine and water and then applied poultices to his thighs. The end was already near when Dr Bruno, finally convincing the others of the efficacy of his favourite cure, got his way and applied 12 leeches to Byron's temples. Two more pounds of blood were drawn.

Byron knew he was dying. "Your efforts to preserve my life will be vain," he declared. "Die I must: I feel it. Its loss I do not lament; for to terminate my wearisome existence I came to Greece.—My wealth, my abilities, I devoted to her cause.—Well: there is my life to her." He became delirious, and, in his fever, imagined he was leading the military charges he would never make. Glory was now just a fevered dream.

The doctors prepared another purge. He was weakened almost to death and said he wanted to sleep. These were his last words. When he had fallen powerlessly back on his pillow, Dr Bruno prepared to bleed him again. And this time he bled him all night long.

The following day, 19 April 1824, at around six o'clock in the evening, a storm broke and tremendous lightning flashed over Missolonghi. To the Greeks, such an upheaval in the heavens could mean only one thing and they began to mutter among themselves that the great man was gone.

It was decided that, after an autopsy, the body should be embalmed and returned to England for burial. Bruno examined the corpse with great interest. He discovered that in some respects Byron's internal organs were those of a very old man. This may have been in part due to inherited weaknesses, but the process had certainly been accelerated by the pace of Byron's life, the constant seeking after sensation and change, that energy and fear of the void which had propelled him through his short and tumultuous existence. Now that turbulent life was stilled. A tin-lined chest was prepared for Byron's body. His heart, brain and intestines were placed in separate containers. His lungs were given to the inhabitants of Missolonghi. The coffin, placed in 180 gallons of spirits, was loaded onto the *Florida*, which sailed on 24 May, successfully avoiding the Turkish fleet and arriving a month later.

The news of Byron's death "came on London like an earthquake". Radicals and literary men throughout the country mourned. The young Alfred Tennyson disconsolately engraved, "Byron is dead" on a rock in the countryside. Half a world away, in America, Harriet Beecher Stowe, having heard her father preach a sermon in which Byron figured as an example of human wickedness, wished she could take on herself a portion of his sins.

Hobhouse made the arrangements for the funeral. The body, when it was laid out in state, was so changed he noted, so distorted, that it barely seemed to be Byron's at all.

The body was borne through London on a black-plumed hearse accompanied by pages and mutes. The coffin itself was covered with a black silk pall. But the great families of England were reluctant to follow the cortège in person. Although radicals and literary men now regarded Byron as a hero, his scandalous personal behaviour meant that fashionable society still ostracized him, while the Greek cause itself was still a problematic issue for the British government. Nonetheless, as a peer, Byron merited certain dignities. Eventually, 47 carriages, each draped in mourning and bearing the coats of arms of their absent owners, followed the procession along Oxford Street and on to the fashionable edges of the capital. Then, for four days, the cortège travelled north, watched at each stopping place by wondering crowds. Finally it reached Hucknall Torkard and was carried to the family vault. Hobhouse had wanted to place the coffin on that of Byron's mother, but it was found to be too flimsy. Instead, Byron's remains were placed on those of the fifth and "Wicked" lord. The poet was at last among his ancestors.

"Remembered Tones"

With his death, the creation of the Byron myth began anew. As with so many myths, facts were less important than the needs the myth itself could be made to serve. Hobhouse, Murray and their circle perversely helped in this. The Memoirs Byron had started in Italy, those manuscript pages which would surprise the reader by showing "that I should have so much to confess, and that I should have confessed so much," were burned by the poet's over-cautious friends. Perhaps the loss of no other work in English literature is more to be lamented. But if the precise details of Byron's life were reduced to ashes and then distorted by rumour, the protean shapes of his art and personality, which offered such a range of images to poets, painters, musicians and philosophers, ensured his brilliant reputation.

Byron burned across his age like a comet. To some he was a portent of moral disaster and chaos. To others his influence whispered of new desires and freedom from traditional cant. Although, at the close of the 20th century, we are apt to look critically at some of the literary enthusiasms which fired the start of the 19th (few great poets produced more bad verse than Byron), it is important to understand why Byron was so influential, and how he attained his mythic status.

Byron's career reads like an anthology of romantic attitudes. Each aspect of his life and work, sometimes subsequently developed by artists of far greater power, added to the lustre of his name. This of

---

Byron's influence across 19th century Europe was of staggering proportions. Schoolgirls sighed over him, poets imitated him, painters illustrated him, musicians were inspired by him, while liberal politicians found him a powerful spokesman for their cause. There was barely a major figure of the romantic movement who was unaffected by Byron. He spoke of sorrow and illicit passion, joy, satire and freedom. From the days of his triumph in London society, Byron was copied by those in the vanguard of fashion. The Whig Thomas Hope, for example, had himself painted in the Turkish manner of "Childe Harold's Pilgrimage".

itself became a guarantee of all that was most "romantic" in romanticism. To allude to Byron was to be in the vanguard of European thought. His concern with political freedom and oppressed peoples, for example, gave heart to struggling nations everywhere. His wit, cynicism and hatred of lies were in powerful opposition to the duplicity of autocratic governments. The heroes of his *Oriental Tales* (poems sufficiently coarse-grained to be translated without too much loss of effect) provided the colour and exoticism, not just of exciting places but of bizarre psychology and irrational passions. The defiance and despair of *Manfred* and *Cain*, and Byron's concern with self-extinction and world destruction, were early expressions of romantic *weltschmerz*. Finally, his life itself, with its dissipation, heroic gesture, and prodigious fecundity of expression, became the very model of the artist's existence at that crucial period in the early 19th century when creators were no longer viewed as the hired servants of the great, but as seers of special insight whose intuitions verged on mystic revelation. Like Rousseau and Chateaubriand, he was a European giant who wore his heart on his sleeve. And it is as a European that Byron is best appreciated.

Nowhere is this clearer than in politics. "The day will come," wrote the Italian patriot Mazzini, "when Democracy will remember all that it owes to Byron." To the poet's countrymen, such effusions still come as a surprise, and perhaps as a source of mild embarrassment, but to follow Byron's trail across Europe and trace the influence of the innumerable translations of his work is to be astonished at the persistence of his political reputation. From Spain to Russia, from France and Germany south through Italy to Greece, Byron was a great shaping force of the Romantic Movement and the hopes of nationalism that accompanied this. His death was an inspiration to patriots everywhere.

Nothing in his life became him like the leaving of it, and the myth of Missolonghi was perhaps Byron's most potent legacy. His statue still looks out across many Greek squares. The winding streets in a score of little towns bear his name. The grand eccentric, who came to the help of Prince Mavrocordatos and died in the squalor of a sickbed rather than in the turmoil of battle, remains a national hero. But how far was Byron truly responsible for the freedom of the Greeks?

The variety of romantic themes explored by Byron helps to account for his European influence. His "Oriental Tales" in particular were widely read. Lermontov translated them, Berlioz wrote an overture which he titled "The Corsair', while Delacroix captured their potent mixture of exotic settings and illicit passion in his "Bride of Abydos".

The events of that historic campaign have all the complexity of international politics, and in the hands of Canning, who had succeeded to the premiership, that complexity became great indeed. Canning himself was no friend of either democracy or despotism. He believed in the English status quo—a form of government so perfect that, in his view, it was England's duty to teach more tyrannical regimes such as the Sultan's respect for the principles of liberalism as Canning conceived them. Popular crusades were anathema to him, for he considered revolutionary fervour to be dangerous. Certainly, the situation in Greece, Canning believed, was far too dangerous for such feelings to be loudly expressed. He therefore rebuffed the Greek delegates who came to seek his protection. Instead, he reaffirmed England's neutrality, and forbade its people to serve in the War of Greek Independence. He did, however, recognize the Greeks as belligerents rather than rebels. Thus, at home, Canning managed to serve the Tories without wholly alienating the Whigs.

On the international front, Canning had larger games to play and he manipulated these with equal shrewdness. He realized that the uprisings in Greece had been partly fermented by Tsar Alexander who wished, by vanquishing the Ottoman Empire, to add it to his own. It was thus in England's interest to protect the Sultan on his Russian border, if not in the Mediterranean. Here, it was British superiority that Canning sought, and, by shrewdly combining with Russia and France, he committed the three powers to jointly compelling the Sultan and the Greeks to accept their arbitration. This delicate balance of influence was to be maintained by their united fleets cruising the Mediterranean under English command. Admiral Sir Edward Codrington's commission was to maintain peace rather than wage war.

Nevertheless, some sort of confrontation was all but inevitable, and, by the end of 1827 the allied forces had surrounded the Turkish and Egyptian fleet in the bay of Navarino. This restricted its manoeuvres at sea, but could not prevent it from serving as a base for outrages on land. Codrington, who had been given wide latitude in the interpretation of his instructions, eventually decided to put a stop to these acts by a demonstration of his power. This developed into a sweeping, if disorderly, bombardment, now called the battle of Navarino, in which the Sultan's fleet was annihilated. Greece at last was free.

Told in this way, the conclusion of the Greek War of Independence makes Byron's role seem a comparatively minor one. He came, died early, and did not fight. But the factual narrative is not the whole story. It is for poets to provide images and shape dreams, and the image of the noble romantic dying for the cause of Greek freedom was so much more powerful than the little Byron actually achieved, that it focussed the aspirations of liberals and patriots not just in Greece herself but across the whole of Europe.

In the 1820s, for example, the young Count Cavour who, along with Mazzini, was the architect of Italian unity and independence, transcribed many passages from Byron's verse into his notebook and declared in wistful, if misspelt English, "What Lord Byron says in defense of the abused Greeks can be said to the justifidation of all the other nations, who groan in bondage, and are reproached for the vices that their tyrants have given them." Cavour's shrewd diplomacy, drawing on the intense feelings Byron had helped articulate, eventually succeeded in making Italy a free and united country.

A more passionate, and in some respects equally influential voice of Italian patriotism was that of Verdi. Like many of the great romantics —Berlioz and Delacroix spring immediately to mind—Verdi was influenced by three major English writers—Shakespeare, Walter Scott and Byron. And it was from Byron (by way of French intermediaries and prompted by his librettists) that Verdi derived the limpid senti-mentalism of his early opera *Il Corsaro*, as well as the more powerful liberal emotions of *I Due Foscari*.

Perhaps no one has described Byron's effect on them more vividly than the French composer Berlioz. In his *Memoirs* he describes his first reading of Byron's *Oriental Tales*. Berlioz was in Rome, and it was his habit to shelter from the sun in the coolness of St Peter's. There, in the silence of a confessional, he read—of all things—*The Corsair*, revelling in the hero's desperate adventures and furiously contradictory feelings. In the intervals of drinking in "that burning poetry", Berlioz stared up at the sublimity of Michelangelo's dome and then down at the pave-ments Byron himself had trod with, as Berlioz erroneously supposed, the Contessa Guiccioli. In such moments Byron became the image of all the frustrated Berlioz would have liked to be: "a poet . . . beloved . . . rich . . . *He* was all three!" The contrast between their states was unbearable, "and I ground my teeth so that the walls of the confessional re-echoed and the souls of the damned must have quaked".

The results of this highly charged contact with Byron were two works. Berlioz's concert overture, *The Corsair*, derives only inciden-tally from Byron's poem (the title was an afterthought) and is in fact a superbly emotive combination of contrasted rhythmic sections adorned with an *adagio sostenuto* passage of great beauty. But if Byron's poem did not provide the programme for Berlioz's work, the Byronic is every-where evident in its exuberance and melancholy reflectiveness. The title indicates the origin of a profound state of artistic awareness.

The second and greater work in which Berlioz paid homage to

Byron is *Harold in Italy*. This piece was prompted by the violinist Paganini, another all but mythical figure of the Romantic Movement (popular rumour had it that the strings on one of his instruments were made from the guts of a murdered mistress), who wished to show his virtuosity on a newly acquired Stradivarius viola. No doubt Paganini had a concerto in mind, but Berlioz responded with a symphony in which the viola obbligato sections, haunting and subtly rhythmic, reflect the sensitive musings of a romantic wanderer, a Childe Harold who is, in fact, Berlioz himself as he recalls his memories and dreams of such typically romantic sources of inspiration as mountains, pilgrims, passionate peasant couples, and brigands' orgies. Paganini never performed the piece—the appearances of the lyrical Harold were too infrequent for his artist's ego—but he later showed his recognition of the work's outstanding beauty by a payment to Berlioz of 20,000 francs.

Byron's influence on French painters was also considerable, and many, inspired by him, created powerful images of the Greeks' longing for freedom. Delacroix's masterpiece, often associated with Byron by being erroneously called *Greece Expiring on the Ruins of Missolonghi*, is in fact an allegory of the new nation's desire for liberty and a manifesto of Delacroix's own political views and artistic aspirations. Greece is portrayed as a sensual and exotic figure rising from centuries of decay to beg her cause with the fashionable audiences who thronged the charity concerts and the exhibition at the Galerie Lebrun, all of which were held *au profit des Grecs*.

Delacroix, the French master of colour and orientalism, painted many other scenes of Greek and Turkish warriors, but as one of the most articulate of 19th century artists—as well as one of the best read—he found in Byron a compelling source of inspiration. Like his admired contemporary Géricault, Delacroix illustrated scenes from the *Oriental Tales*, while the vibrant colours of his *Execution of Doge Marino Faliero* pay tribute to such Venetian masters as Veronese, even as they suggest the republican ideals Byron himself had found in this episode from Venetian history. To the poet Baudelaire, whose own affinity to Byron's diabolism and pursuit of sensation was profound, Delacroix's picture was a memorable expression of contemporary artistic achievement.

The Death of Sardanapalus—the most extreme if not the most satisfactory of Delacroix's essays in the oriental—was prompted by Byron's play of that name, but it is the scene from *Don Juan* entitled *The Drawing of the Lots in the Boat at Sea* that is the supreme example of Byron's fructifying effect on Delacroix's imagination. In this most remarkable of 19th century seascapes, at once gleamingly sombre and frighteningly vast, Delacroix has placed figures at the mercy of the elements and trapped by degrading and bestial circumstance. His figures face the horrors of cannibalism, starvation and almost certain death; but, against the vast and cruel indifference of the sea, they nonetheless attain a heroic stature, thus expressing Delacroix's ideal in painting.

Byron's influence on French literature was equally wide-ranging, if not always so obvious. Many young poets dreamed of waking to find themselves famous with a *dernier chant de Childe Harold*, but the most successful of them were also the most selective. Hugo adopted Byron's Eastern colours, Vigny aspects of his rebellious stoicism, de Musset something of his satire. As late as 1843, the critic Sainte-Beuve could still couple Byron with de Sade as the greatest source of inspiration for modern writers, which might seem a strange comment until one recalls that combination of sadism, orientalism and the erotic in Flaubert's *Salammbô* and *Herodias*. Very early in his career, Flaubert had written that Byron "believed in nothing, unless it was in all the vices", and suggested that his God existed solely for the pleasure of sinning against. Byron, the satanist, was indeed a powerful force.

Such ideas were developed and sensationalized by that strange *poet maudit*, Isidore Ducasse. Publishing his homosexual and sadistic *Chants de Maldoror* under the pseudonym "Comte de Lautréamont"—a name derived from the Byronic hero of a French novel—Ducasse declared he had wished to create something in the style of Byron's *Manfred*, but *bien plus terrible*. Early in this century, the surrealists were to claim Ducasse's work as a precursor of their own.

The French language—and Paris in particular—served as a source for the European-wide dissemination of Byron's influence, especially in the revolutionary years between 1830 and 1848. French was still the international language of the educated, and French translations of Byron were to affect many liberals either exiled in Paris, or reading him in their own suffering countries. Jose de Espronceda, for example, discovered Byron in French translation and emulated the egocentric cynicism of *Don Juan* in his *Diabolo Mundo*, thereby earning the soubriquet "the Spanish Byron".

On the other side of Europe, the melancholy of Byron's oriental tale *Lara* was to inspire the Czech poet Karel Hynek Macha's poem *Máj (May)*, while in a Poland suffering under the cruelties of Russian oppression, Byron was hugely influential. "I climb the mountains with Byron," wrote the Polish poet Slowacki, and, after the failure of the Polish uprising in 1831, when Slowacki went on a long journey to the Near East, he eventually returned with a mournful, patriotic poem very much in the manner of *Childe Harold*, and shot through with reminiscences of Byron himself.

But it was Adam Mickiewicz, the greatest of the Polish romantic poets, who was perhaps most profoundly influenced by Byron. Mickiewicz, indeed, exemplifies the effect Byron was to have on European liberalism. Having painfully worked his way through Shakespeare with the help of a dictionary, Mickiewicz's reading and eventual translation of *The Giaour* proceeded much more easily. Some of the lines from this translation were to become proverbial expressions of his nation's intolerable inheritance of oppression.

For Mickiewicz, Byron's greatness lay not just in the fact that "he had tackled all the basic moral and philosophical questions . . . and . . . cursed and fumed like Prometheus, the Titan, whose shade he loved to evoke so often", but in Byron's willingness to sacrifice his life for Greek freedom. "Do you think," Mickiewicz wrote to a friend, "that poor Byron would have written so many grand strophes had he not been ready to give up his title and London for the Greeks? The secret of his power as a writer lay in just that readiness." There is much wishful self-identification in these views, suggesting the needs the Byron myth could serve. But myth is a powerful force—lines from Mickiewicz's translation recently appeared as a quick, desperate flurry of graffiti on the walls of the shipyards in Gdansk, proving that Byron's words can still inspire hope in places where freedom is a muffled cry.

Nonetheless, Byron's moral values were notoriously more complex than Mickiewicz was prepared to suggest. This is shown by the profound, but very different influences Byron was to exert elsewhere in Eastern Europe.

In Russia, for example, the Decembrist revolutionaries who so opposed the tyranny of Tsar Nicholas I were Byronists. Their poems celebrated restless, gloomy heroes who while they profess that nothing brings them joy and that they are doomed nonetheless declare, "I will die for my land, I feel it and, holy father, I gladly bless my fate." For these men, "Byron who soared in heaven comes down to earth to denounce the oppressors, and in his romanticism assumes a political colouring".

This was certainly also true for the youthful and exiled Pushkin, though from the start his was too powerful a poetic mind to be wholly under Byron's tutelage. *The Fountain of Bakhcisavary* derives much from the orientalism and fragmentary structure of *The Giaour*. *The Prisoner of the Caucasus* portrays a banished romantic individualist, but the precision with which his plight and personality are drawn has more in common with the realism which makes his verse novel, *Eugenii Onegin*, very different to the greater part of *Don Juan* (except, perhaps, in its opening chapter). This fact did not appeal to some of the more romantically inclined of Pushkin's readers.

The outstanding Russian follower of Byron, however, and again a writer of world status, is Mikhail Lermontov. He first came to Byron through contemporary Russian translations of his work, and the influence of the early Pushkin. Then he began to translate such poems as "Fare thee well" himself. At first, it was the English poet's declamatory style which appealed to Lermontov, along with Byron's revolt against cant and oppression, but when Lermontov read Moore's *Life of Byron* he realized that their spirits were akin in their rebellious and gloomy restlessness.

In such poems as *The Dream: An Oriental Tale*, the influence of Byron's early narratives and metaphysical melodramas is clearly apparent as Lermontov develops his concept of the evil genius, the devil born of vice and danger, who fills his victim with spite, making the sufferer a wilful stranger among men and an unbidden guest in heaven.

However, Byron's influence on Lermontov was more extensive than this suggests, for the Russian was one of the very few poets of the first rank who could absorb the kaleidoscopic manner of *Beppo* and *Don Juan* and make of it something that was his own. Lermontov's *Fairy Tale for Children*, though unfortunately incomplete, has just the wit, self-mockery and colloquial vigour of Byron's best work, and it was this affinity that led Lermontov to delight in Moore's 1830 edition of Byron's *Letters and Journals*. The mixture of philosophy and jest, aphorism and incident, subjectivity and ironic observation he found there, appealed to him very deeply. Here was a style that could help shape Russian prose, and its influence is clear in Lermontov's masterpiece, his novel *A Hero of Our Time*.

The time is 1838–1840 in a Russia that is stultified by the failure of the Decembrists' revolt. The hero is Pechorin, a man of intellectual ability, shrewd, energetic but frustrated. He is a man of talent in a period of mediocrity. Trapped in his world-weariness and cynicism, Pechorin squanders his talents in vindictive and trivial love affairs. Witty, aphoristic, yet compelled to destroy, he also realizes, like a Byronic hero, that poisoned idealism has reduced him to his state of gratuitous emotional savagery. In this recognition, and in the deep sense of loss engendered by his failed love affairs, Pechorin is a figure representative not just of his times but of a psychological type of permanent interest. In his frequent analyses of his complex emotions (these are often revealed through a journal that clearly owes much to Byron's confessional style), Pechorin is the first hero of the Russian prose novel. Tolstoy, Dostoevsky and Chekhov all paid tribute to the shrewdness with which Lermontov recreated the Byronic hero, and, in so doing, helped initiate the great tradition of Russian fiction. In such ways, through the development of ideas latent in another artist's work and yet perhaps unguessed by him, literature develops.

With the failure of the Decembrists' uprising, liberalism in Russia was cruelly and largely silenced. In many German-speaking areas, the repressiveness of Hapsburg rule meant that here, too, the ideals of personal freedom could have little part to play in contemporary politics. Instead, entirely different aspects of Byron's work were to influence artists such as Goethe.

Byron himself had derived much from Goethe's work. The passages from the first part of *Faust* that Lewis had translated for him along with those in the writings of his neighbour in Switzerland, Madame de Staël, both had an influence on his *Manfred* mode. When Goethe read *Cain* however, he declared, "Byron alone do I admit to a place at my side". Goethe's relationship with the English poet deepened yet further in the last years of Byron's life (they had a brief correspondence just before Byron left for Greece), reaching its apotheosis in the second part of *Faust*.

In the third Act of that vast poetic drama, an Act which Goethe himself described as a "Classical-Romantical Phantasmagoria", the figure of Euphorion represents a symbolic image of Byron. Euphorion is the child of Helen of Troy (whom we may loosely identify with the "classical") and Faust himself, the medieval, German, and hence "romantic" scholar. Euphorion is thus suggestively symbolic of the struggle in Goethe's own career between the two poles of creative activity: the classic which is apparently ordered, logical and restrained and the romantic which is questioning, dark and mysteriously passionate. Byron seemed to Goethe to bring a new dimension to this problem, and he spoke of the English poet as being "not antique and not romantic, but . . . like the present day itself". It was Goethe's wish "to represent the most recent age of poetry" in his work, and he seized on Byron, whom he regarded as "the greatest talent of the century", for his purpose.

That purpose reveals itself in a complex meditation. Euphorion, vibrant with "eternal music" and as beautiful as Apollo, revels in his energy, a psychological and physical exuberance which, while it expresses all the joy and plenitude of the new force created by the mingling of the classic and romantic strains, is yet touched by something demonic, the restless striving that Goethe rightly detected in Byron's "unappeased temperament and fighting spirit". The winged Euphorion cannot be tied to earth nor to quiet pleasures. He rejoices in the chase of sexual passion, in storm, and finally in war. He must fly ever higher, ever faster. Here indeed is that restless pursuit of stimulation, the "mobility" Byron had acknowledged in himself. But if, for Byron, his restlessness originated in a fear of the void and spiritual inertia, for the German poet, Euphorion's energy is less anguished. It is potent as well as self-destructive, creative yet fatal, an image of genius wrecked by its own undisciplined forces. And, finally, Euphorion's wings cannot support him. Having glimpsed his mission in Greece, he falls dead at his parents' feet. His corporeal substance immediately fades, and only his robe and lyre—the symbols of his art and his legacy to the future—survive him.

The Chorus then sing Goethe's elegy to Byron-Euphorion. It is both an evocation of an individual and a symbol of youth, and a meditation on a rebel and the great cause for which he died. Helen, however, can no longer bear a world where joy is self-destructive and she descends sorrowing to Hades. The marriage of the classic and romantic is over. The child of hope it nurtured is no more. Faust's spiritual search must begin anew—he emerges, Manfred-like, on the mountains.

It was this dark, rebellious world of the metaphysical melodrama that made such a deep appeal to others in Germany. Schumann, for example, identified intensely with Byron's anguish-ridden hero. However, where Byron's play lacks real structural and intellectual coherence, Schumann's *Manfred* Overture, while suggesting its subject's rare and tortured states of mind by its use of an exotic key, its emotional vehemence and strongly syncopated rhythms, remains nonetheless a superbly controlled example of musical architecture. This contrast between violent agitation and intellectual control is deeply satisfying, nowhere more so than in the coda. Here, in a break with most established traditions, Schumann, rather than ending on a grand statement, allows his music to fade away with a searing gesture of romantic despair, a conclusion infinitely more satisfying than Byron's.

Another major German figure of the Romantic Movement also composed an overture to *Manfred*. The philosopher Friedrich Nietzsche first read Byron's poem when he was 13 and declared that in his soul he already knew "all the dark abyss of this work". Later, in *Human, All-too-Human*, he quoted Byron's lines:

> Sorrow is knowledge: they who know the most
> Must mourn the deepest o'er the fatal truth
> The Tree of Knowledge is not that of life.

Both *Manfred* and *Cain* appear to touch on a number of Nietzsche's themes—the rejection of Christian values and the will to power, and so on—but Nietzsche's development of these concepts lies outside the scope of this book, while the similarity between Byron's thought and his is essentially superficial. Byron's genius was for satire rather than philosophy, and since England was one of his prime targets, we should now examine the effect of his life and writing in his own country.

"Sir, I have quarrelled with my wife; and a man who has quarrelled with his wife is absolved from all duty to his country." Thus speaks Mr Cypress, the poet in Peacock's *Nightmare Abbey*, who represented a shrewd portrayal of the melancholy, Germanic Byron during the period of his separation from his wife. Peacock was a most intelligent critic of the romantics—far too intelligent, indeed, not to see that beneath Byron's posturing there lay a real poet with deep intuitions —but by 1818, the year in which *Nightmare Abbey* was published, Byronomania in England was changing to mistrust of the poet's immorality. No country in Europe shrugged off Byron's influence more quickly than his own. Poets who had read and mourned him in their youth largely rejected him in their Victorian maturity. Radical politicians found greater sustenance in Shelley. Though Thackeray and Browning both gained from the *esprit* of *Don Juan*, and the heroes of both *Wuthering Heights* and *Jane Eyre* derive much from those elements of the Byronic hero evident in the gothic novel, by 1822 Byron was already being accused of founding a "school of immorality and pro-faneness". Later in the century, reflecting her creator's tastes, George Eliot's Maggie Tulliver ceased to read Byron when she realized his poems blunted her feelings for normal, everyday life. Matthew Arnold rejected what he called the pageant of Byron's bleeding heart as irrelevant to his pursuit of "high seriousness". Byron's works apparently did nothing to lift the adolescent tribulations of the young John Stuart Mill. He found the poet's melancholy "vapid and uninteresting" and the "vehement sensual passions of his Giaours" unstimulating.

This rejection of Byron by the Victorians does not mean, however, that Byron had no influence in his homeland. One supreme figure of English romantic art was deeply affected by him.

In 1834 Murray published an edition of Byron's poems illustrated with engravings designed by Turner. The artist took great care in the supervision of these and, with his workmen, achieved a flexibility of outline and a subtle gradation of tone that is still pleasing. It is, however, in Turner's watercolours and oil paintings that the relation between these two great romantics is most interestingly displayed. The Byron of the last two cantos of *Childe Harold*, in particular, helped Turner define his complex and often tragic view of man's history and place in the natural world.

The Field of Waterloo, for example, was exhibited in 1818 with stanzas from Byron's evocation of the scene attached. Each is a bitter comment on victory. Turner, in particular, dwells on the futility of carnage. In his painting, a vast night sky broods over a scene from which every aspect of the heroic has been removed. Only the dead and the dying remain, their sacrifice exposed by the lamps of the pillagers, which pierce the mercifully enshrouding darkness. Light comes from the lowest forms of human greed. It is a terrible comment.

A similar though less immediately poignant irony is revealed by two pictures inspired by the fourth, Italian canto of Byron's poem. *Childe Harold's Pilgrimage—Italy* suggests at first all the colour and gaiety that the cult of southern Europe brought to English romanticism, but the epigraph qualifies this first impression:

> Thy very weeds are beautiful . . .
> Thy wreck a glory.

The idyllic scene takes place amid the ruins of a glorious past; behind the joyous foreground stretch both beauty and waste.

To Turner, the painter of light, Venice was a subject of recurring fascination. His interest, however, was not always purely aesthetic. Few paintings of that famous view are more purely beautiful than Turner's *Bridge of Sighs, Ducal Palace and Custom-house, Venice*. Buildings and water, man's works and nature's, appear held in a golden synthesis, a reconcilement of colour and joy. Once again, however, the quotation from Byron which Turner appended points to the irony. The view, for all its loveliness, is of a prison and a palace—symbols of power and repression. Though the light throws over them a brief and dazzling beauty, the Byron quotation hints at the divide between the world man has made and the natural world in which he also lives.

Today, Byron has a commemorative stone in Westminster Abbey. While his mortal remains lie among his dissolute ancestors, his fame is enshrined among his literary peers. This last took many years to attain. For over a century, Byron's personal reputation in England was more important than his poetic achievement. Trapped in its own myth, his was the dark, satanic ghost limping among the more respectable shades of English literature. Only in 1969, nearly 150 years after his death, was Byron's merit officially recognized, and his place in the established order of literature affirmed. It was an ironic victory. Byron is among those English poets who most powerfully and consistently satirized the cant and cruelty of the established order. "God," he once declared, "will not always be a Tory." At his greatest, his sheer vitality expressed itself in laughter and in scorn of those whose political half-truths inflicted a mean half-life on those they supposedly served. He speaks still for freedom, for choice, for change. Such voices we ignore at our peril.

Glossary: Poems

p8   *certes* – certainly

p9   *freeholders* – men of property

     Geordi-an – referring to the Tory machinations of George III and his son

p24   *Berkeley-Ballads* – "The Old Woman of Berkeley" is a ridiculous ballad by Southey

     to shake off toil and trouble – a reference to Wordsworth's poem "The Tables Turned" in the *Lyrical Ballads*

     verse is merely prose – a parady of Wordsworth's argument in his Preface to the *Lyrical Ballads*

     idiot Boy – a further allusion to the *Lyrical Ballads*

     Pixy – a slighting allusion to Coleridge's poems

p25   *Eremite* – hermit

p26   *ee* – eye

     Paphian girls – prostitutes

     mote – might

p27   *leman* – girlfriend

     feere – consort

     Paynim – pagan

p32   *Pharisaic* – hypocritically restrained

p33   *St George's collar* – a Russian military decoration

p35   *Nay* – a pun on the name of Napoleon's field-marshal who led the attack of the Old Guard at Waterloo

     Marinet's affair – Byron's friend Lord Kinnaird had warned of a plot to assassinate Wellington but was badly treated for his pains

p36   *the best of cut-throats* – a quotation from *Macbeth*

     Cincinnatus – a Roman patriot who saved his country without asking for reward

     Sabine farm – the poet Horace's reward from the Roman state

p45   *dull spoiler* – Lord Elgin, the Scottish or Caledonian peer

     Albion – England

     Eld – age

p46   *Alaric* – the barbarian destroyer

p47   Ζωή μου, σὰς ἀγαπῶ. – Byron glosses this as "*my Life, I love you!*"

p49   *Me jam nec faemina* – Byron quotes from memory the first Ode in Horace's fourth book in which the Latin poet declares that love and wine no longer bring him delight

p51   *Cynthia's moon* – the full moon. Cynthia, or Venus, the goddess of love is symbolized by the moon.

p53   *manufacturers* – factory workers

p56   *Or Olu* – a fashionable Regency form of gilding

     Jack Horner – an allusion to the nursery rhyme

p73   *Demosthenes* – an ancient Greek orator

p82   *Philip's son* – Alexander the Great

p83   *king-making Victory* – Waterloo restores the old monarchs of Europe

p84   *eagle* – the standard of Napoleon

     One – Napoleon

     Harmodius – liberated Athens from tyranny

p85   *Brunswick's fated chieftain* – Frederick, the nephew of George III

p86   *Albyn* – the Gallic name for Scotland

     Evan's, Donald's – heroic warriors of the Cameron clan

p92   *Lake Leman* – Lake Geneva

p106   *Janus glance* – Two-faced

p109   *seccatura* – dry, a term of critical abuse

     Improvisatori – storytellers and actors who improvise their material

p111   *Habeas Corpus* – the right to no imprisonment without trial

p118   *Cara . . .* – darling, you are too beautiful and too young to have any need of my help

p122   *temporale* – a storm

p126   *pinions* – wings

     Spahi – ruler

p132   *Cortejo* – the Spanish equivalent of the cavalier servante

p133   *Hidalgo* – aristocrat

p140   *peruke* – wig

p141   *Friar Bacon's brazen head* – the medieval Friar Bacon supposedly made a speaking clock

     chymic – illusory

p146   *some play the devil* – an allusion to Lady Caroline Lamb and her novel *Glenarvon* which was loosely based on Byron's life

p147   *Promethean vulture* – according to mythology a vulture fed daily on the liver of Prometheus

p149   *Ugolino* – Dante describes the scene in which Hugolino is punished by being condemned to gnaw on the head of his enemy for eternity

p157   *freedom's second dawn* – the revolutions in Spain, Portugal and Greece in 1820

     gold – Byron refers to the elaborate precautions taken to prevent the royal corpse from rotting

p158   *pantisocracy* – the idealistic scheme dreamed up by Coleridge and Southey for a perfect community in America

p159   *Wesley* – the great figure of 18th century English Non-conformist Christianity

     King Alfonso – the Spanish ruler declared how he could have avoided some absurdities if he had been consulted at the creation of the world

p160   *his lake* – Southey had made his home in the Lake District

     corks – Byron refers to Southey's floating corpse

     Wellborn – a character in Massinger's 17th century play *A Way to pay Old Debts*

     precisian – a religious pedant

p165   *Scian and the Teian* – Homer and Anacreon respectively

     king – King Xerxes who watched his fleet being defeated at Salamis by the Greeks.

p166   *Pyrrhic phalanx* – a group of tightly-grouped warriors protected by their shields

     Cadmus – the legendary introducer of writing to Greece

     Polycrates – the tyrant of Samos

     Miltiades – the Greek commander at Marathon

     remnant of a line – Byron believed that the Suliotes were descended from the Spartans

     Heracleidan – descendants of Hercules

     Franks – any foreigners resident in Greece

p168   *dollars* – Levantine dollars

p169   *real Simon Pure* – pretending to be the innocents that they are not

     gyves – leg-irons. The quotation is from Henry IV Part 1

p171   *The Spartan borne upon his shield* – dead Spartan heroes are returned to their families in this way

INDEX

Bold figures indicate poems or extracts printed
Italics indicate illustrations
B. = Byron

Acknowledgments

Any student of Byron must acknowledge his debt to two great Byron scholars: Jerome J. McGann, whose continuing seven volume edition of Byron's poems is essential, and Leslie A. Marchand whose 12 volume edition of the letters and three volume biography of Byron are both monuments of 20th century academic endeavour. Selections from the poems and letters included here are both reproduced from these works with grateful acknowledgments to the Oxford University Press and John Murray Ltd respectively.

I would like to thank Jeremy Harwood of The Paul Press for suggesting this work, Sally MacEachern for her kindly patience and finesse as my editor and Lester Cheeseman for his design skills.

Finally I would like to thank my parents who read the draft of the manuscript, made many helpful comments, and sustained me with their enthusiasm.

The Paul Press Ltd would like to thank the following organisations for permission to use their material:

PROSE

John Murray (Publishers) selections from *Byron's Letters and Journals* ed. Leslie A. Marchand

POETRY

© **Oxford University Press** 1980–1988. Reprinted from *The Complete Poetical Works of Byron* edited by Jerome J McGann vols I–VI (1980–1988) by permission of Oxford University Press

ILLUSTRATIONS

Published by permission of the Birmingham Museum and Art Gallery 142
The Bridgeman Art Library 35, 58, 117 (Victoria & Albert Museum, London), 48, 132 (Roy Miles Fine Paintings, London), 57 (Prado, Madrid), 97 (Kunsthalle, Hamburg), 134 (Christie's, London), 76, 158, 176 (Musée du Louvre)
BBC Hulton Picture Library 150
By permission of the British Library 20, 33, 34, 37, 122, 160
Reproduced by courtesy of the Trustees of The British Museum 67, 81, 87, 133
City of Manchester Art Galleries 85
City of Nottingham Museums, Newstead Abbey 9, 92, 115, 131
Derby Art Gallery 94
The Fine Art Society Ltd 32
The Illustrated London News Picture Library 11, 14, 63, 168
John Murray, London 8, 110, 119, 123, 143
Mary Evans Picture Library 24, 30, 31, 46, 53, 54, 62, 89, 130, 144, 159
Musée Calvert, Avignon 114
© **Cliché Musée des Beaux-Arts** 149
Museo Civico Treviso 169
National Museums & Galleries on Merseyside, Walker Art Gallery 147
By courtesy of the National Portrait Gallery, London 17, 45, 84, 88, 93, 145, 175
Oskar Reinhart Collection "Am Romerholtz", Winterthur 136

Reproduced by gracious permission of Her Majesty the Queen 36
South African Library, Cape Town 139
Staatliche Museen PreuBischer Kulturbesitz Nationalgalerie Berlin (West) Foto: Jorg P. Anders 83
The Tate Gallery, London 18, 116
University of London Central Slide Library 47 (Reproduced by permission of the Trustees, The Wallace Collection, London), 75, 146 (Musée du Louvre), 82 (Musée National du Château de Versailles), 87 (The British Museum), 98 (City of Manchester Art Galleries), 118 (City Art Museum, St Louis), 135 (The National Gallery), 148 (© Cliché Musée des Beaux-Arts), 111
Reproduced by permission of the Trustees, The Wallace Collection, London 61, 157
Yale University Art Gallery John Hill Morgan, B.A. 1893, fund 86

Efforts were made to contact all possible holders of copyright material, and failure to include acknowledgement here is no indication of intent to avoid such acknowledgement. Any omissions notified to the publishers will be included in further editions.

Bibliography

Beatty, Bernard *Byron, Don Juan and Other Poems*, Penguin Masterstudies, Penguin Books, Harmondsworth, 1987
Kelsall, Malcolm *Byron's Politics*, Harvester Press, Sussex 1987
McGann, Jerome J (ed) *The Complete Poetical Works of Byron*, 6 vols, Clarendon Press (Oxford University Press), 1980–88
Marchand, Leslie A *Byron: A Biography*, 3 vols, John Murray
   Byron: A Portrait John Murray, 1971
      (rptd. The Cresset Library, 1987)
   Byron's Letters and Journals, 12 vols, John Murray, 1973–82
Martin, Philip W *Byron: A Poet Before His Public*, Cambridge University Press, 1982
Moore, Doris Langly *Lord Byron: Accounts Rendered*, John Murray, 1974
Origo, Iris *The Last Attachment*, John Murray, 1949 (rptd. 1972)
Quennell, Peter *Byron: The Years of Fame*, Collins, 1943
   Byron in Italy, Collins, 1941
Rutherford, Andrew *Byron: A Critical Study*, Standford University Press, 1961 (rptd. 1965)
Trueblood, Paul G *Lord Byron* Twayne's English Author's Series, Twayne Publications, Inc, 1969